Applying
Moral Theories

C. E. Harris, Jr.
Texas A & M University

Applying Moral Theories

Wadsworth Publishing Company
Belmont, California
A Division of Wadsworth, Inc.

For Pat, Alison, and Charlie

Philosophy Editor: Kenneth King
Production: Mary Forkner, Publication Alternatives
Cover Designer: Diane Hillier
Designers: Adriane Bosworth and Richard Kharibian
Manuscript Editor: Patricia Cain
Print Buyer: Ruth Cole

Printed in the United States of America

3 4 5 6 7 8 9 10—90 89 88 87

ISBN 0-534-05898-1

Library of Congress Cataloging in Publication Data

Harris, C. E. (Charles Edwin), 1938–
   Applying moral theories.

   Includes index.
   1. Ethics.   I. Title.
BJ1012.H318   1986   171   85-22532
ISBN 0-534-05898-1

CONTENTS

PREFACE

In spite of the increasing interest in applied ethics, relatively little has been done to make ethical theory more accessible to students and more easily applicable to moral problems. Several features of the book represent an attempt to remedy this defect.

1. A common outline presents each theory, facilitating comparisons.
2. Concept summaries are provided at the end of the shorter chapters and at crucial junctures in the longer chapters.
3. A checklist provides specific directions for applying each theory to moral problems.
4. Examples are used profusely throughout the text, and the checklists are followed in applying each theory to several cases.
5. The same criteria of evaluation are applied to every theory, again facilitating comparison.
6. The final chapter applies all four theories discussed in the book to a single moral problem, illustrating the value of using multiple perspectives in treating a complex moral problem.

Several considerations should be kept in mind in reading this book.

First, this is a book on moral theory, albeit theory oriented toward application. The discussions of particular cases are not intended to be full-scale treatments but, instead, short examples showing how the theories can be applied and illustrating some of the problems encountered in application.

Second, whereas the chapters on egoism, natural law, and utilitarianism are presentations of standard positions, the chapter on the ethics of respect for persons is something of an exception. The reliance on Kant is obvious, but it should not be taken as a straightforward presentation of Kantian moral theory. Many scholars would say that my use of what Kant would call the "contradiction in conception" test is not Kant's, and I do not use Kant's "contradiction in the will" test at all. My interpretation of the means-ends principle relies as much on Alan Gewirth as Kant. I believe the chapter gives a reasonably clear presentation of a deontological position that owes much to Kant.

Third, the book is oriented toward normative ethical theory and pays minimal attention to metaethical issues. Attempts to justify individual moral standards are briefly sketched, and the issues raised by the analysis of the meanings of ethical concepts are not discussed at all. Ethical relativism and scepticism are dealt with in some detail, but the "solution" in the last chapter is suggested rather than worked out in detail. For the purposes of this book, the problems are important primarily from the standpoint of application.

I want to thank all of those who have helped in the preparation of this book, especially those who have given encouragement by saying I was doing something that needed to be done. The following manuscript reviewers provided valuable comments and suggestions: John Arthur, College of Charleston; Edmund Byrne, Indiana University at Indianapolis; Martin Gunderson, Macalester College; Terrance McConnell, University of North Carolina at Greensboro. Special appreciation goes to Kenneth King, Mary Arbogast, Mary Johnson, and Alma Cantu.

C. E. Harris, Jr.

Applying
Moral Theories

I

WHAT IS ETHICS?

In a 1968 study, Raymond Baumhart asked 100 businessmen "What does *ethical* mean to you?" The following responses were typical:

> Before coming to the interview, to make sure that I knew what we would talk about, I looked up *ethics* in my dictionary. I read it and can't understand it. I don't know what the concept means . . . .

> *Ethical* is what my feelings tell me is right. But this is not a fixed standard, and that makes problems.

> *Ethical* means accepted standards in terms of your personal and social welfare; what you believe is right. But what confuses me . . . is the possibility that I have been misguided, or that somebody else has been poorly educated. Maybe each of us thinks he knows what is ethical, but we differ. How can you tell who is right then?[1]

Fifty percent of the businessmen in the survey defined *ethical* as "what my feelings tell me is right." Another 25% defined it in religious terms as what is "in accord with my religious beliefs," and 18% defined *ethical* as what "conforms to 'the golden rule.'" Many of us feel the same concern and confusion when we think about ethics. We recognize that ethics is important in our own lives and in the life of our nation and the world, but we find the subject baffling.

---

[1] Raymond Baumhart, *An Honest Profit: What Businessmen Say about Ethics in Business* (New York: Holt, Rinehart & Winston, 1968), pp. 11–12. Used with permission. Quoted in Manuel G. Velasquez, *Business Ethics: Concepts and Cases* (Englewood Cliffs, N.J.: Prentice-Hall, 1982), p. 6.

One businessman said he looked up *ethics* in the dictionary, but it didn't help him much. If he used *Webster's New World Dictionary of the American Language,* he found this definition:

> *ethics* 1. the study of standards of conduct and moral judgment; moral philosophy. 2. a treatise on this study; book about morals. 3. the system or code of morals of a particular philosopher, religion, group, profession, etc.

If the businessman had been especially enterprising, he might also have looked up the word *moral,* which has a much more elaborate set of definitions. The first definition of *moral* is "relating to, dealing with, or capable of making the distinction between right and wrong in conduct." He might also have found the contrast between *moral* and *ethical* interesting. "*Moral,*" says the dictionary, "implies conformity with the generally accepted standards of goodness or rightness in conduct or character, sometimes, specifically, in sexual conduct." "*Ethical,*" on the other hand, "implies conformity with an elaborated, ideal code of moral principles, sometimes, specifically, with the code of a particular profession." So, in common usage, *moral* has to do with generally accepted standards in a community, whereas *ethical* has to do with principles set out in a book on ethics or in a professional code. This distinction has some validity, although *moral philosophy* would have to be thought of as synonymous with ethics, since it involves a set of specifically elaborated principles of ethics. In fact, in this book *ethics* and *morals* will be used as equivalent terms.

Although they are generally helpful, these definitions do not seem to get to the heart of the puzzlement about ethics or morals. In their statements, the businessmen seemed to be expressing two problems. First, they were confused about the *nature* of ethics. How does ethics differ from science? How does the claim that abortion is wrong differ from the claim that water is composed of two parts hydrogen and one part oxygen? How do ethical claims differ from factual claims, such as the statement that the sun is shining or that Mary has brown hair? Scientific and ordinary commonsense, factual statements seem far removed from ethical statements, but other statements seem much closer. For example, how does the statement that you should knock before entering a room differ from the statement that you should not sexually exploit small children? We shall deal with the question of the nature of ethics in this chapter.

The second issue the businessmen dealt with was the *validity* of ethics. If ethics is merely a matter of what my feelings tell me or what each of us thinks is right, how can I say that ethical opinions are valid or that they have any objectivity? What can I make of the fact that people seem to differ in their ethical evaluations of people and actions? Perhaps I should adopt the philosophy "When in Rome, do as the Romans do." We shall deal with the question of the validity of ethics in Chapter 2.

When you have finished reading this book, you should not have the same puzzlement about ethics that the businessmen expressed. In the first three chapters, we shall discuss the nature and validity of ethics and the structure and evaluation of a moral theory. Then we will consider four moral philosophies that are especially influential in our society. These philosophies are (1) *egoism,* the theory that everyone should do what is in his or her self-interest; (2) *natural law,* the theory that one should do what is in accord with human nature; (3) *utilitarianism,* the theory that one should do what leads to the greatest overall human welfare; and (4) the *ethics of respect for persons,* the theory that one should act in a way that respects the equal dignity of all human beings. You will see how these philosophies are applied to particular examples, and you will be provided with guidelines for applying them to new situations.

This first chapter is devoted to the clarification of concepts. In applying ethical theory to moral problems, it is important to think as precisely as possible. Our discussion will move from broader issues to more specific ones. First we shall differentiate the three major issues in a moral problem: factual issues, conceptual or definitional issues, and moral issues. Then we shall focus on moral statements and distinguish them from other types of statements that express value judgments. Finally we shall narrow the limit still further to focus on some distinctions and concepts within the realm of moral discourse. We shall conclude with an example to which the concepts we have discussed can be applied.

Three Types of Claims Made in Moral Arguments

On January 17, 1912, Capt. Robert Falcon Scott and his four companions reached the South Pole. They had 800 miles to walk back, hauling their sleigh, to their base camp on McMurdo Sound. They died 100 miles short of their destination, and Capt. Scott's diary, found with their bodies the following spring, tells a story of heroism that still fires the imagination.

One of the men in the party, Capt. L. E. G. Oates, became frostbitten. He suffered terribly for weeks and realized he was slowing the party's march and thereby increasing their peril. On March 10 Oates asked the physician in the party, Dr. Wilson, if he had a chance. The physician said he didn't know, but Capt. Scott says in his diary that, in point of fact, Oates had no chance of surviving the march. Scott remarks that he doubts whether the party could make it to safety in any event, but he concludes that they might have "a dog's chance" if Oates were not present.

A few days later Capt. Oates said he could not go on and proposed that they leave him in his sleeping bag. The party refused and finally induced him to come on the afternoon march. He struggled a few miles and that night he was still worse. Capt. Scott gives this account of Oates's death:

> This was the end. He slept through the night before last, hoping not to wake; but he woke in the morning—yesterday. It was blowing a blizzard. He said, "I am just going outside and may be some time." He went out into the blizzard and we have not seen him since.

Scott remarks a few lines later:

> We knew that poor Oates was walking to his death, but though we tried to dissuade him, we knew it was the act of a brave man and an Englishman.[2]

One of the members of the party, Edgar Evans, had already died at the foot of Beardmore Glacier. The other three members of the party, Scott, Wilson, and Bowers, died in their tent of cold and starvation, prevented by the blizzard from struggling the last 11 miles to One Ton Depot, where they would have found food and fuel.

In asking yourself whether Capt. Oates's action was morally right, you must consider three kinds of issues. They are the same types of issues that come up in most moral discussions.

1. Factual Issues. Some questions of fact are relevant to the case. One question is whether Oates's removal from the party would have made a significant difference in the others' chances for survival. Scott thought Oates's absence might increase the chances of survival a little, but not very much. Perhaps Oates thought that, since the party's chances for survival were virtually nil with him along, this difference was important. Another question has to do with Oates's true motives. Was his action motivated primarily by the desire to give Scott, Wilson, and Bowers a better chance at survival, or was it primarily motivated by the desire to end his own suffering? Given the strong sense of loyalty that the members of the party had to one another, we can probably say that the primary motive was the former.

Every moral problem contains factual issues that are relevant to the moral decision being made. When we discuss whether marijuana should

---

[2]See Ann Savours, ed., *Scott's Last Voyage* (New York: Praeger, 1975), p. 155.

be legalized, we must question the medical, psychological, and social consequences of the drug's widespread use. A consideration of the morality of capital punishment must include the question of whether it deters crime. When trying to determine the proper distribution of wealth in our country, we must know the current distribution of wealth. We also must know how many people are poor and how much incentive would be affected by a radical redistribution of wealth.

You can probably think of many other factual issues that are vitally relevant to the moral questions we have posed, but these examples should be enough to convince you that we must isolate those questions of fact that are a part of a moral argument and then attempt to answer them. Awareness of the different types of issues in a moral debate will enable you to see that sometimes the major argument is not really over moral principles at all but, rather, over matters of fact.

2. *Conceptual Issues.* Was Capt. Oates's act an instance of suicide? The answer depends on our definition of suicide. Conceptual or definitional issues are important in many, but not all, moral debates. Conceptual issues differ from factual and moral issues; they cannot be settled by an appeal to facts or by an appeal to moral standards. However, one can give arguments as to which definition is better. These arguments can appeal to many considerations, such as our intuitive sense of how a word should be used or the convenience of one definition as opposed to another.

We might propose to label as suicide any action in which a person does something he knows will end his own life. But this definition is implausible because it would mean that a religious martyr who chooses to die rather than to renounce her faith is a suicide. We do not usually call martyrs suicides. Rather, we say that what they did directly was to hold to their faith in the face of persecution and that their death was only an unfortunate and undesired consequence of their steadfast faith. Can something similar be said of Capt. Oates? Was his action primarily intended to increase the chances of survival of his companions, and was his death only an unfortunate and unintended—even if foreknown—consequence of his action? The answer to this question depends on the extent to which Capt. Oates's action was motivated by the desire to end his own suffering. The fact that Capt. Oates proposed ending his life only when he could not travel further strongly suggests that his motive was not self-interest.

Conceptual issues, or issues of definition, are often prominent aspects of a moral debate. The debate over abortion is probably the best example. Is the fetus a person? The answer depends on how we define *person* and on whether the fetus fits this definition. The issue cannot be decided by an

6 / Chapter I

appeal to medical facts or moral principles alone, but the answer is nevertheless crucial to the abortion debate. When we consider the morality of bombing civilian populations in wartime, we encounter another conceptual issue. Are civilian populations innocent? Are people innocent if they are not in uniform or not directly connected with the war effort? Does it make any difference whether the civilians live in a democracy, where they have some voice in governmental actions, or in a totalitarian state, where they do not? If you want to think about these issues clearly and intelligently, you must recognize when you are faced with a conceptual issue and know how to go about resolving it.

   3. Moral Issues. Some issues in a moral problem are genuine disagreements over moral principles. If Capt. Oates's action was a genuine suicide, was it morally right? Capt. Scott records in his diary that Dr. Wilson had morphine in his medical supplies and that the members of the party debated whether they should end their lives with morphine or wait to die naturally. Would it have been morally wrong to have taken the morphine? The Judeo-Christian tradition has held that genuine suicide is immoral, although many acts that will almost certainly end in one's death are morally permissible. One of the traditional grounds for this belief is that life is a gift of the Creator and that a human being should not take his or her life before the Creator takes it. Some existentialist philosophers argue that the ability to take one's own life is the supreme manifestation of personal freedom. What other considerations are relevant to the morality of suicide? How would you decide the issue?
   Moral questions are, of course, the most characteristic feature of moral debates. You can probably easily call to mind some of the moral issues suggested by the other examples. If the fetus is considered to be a person, is an abortion still sometimes permissible? If civilians are considered to be innocent, is killing them permissible if greater numbers of innocent people can thereby be saved? Does the state have a right to prohibit you from smoking marijuana, even if it is harmful, as long as you know what you are doing? Here we have arrived at the very heart of a moral discussion.
   The first step in facing a moral problem is to distinguish the factual, conceptual, and moral issues. You will often find that, in a discussion of a moral problem, people are not sufficiently aware of the differences among these three kinds of issues. Thus they are also not aware of the important differences in how these three kinds of issues are resolved. Making distinctions is an important part of moral thought. Now we shall look more closely at the nature of the most important statements in moral debates—moral statements.

The Nature of Moral Statements

We all have some intuitive knowledge of what ethics is. We make ethical statements every day. However, we may still find ourselves in a situation like that of the businessmen who were unable satisfactorily to describe ethics. We shall focus on the nature of ethics by looking at the nature of ethical statements. We begin by considering a class of statements of which moral statements are a part—namely, normative statements.

Normative versus Factual Statements. In order to understand the nature of ethical statements, we must first distinguish between normative statements and factual statements. A *normative statement* expresses a value judgment of some kind, and its correctness is determined by reference to a norm or standard. Some examples of normative statements and the standards used to determine their correctness are:

Normative Statement	Type of Confirmation
"Picasso is a great painter."	Aesthetic standard
"Do not use a singular subject with a plural verb."	Grammatical standard
"It is illegal to omit this income from your tax statement."	Legal standard (a law)
"You should not lie to your father like that."	Moral standard
"Stand when a lady comes into the room."	Standard of etiquette

In contrast to normative statements, *factual statements* make claims that are shown to be correct or incorrect by experiment, observation, or research. The following factual statements are listed with the type of experiment, observation, or research that might confirm them.

Factual Statement	Type of Confirmation
"George Washington was the first President of the United States."	Historical research
"The sun is shining."	Observation
"Water is composed of two parts hydrogen and one part oxygen."	Scientific research

Factual Statement	*Type of Confirmation*
"The law you are violating in omitting this income from your statement was passed by Congress in 1978."	Legal research

The distinction between the way normative statements are confirmed (by appeal to a standard) and the way factual statements are confirmed (by appeal to experiment, observation, or research) is of great significance. Most of us feel more comfortable with factual statements because we are better able to determine whether factual statements are true or false. The question naturally arises: How do we confirm the standard to which normative statements appeal? Most moral philosophers think that this distinction leads to a significant truth about the justification of moral statements.

An Important Corollary. Widespread agreement exists in moral philosophy that normative statements, including moral statements, cannot be confirmed by appeal to factual statements alone. A normative statement must always be assumed along with the factual statement in order to produce the normative statement we are trying to confirm.

Let us take a simple example to illustrate this claim. We shall use the type of normative statements in which we are most interested—namely, ethical statements. Consider the following argument:

> The wealth of the United States is at present unevenly distributed among its citizens.
>
> Therefore the present distribution of wealth in the United States is morally wrong.

The first sentence is a simple statement of fact. An economist could determine whether it is true by scientific means. The second sentence is an ethical statement. Most moral philosophers believe you cannot derive the second statement from the first without assuming a moral statement. So let us add the statement:

> An uneven distribution of wealth in a country is wrong.

You may or may not agree with this moral statement; in fact, most people would probably not agree with it. The important point is that the statement must be presupposed in order for the argument to work, so the complete argument now is:

The wealth of the United States is at present unevenly distributed among its citizens.

An uneven distribution of wealth in a country is wrong.

Therefore the present distribution of wealth in the United States is morally wrong.

Moral philosophers have different ideas about the relationship of moral statements to factual statements, and what we have given here is an illustration rather than a proof. Nevertheless, we shall assume hereafter that a moral statement cannot be derived from a factual statement.

This assumption has important implications for ethical argumentation. You cannot justify an ethical claim by an appeal to facts alone. Therefore, if you attempt to support an ethical claim exclusively by reference to facts, something will be missing, even if the facts are relevant to the argument. You should examine your argument to find the ethical assumptions implicit in what you say. Then you should state these assumptions clearly and show why you think they are justified.

Characteristics of Ethical Statements. Now that we have distinguished normative statements from factual statements and drawn an important corollary from this distinction, we must focus more closely on moral statements. How do they differ from other normative statements, such as those in aesthetics or etiquette? How do they differ from non-normative statements with which they have some similarities, such as those in religion? Moral philosophers have not been able to find any single characteristic that is unique to moral statements, but they have found several characteristics that, when taken together, give a good description of moral statements.

1. Prescription of Conduct. Moral statements prescribe conduct. This criterion serves to distinguish moral statements from aesthetic statements. The statement that Picasso was a great painter does not explicitly give direction to behavior, whereas the statement that we should not lie to our parents does; but this criterion is not enough to distinguish moral statements from all others. For example, the statement that we should knock before entering a room also prescribes a certain type of conduct, although we would not classify it as a moral statement.

2. Impartiality. Moral or ethical statements are based on impartial considerations. Philosophers sometimes say that moral standards are based on the reasons that an "ideal observer" or an "impartial spectator" would accept. If we want to make a genuine ethical claim, we must not allow our personal needs to dictate what we call right or wrong. Moral statements are not supposed to advance the interests of one person or group exclusively, but rather to take a universal view in which each person's interests count the same. The implied impartiality of moral statements accounts at least in part for their power. If a moral statement were a mere expression of my own interest, others would have no reason to pay any special attention to it. After all, my interests and yours might not be the same. But, if a moral judgment is genuinely impartial, it stands to reason that you should pay attention to what I say, because you should make the same judgment in the same circumstances.

Keep in mind that some apparent exceptions to this point are not really exceptions when they are properly understood. For example, a request to be treated in a certain way is not necessarily a violation of the requirement of impartiality. Suppose I am a clerk in a bank that is being robbed. I say to the robber who is holding a gun in my face "You should not kill me. I don't deserve to die." Although I am making a statement about killing that applies directly only to me, I am implicitly saying that no one else should be killed in similar circumstances either. Thus the requirement of impartiality has not been violated. Similarly, if I say "It is wrong for you to have done that to me," I intend to convey the idea that even you would consider your action wrong if you looked at it impartially. Impartiality does not distinguish moral statements from most other normative statements; therefore, we must look for other characteristics.

3. Overriding Importance. Moral statements are generally thought to have a particularly serious or overriding importance. Compare the moral statement "You should not lie to your father" with the other normative statements given earlier. A violation of the moral rule against lying is more important than a violation of the rule of etiquette or the rules of grammar. Similarly, a moral judgment is more important than an aesthetic judgment. And ultimately moral statements are more important than statements about law. Most moral and political philosophers in the Western tradition have argued that laws must be evaluated by moral standards. Something is not right simply because it is the law. The belief that laws can be immoral and that moral considerations override legal ones is the foundation of the tradition of civil disobedience. But some people say that religious statements, especially the direct commands of God, override even ethical statements. When Abraham in the Old Testament was told to sacrifice his son, he believed that this command superseded even ethical prohibitions against killing the innocent. Thus, some people do not see overriding importance as a unique characteristic of moral statements.

4. Independence of Arbitrary Authority. Moral statements cannot be established or changed by the decisions of authoritative bodies, nor can their truth be established by a mere appeal to consensus or tradition. That it is impolite to enter a room without knocking is a matter of tradition and consensus, as are the rules of grammar to some extent. But we can always question majority opinion or tradition in a matter of ethics. We can concede to the French Academy the right to determine proper French usage, but we have more difficulty imagining an institution that determines moral propriety. Even religious institutions do not claim to determine morality by decree, but rather to interpret divine law, which exists independently of the institutions. But again this characteristic is not unique to morality. The validity of factual statements is also independent of arbitrary decrees; and many philosophers and artists claim that it is possible to argue rationally about aesthetic judgments, so these judgments are not arbitrary either.

Thus we see that none of the four characteristics is unique to moral statements. However, taken together, they give a good description of the nature of ethical or moral statements, or of the moral standards from which these statements are derived. We shall refer to these characteristics from time to time in the following chapters, especially in our evaluation of a moral theory. If a moral theory fails to do justice to one of these four criteria, this failure must be taken as a mark against the theory.

Concepts in Ethical Discourse

Before we consider additional examples, we should focus on some concepts and distinctions within ethical discourse itself. Two pairs of terms are of special importance: First, many ethical theorists see an important distinction between consequentialist and non-consequentialist theories. They believe that all moral philosophies can be classified into one or the other of these categories and that this distinction is of vital importance in understanding the nature of ethical theories. In *consequentialist moral theories,* actions, persons, or motives are morally judged solely according to the nature of their consequences. The two consequentialist theories that we shall consider are egoism and utilitarianism. Roughly, egoism holds that actions are to be judged in terms of their consequences for a person's self-interest, and utilitarianism holds that actions are to be judged in terms of their consequences for the welfare of humanity in general.

A *non-consequentialist theory* of ethics holds that actions, persons, or motives are to be judged, not by their consequences, but by conformity to moral rules. What these rules are depends on the particular non-consequentialist moral theory in question. But, in any case, the rules are those that follow from what we shall call the basic moral standard—that is, the fundamental criterion for determining what is right and wrong. The two non-consequentialist theories that we shall consider are natural law, which holds that actions are to be judged by their conformity to human nature, and the ethics of respect for persons, which holds that actions should be judged by whether or not they are in conformity with the equal value of each person. Since the morality is to be judged solely by a consideration of whether the relevant moral rules are violated, the non-consequentialist moral theories often appear to be rigid and inflexible.

Most of us are naturally inclined to look to consequences as a way of determining the moral acceptability of an action. "What better way," we might say, "do we have of determining what we ought to do than by looking at the consequences of various alternatives?" Nevertheless, we shall see that the consequentialist approach has severe problems. Furthermore, Hebrew-Christian morality is basically non-consequentialist, so that consequentialism is contrary to the most influential Western tradition in morality.

The second pair of terms we shall define is *right* and *good,* probably the most commonly used ethical words. Two contrasts between these words are worth noting: (1) Goodness can be thought of in degrees, but rightness cannot. Something is either right or not right, whereas an action can be good, better, or the very best thing to do in the circumstances. The word *good* can denote anything from merely morally acceptable to highly morally praiseworthy. (2) *Good* refers to a wider range of phenomena than *right.* *Good* refers to actions and the motives of actions, but it can also describe persons or things. *Right,* on the other hand, refers primarily to actions. We can speak of good people and good things, as well as good actions and good intentions, but we cannot substitute "He is a right man" for "He is a good man." Nor can we say that knowledge or courage is *right,* although we can say they are *good.*

Moral philosophers have long debated over the meaning of *right* and *good.* Following one influential tradition in contemporary moral philosophy, we shall use the word *good* as a general term of moral commendation. Thus to say that a person or an action is good is to commend morally the person or action.

Right, as we have seen, usually has the more restricted meaning of "morally obligatory" or at least "morally permissible," as applied to actions. Because *right* does have special reference to actions, we shall use *right* in the formulation of moral standards, the fundamental criteria for determining what is morally permissible and impermissible for any given moral philosophy. Thus the moral standard will usually read "Those actions are right that . . . ."

We have distinguished moral statements from factual statements and from other types of normative statements. We have also defined some important concepts within the sphere of ethical discourse itself. Now let's look at a case that uses the concepts we have discussed. Remember that we are concerned, not with resolving the issues in this case, but with analyzing them clearly.

A Burn Victim's Desire to Die

In July of 1973, an unmarried 26-year-old-man, whom we shall call James, was severely burned when he and his father set off an explosion from a leaky propane gas pipeline.[3] The father died before reaching the hospital, and James sustained second- and third-degree burns over two-thirds of his body. He is now blind in both eyes, although he might possibly be able to recover sight in one eye. After nine months of treatment, the tips of his fingers have been amputated, his hands are useless, he cannot get out of bed by himself, and the burns are still not healed. In order to keep the open burns from becoming infected, James must be immersed daily in a bath of antiseptic solution. The baths are preceded by injections that make James unconscious, but the dressing of the burns after his bath is still quite painful to him.

James is an intelligent and articulate young man. He has persistently pleaded to be allowed to leave the hospital and go home to die. He says that he will not wait to die a natural death from the infection that would begin in the open burns but would take measures to end his own life. He has recently refused permission for further surgery on his hands.

The physicians have called in a consulting psychiatrist with the intent to have James declared incompetent, but the psychiatrist has concluded that James is rational. James's argument for wanting to end his life is that he has been an active person, has participated in sports, and is fond of the outdoors. He does not find enough value in living blind and as a cripple to make it worthwhile to endure the painful treatments and the problems of adjusting to a new lifestyle. James has asked the physician to help him get out of the hospital, so he can go home and die. Should the physician honor James's request? Let's apply the concepts discussed in this chapter.

Factual Issues. The physician must answer a number of factual questions before he can make a decision. One of the questions is whether James could adjust to his new lifestyle. James says he would never find life worth living as a disabled person, but the physician has access to histories of other victims of catastrophes and will want to make a determination on his own of James's prospects for future happiness. The physician will also want to know the law governing these situations. What can he do legally without incurring unacceptable liabilities for himself or the hospital? You may think of other factual issues that are important in the case.

[3]Adapted from Robert B. White, "A Demand to Die," *The Hastings Center Report,* 5 (June, 1975), pp. 9–10. See also videotape, "Please Let Me Die," by Robert B. White. Used with permission.

Conceptual Issues. Two important conceptual issues arise in the case. The first is whether this proposed action is a case of suicide. Because James wants to end his life by some direct means and out of concern for his own well-being, most people would consider his action to be suicide. The second question, which is more difficult, has to do with the concept of rationality. Is James rational enough to make such a serious decision about his own future? The physician has to have a clear concept of what he means by *rationality* before he can answer this question. Of course factual issues can be raised here as well. The physician might have a clear concept of what it means to act rationally but might still be puzzled about whether James is acting rationally. If he defines *rationality* as involving, among other things, making decisions on the grounds of all available evidence, he might still wonder whether James fully understands the degree to which he will be able to manage his own affairs at home. Nevertheless, having a clear concept of rationality is an important first step in determining whether James is rational.

Moral Issues. This case has two important moral issues. One is the morality of killing oneself. This question is especially interesting because James is not dying. Given sufficient time, the burns will heal and James will be sent home. He should be able to live out his normal lifespan, even though he will be handicapped. The second issue has to do with the obligations and prerogatives of the physician. Does the physician have an obligation to help James get out of the hospital? Does he have an obligation to help James end his life if he is asked to assist? Does he have the right to try to keep James in the hospital if he thinks James is not rational? Does he have the right to try to keep James in the hospital if he disagrees with James's decision to end his life, even if he believes James is rational?

Moral and Factual Statements. Recall that moral conclusions do not follow directly from the facts of the case. For example, the fact that James will recover and can eventually be sent home does not necessarily mean that his ending his life would be wrong, although this consideration is relevant to the issue. The fact that the physician is prevented by law from directly administering a lethal injection to James at his request does not settle the question of whether he should legally be allowed to do so. The fact that the physician may be opposed to all forms of suicide does not necessarily mean that he should act to prevent James from killing himself.

Characteristics of Moral Statements. The moral questions at stake seem to exhibit the four characteristics of moral statements. First, the answers given to the moral questions at issue prescribe the conduct that James and his physician should follow. The statement that it is wrong for James to commit suicide implies that James should not take any measures to end his own life. The conclusion that the physician has an obligation to help James get out of the hospital implies that he should take steps to achieve the goal. Second, the moral statements made about this case are ordinarily made from an impersonal standpoint. If we are making judgments about the case from an observer's perspective, this impersonal standpoint can be assumed. But, even if we take the physician's standpoint, we would presumably ask what should be done based on his moral and professional obligation. Self-interest is not a legitimate consideration unless it would apply to any other physician in the same situation. If injecting James with a lethal drug would result in the physician's incarceration, that consideration would appropriately carry some moral weight. But it would carry moral weight with any other physician in the same situation. Third, the moral issues have a serious and overriding importance. The moral issues are more important than issues of medical etiquette or the aesthetic questions regarding James's burns. They are even more important than the legal issues in the case, because we might conclude that the laws should be changed to accommodate our moral beliefs about what should be done. Fourth, the issues cannot be settled merely by an appeal to authority or to consensus or tradition. Deciding whether it is wrong for James to take his life or whether the physician should help him take his life involves more than taking a vote or determining how the issue would have been decided in the past.

Concepts in Moral Philosophy   We can look at this problem from either a consequentialist or a non-consequentialist perspective. An egoist would ask about the consequences of the alternatives for James's or the physician's self-interest. A utilitarian would ask about the consequences for the general human welfare. Non-consequentialists, such as natural-law theorists and advocates of the ethics of respect for persons, would approach the issues differently. They would ask whether James's or his physician's actions were in accordance with human nature or the respect due the person. We shall leave the steps of this determination for another time; the important point is that the consequences of alternative actions are not the decisive point. For example, by the standards of natural law, James should not kill himself, even if the remainder of his life produces no benefit for him or anyone else.

Finally, in a discussion of the case, we would use the terms *good* or *bad,* intending thereby to commend or condemn the actions, motives, or people involved. We would also refer to the actions of the people involved as *right* or *wrong,* intending thereby to classify them as morally obligatory (permissible) or as morally impermissible. The concepts and distinctions we have discussed in this first chapter, then, are an essential part of our moral discourse.

CONCEPT SUMMARY

An important part of ethics is making distinctions. When analyzing a moral problem, you should first distinguish between questions of fact, questions involving the definitions of concepts, and questions that directly involve moral principles.

Moral statements themselves are a type of normative statement, as are statements in such areas as aesthetics, etiquette, law, and grammar. Normative statements differ from factual statements in that normative statements make value judgments that appeal to norms. Most moral philosophers believe that moral statements cannot be derived from factual statements. An important corollary of this belief is that moral statements cannot be justified by an appeal to facts. This point is important in moral arguments.

Several characteristics, taken together, give a good description of moral statements. Moral statements prescribe conduct, they are based on impartial considerations, they have overriding importance, and they cannot be established or changed by the decisions of authoritative bodies, nor can their truth be established by a mere appeal to consensus or tradition.

To understand a moral theory, you must know whether it is a consequentialist theory (one that judges actions, persons, or motives according to their consequences) or a non-consequentialist theory (one that judges actions, persons, or motives by their conformity to moral rules). Egoism and utilitarianism are consequentialist theories, and natural law and the ethics of respect for persons are non-consequentialist theories. We shall use the word *good* as a general term of moral commendation and the word *right* to mean "morally obligatory."

II

ARE MORALS RELATIVE?

For eighteen months Del Monte Corporation tried to buy a 55,000-acre banana plantation in Guatemala, but the government refused to allow the sale. Del Monte officials made inquiries and asked for meetings, but nothing happened. Then they hired a "business consultant" for $500,000. The "consultant" was a wealthy businessman who frequently contributed to political parties in Guatemala.

The businessman feared that disclosure of this relationship with a large U.S. company would diminish his influence in Guatemala and perhaps even provoke left-wing threats against his life. So he demanded and received company assurances of anonymity. To further protect him, Del Monte paid him outside the country. It charged his fee to general and administrative expenses on the books of several Panamanian shipping subsidiaries. His fee was entirely dependent on his ability to get the Guatemalan government to allow the sale of the plantation.

Suddenly the Guatemalan government reversed itself and permitted the sale. Now Del Monte owns the profitable banana plantation, for which it paid $20.5 million, and the "business consultant" is considerably richer.[1]

In many parts of the world, some forms of bribery or payoff are a common and accepted practice. The practice even has names: in Arabian countries it is called "Baksheesh," and in Latin American countries it is called "La Mordida." Everything from large transactions requiring government approval, such as Del Monte's purchase of the plantation, to getting a small-business license or renting an apartment may require it. Many of the government officials who accept the payoffs are poorly paid, and payoffs are a legal and accepted way of augmenting their salary. Yet, in the United States

---

[1]"Del Monte Corp. Finds a Foreign 'Consultant' Can Help a Great Deal," *Wall Street Journal,* July 14, 1975, p. 1.

and in most industrialized countries, such practices are regarded as unethical and are usually illegal.

These examples illustrate how many people, including some of the business managers discussed in Chapter 1, feel about ethics: "Morals are relative." "When in Rome, do as the Romans do." For the Del Monte officials to employ the "business consultant" was entirely proper because business is conducted in this way in Guatemala and morals are always relative to a particular culture. Some relativists even say that morals are relative to a particular class of people.

An important point to keep in mind is the fact that relativists always maintain that moral truth is relative *to* something—a culture, a class, an individual, or a set of principles. The moral relativist does not believe that ethics has no truth but, rather, that it has many truths. Even if no absolute and universal moral truth is objectively the same for everyone, people do make moral judgments that distinguish right from wrong. The relativist believes it is unreasonable to say that people are wrong in making such judgments. Why not say that each individual or each society should find its own moral truth and live by that truth?

In spite of its apparent simplicity and plausibility, moral relativism is a treacherous terrain with many pitfalls. We shall explore some of this terrain by first considering some weak arguments for moral relativism. In doing so, we shall also clarify what the moral relativist believes.

Weak Arguments for Moral Relativism

1. Actions That Are Right for One Person Are Not Always Right for Another Person. Some people try to use the fact that people behave differently as an argument for ethical relativism. Consider the following statement:

She is gay and I am straight, so morals are relative.

Although it may be true that you and she act differently, your situation and hers may have some morally relevant difference. Thus she may find it natural to be attracted to people of her own sex, whereas you do not. You may both agree that people should practice the form of sexuality that most fulfills them, provided it does not harm others. This case carries no disagreement over moral principles, but rather a difference in the sexual orientation of two people.

The statement that different circumstances and conditions sometimes call for different types of behavior is a weak argument for ethical relativism.

One of the essential conditions of any type of moral relativism that should really concern us is that two people must disagree over *moral principles,* not simply over behaviors appropriate to those principles. If you and she disagree over the morality of homosexuality, you have a much more important type of disagreement, which leads us to the second argument.

2. People Disagree over Moral Principles. If your friend and you disagreed over the thesis that people should practice the form of sexuality that most fulfills them, provided it does not harm others, we would have a disagreement over moral principles. She may believe that homosexuality is a morally permissible form of behavior and you may not. The disagreement between Americans and Guatemalans over the propriety of bribery is probably a disagreement over moral principle, although this determination may not be easy to make.

Some of the most dramatic illustrations of disagreement over moral principles are found in the study of other cultures. Attitudes of various cultures toward the suffering of animals reflect a basic disagreement in moral principles. In Latin America a chicken is plucked alive with the thought that it will taste more succulent. The Hopi Indians do not object in the least to their children's "playing" with a bird by tying a string to its legs, even though this "play" often results in broken legs, wings being pulled off, and usually the death of the animal. As one Hopi put it, "Sometimes they get tired and die."[2] We can cite many other examples of apparent disagreement over moral principles: The Romans approved of infanticide, whereas we do not. People exhibit vast differences in attitudes toward adultery, premarital sex, property ownership, violence, the expression of hostility, and many other issues.

But the mere fact of disagreement over moral principles does not prove the truth of moral relativism. First, closer examination often shows that many apparent disagreements in moral principle are actually disagreements over facts. A culture's routine killing of parents before the onset of senility may be due to a belief that a person spends the afterlife in the condition in which he or she dies; this misconception leads them to end their parents' lives for what they believe to be a good cause. Many Guatemalans probably believe that their way of doing business is more sociable and more in agreement with their temperament than the mechanical, impersonal American way.

Nevertheless—and this second point is the more critical one to be made against the argument for moral relativism—it may be that one side in the disagreement is simply wrong. The Hopi children may be engaging

---

[2]Richard Brandt, *Ethical Theory* (Englewood Cliffs, N.J.: Prentice-Hall, 1959), p. 103.

in morally unjustifiable conduct in their "play" with birds. The Guatemalans' business method may represent a type of moral corruption that actually hinders their society. In any case, the mere presence of moral disagreement does not demonstrate the truth of moral relativism any more than disagreement over facts demonstrates that relativism applies to factual beliefs. If I believe there is life on Mars and you believe there isn't, we cannot say that my belief is true for me and your belief is true for you. One of us is mistaken.

3. Individuals Are Sometimes Equally Justified in Making Conflicting Moral Judgments. This argument is closer to being a significant argument in favor of moral relativism. However, the situation in which people have equally good reasons for holding conflicting beliefs is not unique to ethics. Scientist A may hold one hypothesis about the origin of a disease, and Scientist B may hold a different and incompatible hypothesis. Both scientists may have equally good evidence for their views, but we cannot conclude that Scientist A's hypothesis is true for him and Scientist B's hypothesis is true for her. Instead we say that the evidence is inconclusive, because we know that at least one of the hypotheses is incorrect. The same thing could be true in ethics. When people have equally good reasons for holding different ethical beliefs, at least one of them may be wrong.

This argument serves to clarify the nature of moral relativism and to suggest another argument in its favor. The essential claim of *moral relativism* is that different ethical principles are correct for different people.[3] This claim suggests a stronger argument in favor of moral relativism than any presented thus far—namely, an argument from moral scepticism. The essential claim of *moral scepticism* is that we cannot know that any ethical principles are correct. Moral scepticism does not prove the truth of moral relativism; the fact (if it is a fact) that we cannot know which ethical principles are correct does not immediately lead to the conclusion that different ethical principles are correct for different people. The moral sceptic might just hold to her scepticism and maintain that morality has no truth at all, or at least that we cannot know the truth if there is any to know. However, the relativist is impressed with the fact that people believe their own moral principles to be correct. If we combine the fact that people do believe their own moral principles are correct with a belief that we cannot know which ones are correct (moral scepticism), we can plausibly conclude that different ethical principles are correct for different people (moral relativism). Therefore we must look at the arguments for moral scepticism.

---

[3]See J. W. Cornman, Keith Lehrer, and George Pappas, *Philosophical Problems and Arguments: An Introduction,* 3rd ed. (New York: Macmillan, 1982), p. 270, for a similar definition.

Arguments for Moral Scepticism

The moral sceptic has no easy and direct way to prove her case. Because the claim is that moral principles cannot be proved to be correct, the sceptic would have to refute every possible attempt to prove the correctness of a set of moral principles and then show that she had canvassed all of the possibilities. Neither can be proved, so we must be content with an incomplete argument that at most suggests the truth of moral scepticism. We shall consider sceptical arguments against two of the most common attempts to justify moral principles—namely, the appeal to religious authority and the appeal to moral intuitions about what is right. Then we shall consider a more general argument in favor of moral scepticism. If these arguments are valid, the moral sceptic will have made a good start toward establishing her case.

1. Religion Cannot Give a Satisfactory Foundation to Ethics. The view that morality is in some sense based on religious authority is a persistent theme in the history of philosophy and is shared by many nonphilosophers as well. In a psychological or motivational sense, morality is based on religion when people's faith is what *causes* them to be moral. Religion can give either a positive or a negative motivation to morality. As positive motivation, the hope of eternal reward, the influence of fellow believers, the love of God, and the examples of great religious figures can lead to morally praiseworthy action. As negative motivation, the fear of punishment, guilt, and the disapproval of one's fellow believers can be powerful deterrents to certain types of behavior. The use of religious motivation to produce ethical conduct is an important influence in the lives of many people. But, although the presence of these religiously induced emotions may causally explain why some people behave ethically, it does not give good reasons for the validity of moral principles. Fear and hope, for example, can often lead to immoral behavior.

To find these reasons we must turn to the logical sense in which religion can provide a foundation for moral beliefs. Here the argument is that what distinguishes right from wrong—what gives "objectivity" to moral judgments—is the relationship of moral judgments to a religious origin. But what precisely is this relationship? This issue is raised in one of the early dialogues of Plato, the *Euthyphro,* when Socrates asks a question that can be paraphrased as: Is something good because God loves it or does God love it because it is already good? Socrates presents the two major positions that can be taken on the relationship of moral principles to divine authority. The moral sceptic believes that neither option provides a sound basis for maintaining that divine authority can provide a foundation for moral beliefs. Let us consider how the moral sceptic would make such an argument.

The first alternative presented by Socrates' question is that something is good behavior because God loves it; that is, God's love or approval of a type of behavior is what *makes* it good. Or, to rephrase, something is right because God commands it; God's command to do something is the reason the action is right. The moral sceptic can make a number of arguments against this alternative.

First, many philosophers believe that, if we derive our moral beliefs from divine commands, we give up moral autonomy or independence. We base our morality on superior power rather than moral conviction. Acting as a genuine moral agent involves being self-directed; a person behaves in a certain way because he or she *sees* that the way is right. Subservience to divine commands requires replacing autonomy with mere obedience, which is morally wrong.[4]

Second, the view that God's approval is what makes something right can also be socially dangerous. If a person's actions are governed by divine decree, God could command his followers to do anything and they would have no recourse but to obey. What, then, if God commands that innocent children be tortured or that "the enemies of God" be put to death? The refusal to adhere to commonly accepted moral precepts in the face of supposed divine commands to the contrary could produce social chaos.

Third, the idea that something is good because God loves it seems incompatible with the language that religious believers themselves often use, such as "Praise the Lord, for He is Good." If whatever God commands is good, then presumably whatever He does is also good, since God would not act against his own commands. So praising God for his goodness is simply praising Him for being obedient to his own commands, which are by definition good. This reasoning is almost as silly as praising the standard meter stick for being one meter long! This objection suggests that at least the word *good* does not mean the same thing as "being in accord with God's commands."

Fourth, the philosopher Peter Geach has argued that it is impossible for our knowledge of all moral precepts to depend on divine commands.[5] If lying is not intrinsically wrong (that is, wrong in and of itself, apart from God's command not to lie), we have no reason to accept God's commands

---

[4]This argument has been challenged recently. See Philip Quinn, *Divine Commands and Moral Requirements* (Oxford: Clarendon Press, 1978), Chapter 1.

[5]Peter Geach, *God and the Soul* (New York: Schocken Books, 1969), pp. 110–120.

as true, for God could be lying to us about what he actually commands. Evidently some things (such as lying) must be wrong independently of God's commands, and if some things are, why not all of them?

Those who believe that God's approval makes something right or good can respond to these criticisms, some of which are philosophically more important than others. But, taken together, the criticisms are strong enough to cause one to seriously question the view that moral principles should be based on divine commands. Many religious thinkers have also rejected this position. The Jewish scholars who wrote the Talmud did not take divine commands as the reason for action; if God commanded them to steal and murder, they would not be obligated to do so. By their nature, humans know what is right and wrong, and revelation is needed only in order to avoid all uncertainty over the application of moral precepts. Similarly, Moses Maimonides and other medieval Jewish thinkers refused to identify the good with the will of God.[6] The Catholic tradition generally takes a similar, though more qualified, stand. According to St. Thomas Aquinas, "to say that morality is determined simply by God's will is to suggest that God's will may sometimes not follow order and wisdom; and that would be blasphemous."[7]

We are forced, then, to view Socrates' other option—namely, that God loves or approves of something because it is already good. According to this option, the source of moral truth is independent of the arbitrary decrees of God. Aquinas suggested that morality is based primarily on God's "wisdom" rather than on His arbitrary will; that is, moral principles are somehow contained in God's intellect, but He did not arbitrarily determine them and cannot arbitrarily change them. Moral principles thus have an existence and validity that is in some way independent of God. You might wonder how a person who believes this alternative can argue that morality is based on religion at all, if in fact God does not decide what is right or wrong. But those who maintain this position can still say that religious revelation is the best source of moral knowledge. If God communicates to human beings what is right and wrong, this communication may still be our best source of moral knowledge, even though it is not based on the decrees of God. Surely God has a better way of knowing moral truth than men, and men may not have any reliable method at all. However, the sceptic can make objections to this position too.

---

[6]See Louis Jacobs, "The Relationship between Religion and Ethics in Jewish Thought," in *Religion and Morality,* ed. Gene Outka and John P. Reeder, Jr. (New York: Anchor Books, 1973), pp. 155–172.

[7]Thomas Aquinas, *De Veritate,* 23.6. Quoted in Eric D'Arcy, "Worthy of Worship: A Catholic Contribution," in Outka and Reeder, p. 191.

First, we still have the problem of determining how God communicates moral knowledge to man. Do we look to the Bible, the Koran, or some other religious document? After we decide on a source of revelation for moral truth, how do we decide on its proper interpretation? The religions of the world differ significantly on moral issues, such as the justifications of violence or the proper treatment of animals. Even within Judaism and Christianity, important moral disagreements exist. Consider how religious authorities in our own country disagree over the morality of such issues as war, abortion, sterilization, and birth control. If religious authorities cannot agree on what God's "wisdom" says, how can they expect us to have any confidence in religion as a basis for our moral beliefs?

Second, both alternatives have the initial assumption that belief in God is rational. The sceptic will quickly point out that judging the validity of religion as a basis for morality depends on first giving a satisfactory answer as to the validity of religious belief itself. The sceptic will argue that the so-called proofs for the existence of God have difficulties and perhaps even say that we have no good reason to believe in God at all, much less base our moral beliefs on this foundation. Furthermore, the evil and suffering in the world provide a serious challenge to the belief that an all-good, all-knowing, and all-powerful God exists. Is it possible to reconcile the belief in such a God with sickness that takes the life of a young child or natural disasters that decimate whole populations? Perhaps we should look at another attempt to give a foundation for belief in the objectivity of moral principles.

2. Intuition Cannot Give a Satisfactory Foundation for Ethics.
People may also attempt to justify moral beliefs by an appeal to moral intuitions. Intuition is a faculty by which people can supposedly directly know moral truth, but intuitionists disagree over the nature of this faculty. Some have maintained that intuitions are feelings or "sentiments": A virtuous action produces in us a feeling of pleasure, and a vicious action produces a feeling of pain or uneasiness. Of course, these feelings of pleasure or pain are distinctive; namely, they are detached and not related to self-interest or personal gain. However, other intuitionists have held that moral intuitions are more like rational knowledge than like sensations and that what we perceive through moral intuition is a certain "fitness" that the right actions have; certain actions seem to be the "right" course to take in the circumstances. But the moral sceptic can point out specific difficulties with the appeal to intuition that are difficult to answer.

First, intuitionists cannot propose any procedure for choosing between competing moral principles when both claim to be based on intuition. Suppose I say that taking innocent lives is always wrong, and you say that sacrificing an innocent person might be justified to avoid some great evil. For example, if an evil tyrant were to threaten our nation with nuclear destruction unless one of his enemies (who had actually done no wrong) were handed over to him, you would say we should give in to his demand, whereas I would say that giving in to his demand is immoral, even if the consequence is nuclear destruction. Now, if we both defend our claims by an appeal to moral intuition, how can we determine who is right? We might introspectively examine our intuitions, and each of us might then report that our claim is right. Then what would we do? Moral intuitionism seems not to provide what we seek—namely, a method for objectively determining right and wrong.

Second, some forms of intuitionism seem to misinterpret the relationship of moral properties to nonmoral properties. Ordinarily we say that a person is good (or bad) *because* he or she has certain characteristics. For example, I say Mrs. Jones is a good person because I believe she is kind to those in distress, she devotes herself to the care of her children, she is tolerant of those with differing views, and so on. If she did not have these characteristics, or some other characteristics that I consider good, I would not call her a good person. But some moral intuitionists view quite differently the process of ascribing goodness to a person or to an action. They believe that our moral intuition enables us to intuit directly that a person is good *without any knowledge of his or her characteristics.* This belief has the strange consequence that, if we consider two people who have exactly the same characteristics, we might intuit that one person is good and the other is not. Mrs. Brown could be kind to those in distress, devote herself to the care of her children, and be tolerant of those with differing views. Yet, if we did not intuit the goodness of Mrs. Brown apart from these qualities, we could not call her good, despite the fact that she has the same qualities as Mrs. Jones, whom we call good. This peculiar result of any form of intuitionism that holds we can intuit the goodness or badness of people or actions independently of their observable characteristics has led many moral philosophers to reject intuitionism.

3. The "Infinite Regress" Argument. Let us briefly consider a third, more general argument for moral scepticism. If we examine the methods of two different ethical standpoints for determining what is right or wrong, we will find that "valid" or "good" reasons for a moral judgment are defined in different ways. For example, the person who argues that the taking of innocent lives is always wrong, regardless of the consequences, may define as "good" reasons in moral argument those reasons that appeal to moral principles, such as those having to do with respect for the person. Those who argue that sacrificing an innocent person might be justified to avoid some great evil will probably define as "good" reasons in moral argument those reasons that appeal to the greatest overall human well-being or utility.

The sceptic maintains that, in order to determine which of these two methods of deciding moral truth is correct, we must have a neutral third method. This method would enable us to give reasons for accepting one of the first two methods and rejecting the other. But such a third method would only offer its own criteria of "valid" reasons, perhaps in contrast to a fourth method that would offer a different set of evaluational criteria. We would then need a fifth method for determining whether the third or the fourth method is correct. Since we cannot endlessly seek methods to justify other methods, we eventually make an arbitrary and unjustified decision to accept one method and reject all others. But no genuine claim to moral knowledge can rest on an arbitrary decision, so we have no way to determine which method to use in deciding whether innocent lives can justifiably be taken and no way to judge any other conflict of moral principles.[8]

We can respond to this argument, as well as to the arguments against religion and intuition, as a basis for morality. Even if we do not have conclusive responses to these arguments at the present time, we might have them in the future. Nevertheless we must admit that the moral sceptic has made an impressive argument for her position. Do we have any reasons to doubt the truth of moral scepticism? Yes, we have reasons, especially to doubt moral scepticism in some of its more radical forms.

Doubts about Radical Moral Scepticism: A Middle Way?

Many moral sceptics believe they can explain why the attempt to validate a given set of moral principles has been fruitless: Ethical judgments are nothing more than expressions of feelings or attitudes.[9] If this account of moral judgments is proper, it is no wonder that rational arguments about them are inconclusive. In the strict sense, rational argument about them is impossible. You cannot argue about why you do or do not like oysters: Either you do or you don't. Admittedly, we do give "reasons" of a sort for why people should have negative feelings toward murder or theft, for example. But

---

[8]See Paul W. Taylor, *Principles of Ethics* (Encino, Calif.: Dickenson, 1975), pp. 25–26.

[9]See, for example, C. L. Stevenson, *Ethics and Language* (New Haven, Conn.: Yale University Press, 1944).

some radical moral sceptics believe these reasons are nothing more than attempts to sway people's emotions, as when a mother scolds her child by saying "Aren't you ashamed of yourself for stealing those cookies!" When I say "Stealing is wrong," I am expressing my negative feelings toward stealing.

The radical moral sceptic also believes that we can argue over the facts involved in moral debates. If we are considering the morality of smoking marijuana and we have a negative feeling about fatal car accidents, we may want to argue over the issue of whether marijuana causes fatal accidents. In a factual argument, it is appropriate to cite statistics, consider the relevant medical evidence, and use any other relevant facts. But these factual arguments are relevant only because we have a negative feeling about fatal car accidents.

This interpretation of the nature of moral judgments—that they are expressions of feelings or personal tastes—provides a basis for understanding the true nature of the appeal to intuitions and the commands of God. In consulting our "intuitions," we are really consulting our emotions. When we say our intuition tells us that something is wrong, we are merely expressing our feelings about the issue. Similarly, when we say that God commands us to act in a loving way toward others, we are expressing our positive feeling about loving behavior.

We do, however, have reason to believe that the radical moral sceptic's account of morality is incorrect. Feelings or tastes on the one hand and moral judgments on the other are clearly distinguished, because our feelings toward an issue can vary independently of our ethical judgment. Consider the following illustration.[10] Jane is ready to go to college, but her mother wants to purchase a new house with most of the money the family has saved for Jane's education. Jane's mother says to Jane's father:

> I know we ought to save our money for Jane's education, but I want that new house while you and I are still young enough to enjoy it. So let's take at least three-fourths of the money we have saved and make a down payment on a house in Memorial Forest.

Jane might agree with her mother ethically but have a negative attitude toward the idea of buying the house:

> I agree that you ought to save the money for my education, so please save it rather than spending it on the house in Memorial Forest.

---

[10]This argument is adapted from Kurt Baier, "Fact, Value, and Norm in Stevenson's Ethics," *Nous,* 1 (May, 1967), pp. 139–160.

Or Jane might agree with her mother both ethically and in attitude:

> Although I cannot honestly deny that you have an obligation to save the money for my education, I want you and Dad to have the new house while you are still young enough to enjoy it.

Or, finally, Jane might disagree with her mother both ethically and in attitude:

> I don't believe for a moment that it would be wrong to use the money to buy a new house. After all, you and Dad have worked hard all your lives, and I am old enough to take care of myself. But I still wish you would keep the money for my education.

Jane's feelings about the proper use of her parents' savings can be different from her moral beliefs. Not surprisingly, therefore, most moral philosophers have rejected the radical moral sceptic's account of morality as nothing more than an expression of feeling, in which rational arguments have no place. When we say that Hitler was an evil man, most of us think we are expressing more than personal tastes, such as when we say "I don't like oysters." Furthermore, ethical argument is more than just trying to manipulate people's feelings, for we recognize certain standards in determining what counts as a legitimate reason in an ethical argument. Jane believed that it would not be wrong for her parents to use most of their money for a new house because she felt she was old enough to take care of herself. If she had given as her reason the fact that she was not a pretty girl, we would be puzzled. We would have a hard time understanding how this consideration would count as a reason that is relevant to her parent's belief about the morally proper use of their money.

What, then, can we say about the question of the relativity of morals? Are morals relative? Most moral philosophers today would probably be uncomfortable with a simple yes or no answer to this question. The arguments we have just given do not prove that moral scepticism is false, although they do cast doubt on the more radical versions of moral scepticism. Insofar as moral scepticism is the strongest basis for moral relativism, the arguments also give some reason to question moral relativism. However, they by no means prove the usual alternative to moral scepticism and relativism—namely, more absolutism. *Moral absolutism* is the view that a single, objectively valid set of moral principles applies to everyone. A great deal of uncharted territory lies between the extremes of absolutism on the one side and complete relativism and scepticism on the other, and we do not yet have the necessary tools for charting this territory. Supplying some of these tools will be the primary function of the next chapter.

CONCEPT SUMMARY

Moral relativism, a pervasive belief in our society, is the view that different ethical principles are correct for different people. Relativists do not deny that moral truth exists, but they believe that moral truth is relative to a culture, class, individual, or set of principles. Several unconvincing arguments for moral relativism are proposed: Actions that are right for one person are not always right for another person; people disagree over moral principles; different people are sometimes equally justified in making conflicting moral judgments.

A more persuasive argument for moral relativism is based on moral scepticism, which is the view that we cannot know that any ethical principles are correct. The moral sceptic can make a persuasive argument that the appeal to religious authority and to moral intuition is not a good foundation for moral principles. The sceptic can also give an "infinite regress" argument for her position. These arguments do not prove that a foundation for moral principles cannot be provided, but they suggest that the moral sceptic may be on the right track.

However, we have reason to believe that the more radical versions of moral scepticism are also incorrect. Many radical moral sceptics say that moral judgments are nothing more than the expression of feelings, but we can show that our feelings toward an issue can vary independently of our ethical judgment. Furthermore, reasons have more place in ethical discussion than the radical sceptic is prepared to admit, which suggests that the truth lies between radical relativism and scepticism on the one hand and moral absolutism on the other hand.

III

THE STRUCTURE AND EVALUATION
OF MORAL THEORIES

Socrates has as much right as anyone to be called the patron saint of philosophy. Few people have represented the ideal of philosophy more forcefully or eloquently, either in their words or in their lives. His conception of the nature and function of philosophy was closely connected with his personal "mission" in life: to coax and cajole the people of Athens into examining their values and beliefs. Socrates would engage individuals in conversation and get them to state their beliefs on some topic. Then he would examine these beliefs, pointing up difficulties and often leading people to reformulate their beliefs or perhaps abandon them altogether. Socrates described the dialogue in this manner:

> I shall question him and cross-examine him and test him. If I think that he has not attained excellence, though he says that he has, I shall reproach him for undervaluing the most valuable things, and overvaluing those that are less valuable. This I shall do to everyone whom I meet, young or old, citizen or stranger, but especially to citizens, since they are most closely related to me.[1]

A little later Socrates gives what might be considered the theme of his philosophical mission: "An unexamined life is not worth living."[2]

Socrates tried to teach people to engage in critical reflection on their beliefs and values. *Critical reflection* involves attempting to give reasons for one's beliefs and values, examining those reasons, and being willing to modify or even abandon convictions that do not withstand rational scrutiny. This task is often very difficult and painful, as Socrates knew all too well. Sometimes those to whom he was talking would simply decide they had

---

[1]Plato, *The Apology,* 29–30.
[2]Plato, *The Apology,* 38.

something better to do than listen to him. At other times they would become angry at having been shown in public to have beliefs that were not well-founded. Many people also felt that Socrates was undermining the morals of the state by coaxing people to question their most fundamental beliefs, and he was finally put to death on a charge of "corrupting the youth." Nevertheless, the kind of critical reflection that Socrates sought to stimulate is the very center of the philosophical enterprise, and it is an essential task for anyone who wants to claim that his or her beliefs are rationally justified.

Critical reflection on moral principles is the only way to determine whether moral scepticism and moral relativism have any truth. It is also the only way to determine which moral principles you want to use in making moral decisions in your own life. So critical reflection has a usefulness quite independent of the question of moral scepticism and relativism. It is an essential component of being a morally responsible person. In this chapter we shall consider some conceptual tools you can use in critically reflecting on your moral principles. The first set of tools is a group of concepts that will help you set up a moral theory. A *moral theory,* which can also be called a *moral philosophy,* is a systematic ordering of moral principles. The second set of tools is a series of criteria for judging the adequacy of a moral theory.

The Three Levels of a Moral Theory

How does a person engage in critical reflection about moral principles? By its very nature, critical reflection about ethical principles is systematic. In justifying one moral claim, you will find yourself appealing to other moral claims and then to still other moral claims, so that in principle you might be forced to reveal your most basic moral commitments in justifying a single ethical claim. Let us consider a simple illustration. Suppose I make the statement

"Capital punishment is wrong."

In attempting to justify this moral statement, I make the following factual claim:

"Capital punishment is discriminatory. That is, if you are condemned to death, you are more likely to be executed if you are poor or are a member of a racial or ethnic minority group."

We have already seen that moral claims cannot be derived from facts alone; so, in order to justify the original moral claim, I must add another moral claim:

"Discriminatory actions are wrong."

But where does this moral claim come from? I might justify it by saying:

"I would not want to be discriminated against in this way if I were condemned to death. I would at least want fair treatment."

But even this claim does not justify my judgment that discrimination is wrong without still another moral claim:

"In order for a principle of action to be right, I must be willing to have the same principle applied to me in similar circumstances."

If you asked me why I believed this claim, I might say that this reasoning is just a basic belief I have about how one determines what is right and what is wrong. So an attempt to defend my beliefs about capital punishment has led me back through increasingly general principles to one of my ultimate moral commitments.

This order of reasoning from moral judgments, through more general moral principles, and finally to a basic moral principle, gives the outline of any moral theory. A moral theory has three levels: The level that you eventually arrive at when you trace your moral convictions back to your most basic moral principles is the moral standard. The intermediate moral principles are moral rules. The moral statement that begins the discussion is a moral judgment. We shall discuss each of these levels, beginning with the moral standard.

The First Level: The Moral Standard.

A *moral standard* is the basic moral principle—the principle that provides the criterion for determining right and wrong for a theory. In the example, since we were reasoning from the moral judgment back to basic principles, the moral standard was the last moral principle stated: "In order for a principle of action to be right, I must be willing to have the same principle applied to me in similar circumstances." In order to have uniformity in the statement of the moral standard (MS), each moral standard will begin with the wording "Those actions are right that . . ." or with some closely analogous formula. (The statement of the egoistic standard will begin slightly differently.) The rest of the statement will supply the criterion that right actions must satisfy. The moral standard of the first moral philosophy we consider, ethical egoism, is:

> MS: Actions are right if and only if they produce consequences that are at least as good for the self-interest of the egoist as the consequences of any alternative action.

Each moral standard has certain terms that must be defined before the standard can be applied. In the egoistic moral standard, the crucial term is *self-interest*. Without clarification of this concept, the moral standard is useless. I cannot know which actions to pursue and which to avoid if I do not know what my self-interest is.

Often additional distinctions and definitions must be given before a moral standard can be used. The egoist, for example, must distinguish between long-term and short-term self-interest and then decide which goal he will pursue. The utilitarian must distinguish between rule utilitarianism and act utilitarianism and determine which kind of utilitarianism he wants to pursue. The natural-law theorist must define the principles of "double effect" before the ethics of natural law can be applied.

The Second Level: Moral Rules. The second or intermediate level consists of general moral principles derived from the moral standard. These moral principles could justify many particular moral judgments. They apply to a wider area of conduct than moral judgments, but not to as wide an area as the moral standard. We shall call these intermediate moral principles moral rules. A *moral rule* (MR) delineates a class of actions that is right or wrong based on the criterion stated in the moral standard. The moral rule in the example was

> MR: Discriminatory actions are wrong.

Using his moral standard, the egoist may derive moral rules that denote kinds of goals he should pursue in order to achieve his self-interest. One such rule might be

> MR: I should enhance and preserve my physical health.

Physical health is a necessary prerequisite to achieving one's self-interest.

A moral theory has many moral rules, whereas it ordinarily has only one moral standard. A useful first step with moral rules is to divide them into rules for personal ethics and rules for social ethics. *Personal ethics* has to do with the relationship of individuals to other individuals. *Social ethics* has to do with the relationship of individuals to groups and of groups to other groups. Personal ethics can be further subdivided into *duties to self* and *duties to others.*

Regarding duties to oneself, the question to be asked is: What character traits and personal goals contribute most to the realization of the ideal set forth in the moral standard? An egoist may find, for example, that he needs to develop his capacity to look at things rationally and calmly in order to determine what will lead to his own self-interest. So the obligation to develop the character trait of rationality follows from the egoistic moral standard. An advocate of natural law may find that she has an obligation to preserve and enhance her own physical health in order to better realize the natural tendency that she and every other living organism has toward self-preservation.

Duties may be negative as well as positive. As an egoist I have a duty not to destroy my own health or to sacrifice myself to the welfare of others. Traditional natural-law theorists believe I have a duty to myself not to commit suicide and not to practice forms of contraception that violate my procreative function.

Some of the most important duties to others are negative. Most moral theories, for example, imply that in general we have duties not to lie to another person and not to perpetrate theft, fraud, or physical violence on them. Besides the duty not to harm others, however, some moral theories may imply the positive duties of preventing harm to others and even of doing good to others. Finally, family and sexual ethics are an important subcategory of duties to others.

Many important moral issues that all of us face as citizens fall into the category of social ethics rather than personal ethics. It is important, therefore, for any morally sophisticated person to work out ideas—consistent, of course, with his or her general moral philosophy—concerning the proper relationship of societies to one another and to individuals. The most general question to be answered is: What kind of social order is best suited to the realization of the goals set out in your moral philosophy? We can take two broadly differing approaches to answer this question.

One approach, represented in its extreme form by libertarianism, advocates what one libertarian calls the "minimal state"; that is, the state should limit its functions to protecting citizens from violence, theft, and fraud and providing some mechanism for arbitrating disputes among citizens. Otherwise individuals should be left alone to pursue their own goals with a minimum of governmental interference. For the most part, the egoistic tradition is sympathetic to the libertarian way of answering questions about social policy.

The other approach advocates a more active role for the state, one in which the state has a positive responsibility to promote the welfare of individuals or to promote some larger societal goals. Utilitarians for the most part have held that the state should take an active role in implementing policies that lead to the general welfare of the public.

The Third Level: Moral Judgments.

Moral judgments are moral evaluations of individual people or actions, or at least of more specific classes of actions or people than those treated in moral rules. In the earlier example the moral judgment was "Capital punishment is wrong." A moral judgment can also apply to an individual action or person, as in "The execution of James Robertson was wrong" or "James Robertson was a really evil person." Sometimes we cannot easily decide whether a statement is a moral rule or a moral judgment. For example, the statement "Discriminatory actions are wrong" might be considered to be a moral rule in some contexts and a moral judgment in others, depending on whether it is the conclusion of a chain of moral reasoning. As long as a moral statement is the last statement made in a chain of reasoning and makes an evaluation of a specific class of actions or people or of an individual action or person, we shall call it a moral judgment.

Three types of moral judgment can be made about an action, and a fourth type is sometimes relevant. Some judgments designate actions that are *morally obligatory*—that is, actions that are right to do and wrong not to do. If the alternative to the action violates the moral standard, the action itself is morally obligatory: we cannot be morally justified in refraining from performing the action. In most moral theories the judgment that parents ought to care for their children designates an obligatory action, because the alternative to the action (that parents ought not to care for their children) violates the moral standard. If you are an egoist, it is morally obligatory for you to protect your property from theft, because the alternative to the action (failing to protect your property from theft) violates your self-interest.

Other judgments designate *forbidden* or *morally impermissible* actions—those that are wrong to do and right not to do. Actions that violate the moral standard fall into this category. A valid example for most moral philosophies is the judgment that the commission of murder is morally impermissible, because this action violates most moral standards. For advocates of traditional natural-law moral philosophy, the decision to use "artificial" forms of contraception is morally impermissible because such use is contrary to the value of procreation.

Third are judgments that are *morally permissible*. We might also refer to morally permissible actions as morally neutral actions, because they do not themselves violate the moral standard, nor do the alternative actions violate the moral standard. Because morally obligatory actions are also permissible, we might refer to this class of actions as merely permissible actions. However, for convenience we shall call them morally permissible actions.

Permissible actions can be trivial or nontrivial. *Nontrivial* permissible actions are those that have important consequences, whereas *trivial* permissible actions are those that have relatively unimportant consequences. The decision to undergo a risky operation that might prolong your life a few more months and the decision to refuse the operation and die a few months sooner may in some cases be equally permissible by your moral philosophy. For example, as an egoist, you might conclude that the advantages of living a little longer would be equally balanced by the pain you would suffer even after the operation. If you had no other relevant considerations, both the decision to have the operation and the decision not to have it would be nontrivially morally permissible. On the other hand, the decision to wear blue jeans rather than dress slacks would in many cases be trivially morally permissible.

The final type of judgment is not usually as important as the other three, but it is essential in understanding the moral status of some actions. Sometimes moral philosophers designate an action as *supererogatory*— that is, "above and beyond the call of duty." Supererogatory acts can be acts of either omission or commission. Supererogatory acts of omission are actions that are good not to do but that are morally permissible to do. When a businessman refrains from demanding immediate and total payment of bills from a company in financial distress, he is doing something morally praiseworthy. However, it is still morally permissible for him to demand payment of a rightful debt. The decision not to demand immediate payment would be a supererogatory act of omission.

Supererogatory acts of commission are actions that are good to do but that are morally permissible not to do. It can be argued, for example, that a corporation is not morally obligated to perform such meritorious actions as contributing to the arts or helping solve the problems of inner-city unemployment and urban blight. For a corporation to perform these kinds of actions would be supererogatory. Others believe corporations have a moral obligation to do these kinds of things. Therefore the question of whether these kinds of actions on the part of corporations are obligatory or supererogatory is often morally significant.

Acts of supererogation are commonly thought to be the actions of saints and heroes. However, some acts of kindness and generosity, although they are more than what duty requires and hence are supererogatory in the strict sense, are certainly not the actions we associate with saints and heroes. Contributing small change to the Home for Little Wanderers may not be a duty, but neither is it saintly or heroic. Giving one's life in the line of duty may be heroic and yet not supererogatory. So we need to distinguish between trivial and nontrivial supererogatory actions. *Nontrivial super-erogatory* actions go beyond what is morally required and also involve the elements of risk and self-scarifice. *Trivial supererogatory* actions do not involve the elements of risk and self sacrifice. When an engineer risks his career to expose corruption or bad engineering in a public project in which he is not directly involved, he may not be doing something he has a positive duty to do, especially if the problems do not pose a serious threat to life. But he is certainly engaging in a nontrivial supererogatory act. Similarly, a lawyer who risks his professional career and perhaps his life by exposing and prosecuting gangsters engages in action that is risky, highly meritorious, and yet not morally required. It is, then, a nontrivial supererogatory action.

The following is an outline of the elements of a moral theory:

I. Moral standard
   A. Definitions of crucial terms
   B. Other relevant distinctions and principles

II. Moral rules
   A. Personal ethics
      1. Duties to self
      2. Duties to others
   B. Social ethics

III. Moral judgments
   A. Is the action morally obligatory?
   B. Is the action morally permissible?
   C. Is the action morally impermissible?
   D. Is the action supererogatory?

I will follow this outline in presenting the four moral theories we shall be considering—namely, the ethics of self-interest, the ethics of natural law, the ethics of utilitarianism, and the ethics of respect for persons. The only modification will be in the third section of the outline. Because moral judgments can be made only about particular cases, we shall discuss specific cases to which the moral theory will be applied. We will ask whether actions are obligatory, permissible, or impermissible, but we will not consider the category of supererogatory actions, unless it is directly relevant. I will furnish a "checklist" that will help you apply the moral theory to specific cases, and I will follow this checklist in discussing the cases presented. This organization should enable you to apply the theory to other moral problems as they arise in class or in your own experience.

Four Criteria for Evaluating a Moral Theory

Having looked at the structure of a moral theory, you are now ready to consider the second set of tools necessary to evaluate your moral beliefs—namely, criteria for evaluating a moral theory. Moral philosophers do not have an agreed-upon set of standards for judging a moral theory. However, consistency is a generally accepted standard for evaluating any theory, so it seems appropriate to apply it to a moral theory as well. The other three criteria we shall employ seem especially appropriate for a moral theory. They are: agreement with your prior moral beliefs, usefulness in resolving moral dilemmas, and the adequacy of the justification of the moral standard.

Criterion 1: Consistency. Is The Theory Consistent? We can usually agree that any rationally acceptable theory should be *consistent;* that is, the statements in the theory should not contradict one another. A scientific theory that is inconsistent would be seriously questioned or even discarded before experimental testing. If a theory regarding the origin of a disease holds both that the disease is caused by a bacterium and that it is caused by a virus, a scientist would probably not even go to the trouble of testing the theory experimentally. In fact, the theory would be difficult to test, because so many different results would be compatible with it.

An ethical theory can be inconsistent in several different ways. Egoism, for example, is often criticized for having an internal inconsistency within the moral standard itself. On the one hand, the moral standard directs us to do what leads to our own self-interest. On the other hand, it implies that we should be willing for others to be egoists also. Since others' pursuit of their own self-interest may conflict with ours, it would seem that we should not want others to be egoists and, in fact, should actively discourage others from pursuing their own self-interest. Many critics of egoism view this topic as an internal inconsistency within egoism.

Critics of natural-law morality argue that a conflict exists between two principles used to implement the moral standard—the *principle of forfeiture* and the *principle of double effect.* This inconsistency is not within the moral standard itself, but in the two principles used to apply the standard. I can fully explain this alleged conflict only after we have discussed natural-law theory.[3] But perhaps it is sufficient to say that the presumed conflict is between the teaching that human life can never be taken directly and the

[3]See pp. 73–75.

teaching that human life can be taken directly when the person has forfeited his or her innocence.

We cannot say that an inconsistency within moral theory means it should be abandoned altogether. Perhaps no moral theory is fully consistent and perhaps it is impossible for humans to hold to a single moral theory consistently. But the concept of consistency is an integral part of the concept of rationality itself, and thus we must regard an internal inconsistency as a significant weakness in a moral theory.

Criterion 2: Plausibility. Does the Moral Theory Produce Moral Judgments That Agree with Our Prior Moral Beliefs?

One way to evaluate a moral theory is to work out its implications for particular moral issues and then compare these implications with our most strongly held moral beliefs. For example, consider a moral theory such as natural law, which holds that it is always wrong to take innocent human life directly. This principle implies that administering an injection to end the life of a dying cancer patient who requests to be put out of his misery is immoral. But you may believe that such an action is not immoral and is in fact an act of mercy. If so, a conflict exists between natural-law moral theory and your own prior moral beliefs.

In the face of such a conflict, you have four options: you can (1) give up your belief that mercy killing is sometimes morally permissible, (2) reject natural-law moral theory altogether, (3) try to show that natural-law moral theory does not really condemn mercy killing, or (4) admit that in this instance your moral theory and your moral beliefs conflict. If you are strongly committed to natural-law moral theory—perhaps because you are a conservative Roman Catholic—you may choose the first option or one of the last two. If you have strong reasons to question natural-law moral theory, you may choose the second option.

Keep in mind that agreement with your prior moral beliefs is not an absolute test of a theory's validity. If a moral theory conflicts with your prior moral beliefs, it may be your moral beliefs that are wrong rather than the theory. But a conflict of this nature should at least alert you that something is wrong.

Criterion 3: Usefulness. Is the Theory Useful in Resolving Moral Dilemmas?

Moral theories are of little practical use if they cannot help us resolve moral conflicts, either within our own thinking or between us and others. A moral theory can fail to help us achieve this goal in at least three ways.

First, the crucial terms in a moral theory can be so ambiguous that the implications of the theory for practical moral questions are also unclear. The definition of *natural inclinations* presents a problem for natural-law theorists, but the moral implications of natural-law theory depend directly on the understanding of this term.

A second way in which moral theories can fail to be useful is by failing to provide guidelines for arbitrating conflicting moral directions given by the theory itself. For example, one of the primary functions of morality is to provide a peaceful means of resolving interpersonal disputes, but an egoist can only admonish each person to do what is in his or her own self-interest. Because this advice does not aid in resolving conflicts of interest, but in fact intensifies the conflicts, ethical egoism does not measure up well by the third criterion. The ethics of respect for persons does not always provide a way of resolving conflicts of duties and thus also has difficulties with the third criterion.

Third, a moral philosophy can require information for resolving moral problems that is difficult to obtain. This problem is especially acute in the two consequentialist moral philosophies—egoism and utilitarianism. Critics of consequentialism may argue that the egoist often doesn't have enough factual knowledge to know what actions will lead to his long-range self-interest and the utilitarian does not have enough factual knowledge to know what actions will lead to the general welfare. For example, can the utilitarian know the long-term effects on a society of the widespread practice of extramarital sex? Will it lead to better sexual adjustment? Will it make marriages more stable or more unstable? Without an answer to these questions, we cannot determine the morality of premarital sex from a utilitarian standpoint.

Criterion 4: Justification. How Well Can the Moral Standard Be Justified?

Every moral theorist provides some reason for accepting his or her moral standard rather than another. We have already discussed two of the most popular ways of defending a moral standard—by an appeal to religion or by an appeal to moral intuitions. Many moral philosophers believe these methods are faulty, but we have many other ways to justify accepting a moral standard. Note that the method of defending a moral standard must be fundamentally different from the method of defending moral rules or moral judgments within a theory. Moral rules and moral judgments can be defended by reference to the moral standard, but the moral standard cannot be defended by making reference to a higher moral standard. Thus, a strict proof of a moral standard cannot be given. At best, a moral philosopher can show reasons why it is plausible to accept one moral standard rather than another. We shall consider some of these arguments when we analyze each of the four theories.

CONCEPT SUMMARY

To evaluate moral principles we first place them in the context of a larger theory and then evaluate the theory. A moral theory has three levels: (1) The moral standard is the basic criterion for determining right and wrong. (2) A moral rule is a moral principle that marks a class of actions that is right or wrong. Moral rules give direction for the relationship of individuals to other individuals (personal ethics) and the relationship of individuals to groups or of groups to other groups (social ethics). (3) Moral judgments are moral evaluations of either specific classes of action or persons or particular actions or persons. Moral judgments can evaluate actions as obligatory, permissible, impermissible, or supererogatory. This outline of a moral theory will be followed in presenting the four moral theories discussed in this book.

The four criteria for evaluating a moral theory are consistency, agreement with prior moral beliefs, usefulness in resolving moral dilemmas, and the adequacy of justification of the moral standard. These criteria will be applied to each of the four moral philosophies that we shall consider.

IV

THE ETHICS OF SELF-INTEREST

Suppose your area is finance and you are the protégé of a first-rate manager. Sixteen months ago he brought you with him when he became the chief executive officer of a manufacturing firm whose equipment and plants are becoming outdated. The board of directors is split between those who want to revitalize the plant and those who want to milk the firm for the profits they can get out of it in the relatively near future. Your boss was brought in because board members dedicated to revitalization won out in a close vote after a long fight. Over the past year, you and your boss have developed a seven-year plan for the renovation and growth of the firm. Since your plan involves large capital expenditures, you are worried that it will greatly lessen investor interest and so you have been working out the most favorable way of reporting these development costs.

Your boss unexpectedly announces that he has been tentatively offered the top job in a great corporation. The rewards and challenges of the new job are simply too much for him to pass up, and he would like you to come with him. Before making a formal offer, though, the chairman of the new firm wants to see some "good figures" in the next financial statement of your present firm. She only cares about good bottom lines; no one is going to worry about the details. Your boss really wants the new job, so he has decided to scrap the seven-year plan. He wants you to look into the possibility of selling off various segments of the firm, or selling off some of its securities, and including such revenue in the reported profits. He does not want you to do anything illegal, but he is confident that, with your knowledge of "generally accepted accounting procedures," you will be able to find a way to make the firm's next income statement look very good indeed.

How should you react to the request? The "quick fix" policy your boss now wants you to adopt clearly will not be in the long-range interests of either the stockholders or the employees of your present company. On the other hand, the policy will allow you and your boss to advance to the new corporation, at which the financial rewards are much greater.[1]

This case illustrates the conflict between an individual's self-interest and the self-interest of others—a conflict played out over and over again in our society and in our individual lives. Many people adopt the position that self-interest comes first. All of the moral philosophers we shall consider give self-interest a place, but is it legitimate to make one's own welfare the supreme criterion of right or wrong? What implications for individual conduct and for social policy does a moral philosophy based on self-interest have? These questions are the kind we shall be addressing in this chapter.

Egoism—the philosophy that self-interest is the highest good—has a long history. Ancient Greek philosophers, such as Plato, wrote about it. But our modern emphasis on the individual in competition with other individuals has given egoism special prominence. The first major philosophical representative of modern egoism—and still one of the most interesting and philosophically acute egoists—was the Englishman Thomas Hobbes (1588–1679).

Hobbes is an egoist in two senses, which must be clearly distinguished. He is a *psychological egoist,* believing that all human behavior *is* in fact motivated by self-interest; our human nature is so constituted that we will always act egoistically. He is also an *ethical egoist,* for he believes that all human conduct *should* be motivated by self-interest; that is, the moral standard should make one's own welfare the criterion of right conduct. Egoism for Hobbes is thus the correct moral philosophy, as well as the only one our psychology will allow us to adopt. Hobbes's book *Leviathan* contains a classic account of the egoist's approach to morality.

Among contemporary popular writers, Ayn Rand is the best-known advocate of egoism. In her novels, such as *The Fountainhead* and *Atlas Shrugged,* and in her more philosophical works, like *The Virtue of Selfishness* and *Capitalism: The Unknown Ideal,* she advocates egoism as the most adequate moral philosophy. Although we are not concerned with a scholarly exposition of their views, we shall use Hobbes's and Rand's ideas in describing egoism.

The Egoistic Moral Standard

The simplest formulation of the egoistic moral standard is that those actions are right that contribute to a person's self-interest. Although this formulation

---

[1]Adapted from a case supplied by R. G. Wengert. Used by permission of R. G. Wengert.

is useful in conveying the basic idea of egoism, it has at least two problems that make it an inadequate basis for a serious discussion.

First, it does not provide a method for deciding which action is right when several alternative actions would each contribute to the egoist's self-interest. If one act produces 10 units of good for the egoist and another act produces 50 units of good for him, both of the acts would be right by this moral standard. Thus an act cannot be the correct one for the egoist simply because it contributes to the egoist's self-interest. The moral standard must prescribe that the course of action to be followed is the one that will produce the *best* consequences for the egoist.

A second problem with the moral standard is that it does not take account of situations in which no action available to the egoist contributes in a positive way to his self-interest. If you, as an egoist, are faced with several alternatives, all of which will detract from your self-interest, you will want to do whatever harms you the least. That action would be the right action in those unfortunate circumstances, even though it would not contribute to your self-interest.

The following formulation of the egoistic moral standard meets these two objections:

> MS: Actions are right if and only if they produce consequences that are at least as good for the self-interest of the egoist as the consequences of any alternative action.

The Definition of Self-Interest. In developing the egoistic position, we must first define *self-interest,* the crucial term in the moral standard. As you might expect, egoists differ in the way they define this term. Some egoists define self-interest in terms of pleasure, power, fame, social prestige, or even physical survival. Others define it in terms of happiness or self-realization. Our definition should be relatively neutral, allowing the individual to give his or her own particular definition. Therefore, we shall define self-interest as the achievement of the "good life" for oneself, leaving it to the individual egoist to determine the exact implications. The good life might include having an interesting and rewarding career, a satisfying family life, a high social position, and enough wealth to allow for sufficient leisure time. Others might define the good life in less conventional ways, but in any case they must formulate a hierarchy of the various elements or goods in the conception of the good life, otherwise they cannot determine which good should be pursued when various goods conflict. For example, in the definition of the good life we have just sketched, career goals might conflict with a desire for leisure time or physical pleasure. I may want to go to a party tonight, but I may also realize that, unless I do well on an upcoming test, I may not achieve my career goal of becoming an engineer. I must make a choice based on my hierarchy of goods as set out in my definition of the good life.

One way of forming a hierarchy of goods is to determine which goods are the most inclusive; that is, which goods are important in obtaining other goods. For example, a successful career not only is satisfying in itself and thus a good in its own right, but it also provides a way of achieving other goods, such as wealth, social position, and pleasure. So an egoist may well choose to place career goals ahead of pleasure in the hierarchy of goods to be pursued. Thus I may decide to study rather than go to the party, because studying is essential to achieving my higher and more inclusive goal of becoming an engineer.

Short-Range versus Long-Range Interests. Although it is possible to be a short-range egoist, the egoist more than likely will be more concerned with the fullest realization of her goals over a lifetime rather than during only a short period of time. She will measure the good life by long-range realization of self-interest rather than by short-range gratifications. The ego-ist seeks to achieve the greatest total amount of pleasure, for example, rather than pleasure in any given instance. The same can be said for all of the other goods that comprise the good life. Thus the egoist must develop powers of self-control and long-range planning to pursue her goals effectively.

How an egoist defines her conception of the good life and its hierarchy of goods is a highly personal matter, but anything she does must be justified as either an aspect of the good life or a means to that end. The consistent egoist will do nothing to obstruct her goal of achieving the good life, nor will she do anything that does not positively contribute to that goal. Thus, as an egoist I will do nothing merely to help others or to contribute to the good of society, although I might help others and contribute to the good of society if I can see those actions as ultimately benefiting me in some way.

Before we examine the personal and social ethics of egoism, let's look at the procedure an egoist should follow in determining what to do.

Checklist for Applying Ethical Egoism

_____ 1. Determine the consequences of the action and the consequences of alternatives to the action as they affect your self-interest. (This step presupposes that you have defined your self-interest and decided whether to maximize your long-range or short-range self-interest.)

_____ 2. Choose the action that produces consequences that are at least as good for you as the consequences of any alternative action open to you.

a. An action that promotes your self-interest as much as possible or detracts from your self-interest as little as possible is morally obligatory.

b. An action that fails to promote your self-interest as much as some alternative action open to you or that detracts from your self-interest more than another action open to you is morally impermissible.

c. If each of several actions contributes to your self-interest at least as much as any other actions, or detracts from your self-interest as little as any other actions, all the actions are equally morally permissible.

CONCEPT SUMMARY

Egoism as a moral philosophy originated in ancient Greece, but the modern emphasis on the individual in competition with other individuals has given it special prominence. The egoistic moral standard states that actions are right if and only if they produce consequences that are at least as good for the self-interest of the egoist as the consequences of any alternative action. Each egoist must personally define self-interest and propose a hierarchy of goods within that definition. Most egoists will be concerned with the fullest realization of their self-interest over a lifetime rather than during only a short period of time.

The Personal and Social Ethics of Egoism

In applying the ethics of self-interest thus far, we have resolved moral problems by referring back to the egoistic moral standard. But it is helpful to know generally what the implications of egoism are—that is, what kind of personal and social ethics the egoistic moral standard supports. This section is devoted to accomplishing this task.

We have seen that for the egoist all duties are ultimately duties to self. All moral obligations to others and to the society must be justified as leading to the egoist's own self-interest. Therefore we can state a general rule governing duties to self: As egoists we should do whatever leads to our own long-range self-interest. Yet egoistic philosophy is able to justify seemingly non-egoistic personal duties to others. Egoism also has a theory of how society and government should be ordered so that people can pursue their own self-interest to the maximum.

Duties to Self. What are some of the particular duties that the egoist owes to himself? One such duty, suggested by Ayn Rand, is to identify those character traits that will contribute to the good life for oneself. The egoist has an obligation to develop those character traits to the fullest. One of the character traits important for the egoist is *rationality.* To achieve one's long-range egoistic goals, a person must not be unduly swayed by emotions of the moment. A person must learn to analyze the consequences of actions and rationally assess the most prudent course of action. A second desirable character trait is *self-discipline.* After the egoist has rationally determined the most prudent course of action, he or she must have the self-discipline to pursue this course, even if it means foregoing temporary satisfactions. Third, the egoist will generally find that *industry* (willingness to work hard) will help in achieving egoistic goals. You can probably think of other character traits that would be important in realizing the kind of egoism you find most plausible.

In addition to the development of certain character traits, the egoist has a duty to perform any other actions that contribute to his conception of the good life. For example, knowledge and formal education will generally contribute to a person's realization of the good life, both by helping him to pursue a rewarding career and by enabling him to understand the world and enjoy leisure time. Physical health and emotional stability are generally necessary ingredients in the good life, and the rational egoist should do what he can to pursue those goals. In addition, an egoist will generally behave in a socially acceptable way. In most cases the egoist will not find it to his advantage to flaunt social conventions—at least not publicly. He will, out of self-interest, not want to appear to be an undesirable member of society. We shall consider this topic in more detail when we turn to the egoist's obligations to others.

Contrary to what one might initially think, occasions may arise in which an egoist can risk his life without violating his duties to himself. Taking considerable risks may well be justified if the risks are essential to achieving a coveted goal. If an egoist is trapped in a dictatorship where freedom of thought and action are suppressed and the conditions necessary for self-realization are lacking, he might well risk his life to escape or to overthrow the dictatorship. An egoist might even commit suicide if conditions of life prevent meaningful self-realization. If he were dying in agony of an incurable disease, he might decide he had nothing to gain by prolonging his life and end it of his own accord. Nothing in such an action is contrary to the principles of egoism.

Duties to Others. All of an egoist's duties to others must be justified as ultimately benefiting himself, and many apparently non-egoistic actions can be justified from an egoistic standpoint. Suppose you are a wealthy man whose wife is dying of a disease that can be cured only at great expense. You might justify spending your entire fortune to save her if her life is important to your happiness.

Many other actions that help others can be justified on egoistic grounds. I may become the chairman of a fund-raising drive for the local charity hospital because I know this action will help my career at the bank. The bank, after all, likes its officers to have a high profile as outstanding members of the community. I will cultivate friendships and go out of my way to help my friends, because I know that this method is the only way to have friends, and friends are important to my idea of the good life. I will also provide for my family and be a responsible parent because the welfare of my children is important to my own happiness. You can no doubt give other examples of duties to others that can be justified on an egoistic basis.

Social Ethics. The egoist approaches the social and political order by asking herself what social policies will allow her to pursue her own self-interest to the maximum extent. Obviously, the way a person defines her self-interest is crucial in determining these policies. We cannot possibly elaborate the political and social implications of every type of egoism; however, we can discuss some premises.

Most egoists seem to regard themselves as more capable than the average person, so that in any fair competition they could come out ahead of most of their fellow human beings. Therefore egoists seek a social environment in which they have the maximum freedom to exercise their abilities in competition with others. For them, the ideal state should protect individuals against physical violence, theft, and fraud, but this protection should be its only purpose. Any extension of the powers of government beyond this function of protecting basic rights is illegitimate.

This political philosophy, known as libertarianism, is the social and political position advocated by Ayn Rand. Without question, though, the most sophisticated recent version of this view is expressed by Robert Nozick in *Anarchy, State and Utopia.* Although Nozick does not base his libertarianism on egoism, his description of the "minimal state" matches the kind of government that egoists might desire:

> Our main conclusions about the state are that a minimal state, limited to the narrow functions of protection against force, theft, fraud, enforcement of contracts, and so on, is justified; that any more extensive state will violate persons' rights not to be forced to do certain things, and is unjustified; and that the minimal state is inspiring as well as right. Two

noteworthy implications are that the state may not use its coercive appa-
ratus for the purpose of getting some citizens to aid others, or in order
to prohibit activities to people for their *own* good or protection.[2]

The justification of the minimal state from the egoistic standpoint is
that the only way the egoist can secure liberties for herself is to agree to a
similar respect for the liberties of others. Thomas Hobbes argues that even
a group of egoists would finally agree to make the transition from a "state
of nature" or anarchy, in which no government exists, to some form of civil
society that enforces law and order, because they would find a society more
conducive to their own self-interest. While Hobbes's civil society is by no
means a libertarian minimal state, a contemporary egoist might use some
of Hobbes's arguments to justify a minimal state. Ideally, of course, an egoist
would prefer greater freedom for herself and less freedom for others, but
this arrangement has little chance of being accepted. Therefore she agrees
to a libertarian minimal state for all. Let's consider some characteristics of
the libertarian state.

First, the minimal state will have the two explicit limitations to which
Nozick refers. There will be no enforced benevolence—that is, "getting
some citizens to aid others." Even though voluntary benevolence is perfectly
permissible (and we have seen that the egoist may sometimes want to help
others for her own benefit), the state has no right to tax one person to
support another. No welfare programs will aid the disadvantaged; the only
possible exceptions might be programs that counteract a clear and present
danger to civil disturbance or that aid victims of natural and war-related
disasters. Even an egoist might prefer to spend tax dollars on relief for the
poor rather than have riots in the streets. And even egoists who believe
they would never be among the poor might wish to be helped in case of a
disaster over which they had no control.

Similarly, the state will not engage in paternalism—that is, forcing
persons to do or not do something "for their *own* good or protection." The
state will not require people to use seat belts or wear crash helmets, even
though such use would be for their own protection. It will not require
people to put away part of their income for retirement. However, a voluntary
social security program, in which persons receive after retirement the contributions they made to the program, plus interest, would be acceptable, as
long as one person's earnings were not distributed to others. In opposing
all strictly paternalistic laws, the libertarian will examine carefully the laws
against the use of drugs such as marijuana and even heroin. The minimal

[2]Robert Nozick, *Anarchy, State and Utopia* (New York: Basic Books, 1974), p. ix.

state can prohibit the use of drugs only to the extent that they cause crime that limits the rights of others. In fact, any law must be rejected that can only be justified paternalistically.

Second, since the only justification for coercion by the state is the protection of individuals from one another or from other states, the minimal state will not prohibit conduct simply because someone thinks it is immoral. Thus no laws will be made against pornography unless lawmakers can show that pornography substantially increases sex crimes and thereby threatens the basic rights of others. Similar considerations apply to laws against homosexuality, premarital sex, or other kinds of sexual behavior that some people consider immoral. Laws forbidding certain kinds of commercial activity on Sunday must be eliminated. Laws forbidding people from having more than one spouse would have no justification in the minimal state. You can probably think of other laws that must be eliminated for the same reason.

Third, egoists generally believe that their moral position is most compatible with laissez-faire capitalism. Capitalism is an economic system characterized by private accumulation of capital, private ownership of the means of production, and a free market system. An economic system compatible with egoism will grant maximum freedom for an individual to pursue her own self-interest in terms of profit, as long as she does not violate the basic rights of others. If self-interest is the most fundamental motivational force in human personality, as psychological egoists believe, then we should not be surprised that capitalism is the most dynamic and productive economic system, for it effectively harnesses the natural egoistic tendencies of all human beings. It may also be true, as many advocates of capitalism, like Adam Smith, have believed, that the pursuit of self-interest also benefits others by generating jobs and wealth. But the motive of the individual egoist is not altruistic, nor should it be.

CONCEPT SUMMARY

The general rule governing an egoistic account of duties to oneself is that a person should do whatever leads to his or her long-range self-interest. Duties to oneself include developing character traits, such as rationality, self-discipline, and industry, that enable a person more effectively to pursue one's self-interest. The general principle governing the egoist's approach to social ethics is that the state should allow the individual maximum freedom to pursue self-interests. This principle has led many egoists to embrace libertarianism, a political philosophy that advocates minimal interference in an individual's conduct, the elimination of enforced paternalism and benevolence, and laissez-faire capitalism.

Applying the Ethics of Self-Interest

Now we shall examine, from the egoist's standpoint, several cases involving a moral decision. These three examples will help you understand how an egoist would analyze a situation requiring moral choice and would formulate an answer as to what he or she should do. We shall follow the methodology outlined in the checklist. We shall also make reference to the distinction between factual, conceptual, and moral questions when this distinction seems useful.

Case 1: The Aircraft Brake Scandal

In 1967 the B. F. Goodrich Company submitted the lowest bid for an aircraft brake to LTV Aerospace Corporation and thereby was awarded the contract. Goodrich engineers soon discovered that the brake designed for the contract was too small to stop the airplane safely. Instead of admitting the error and redesigning the brake, lower-level management personnel decided to falsify the laboratory test results and proceed with construction of the original brake. During tests of the brake on an airplane, several near-crashes occurred. After failing to get any cooperation from their superiors in correcting this situation, a young engineer whom we shall call Searle Lawson and a technical writer, Kermit Vandiver, went to attorneys and later to the FBI with the story of the falsified laboratory tests. These two men lost their jobs as a result of their protest. Employees who went along with the misrepresentations kept their jobs and never experienced any retribution, even after the scandal became public.[3] If Lawson and Vandiver had been egoists, what should they have done?

1. First we must determine the consequences of the actions open to the two men. On the one hand, they could have kept quiet like most of the other employees; they would no doubt have saved their jobs and probably would have suffered no retribution when the scandal came to light. On the other hand, they could have chosen the course of action that they did in fact elect and suffered the consequences of being fired. If Lawson and Vandiver had been egoists and libertarians, they would have advocated a legal system with prohibitions against fraud, so they would be in favor of legal restrictions against the kind of misrepresentation practiced by their company. Yet as egoists they would be willing to break the rules if such action were in their long-term self-interest, especially if they could break the rules while others continued to obey the laws against fraud.

---

[3]Kermit Vandiver, "Why Should My Conscience Bother Me?" in *In the Name of Profit*, ed. Robert L. Heilbroner et al. (Garden City, N.Y.: Doubleday, 1972), pp. 3–31.

2. If Lawson and Vandiver had been egoists, they probably should have decided that revealing the problem was contrary to their self-interest, especially if they defined self-interest in terms of career advancement. Therefore they would conclude that making the information public was morally impermissible.

Case 2: The Legalization of Homosexual Acts between Consenting Adults

In 1957 the Wolfenden Committee in Great Britain recommended that Britain's laws on homosexuality should be liberalized, so that homosexuality between consenting adults would no longer be a crime. Sir Patrick Devlin, who served on the Queen's Bench, objected to this recommendation, arguing that legalization of such activities could cause the disintegration of the social order. Devlin believed that agreed-upon moral values are a part of the binding force that holds society together and that the view that homosexual acts are wrong is a widely shared value in our society. To tamper with the moral consensus on such issues is to tamper with the social fabric. Therefore, homosexual acts between consenting adults should not be legalized. What position would an egoist take on this issue?

1. If the egoist is a homosexual, then he or she will have a strong reason for advocating the legalization of homosexual acts between consenting adults. But let's assume that the egoist is not homosexual. What position is most consistent with his or her moral philosophy? The egoist would be concerned with Devlin's claim that legalizing homosexuality can threaten the social fabric; if the social order is generally in accord with the principles of the minimal state, the egoist would want to see it preserved. But an egoist will require solid evidence that legalizing homosexual acts would contribute substantially to social disintegration, and this evidence is difficult to obtain. One reason is that we cannot easily establish causal relationships between two historical events in order to say that one event (say, a change to a more tolerant attitude toward homosexuality) might cause or even contribute to another event (say, disintegration of the social order). Another reason is that we often have difficulty distinguishing between social disintegration and mere social change. The social changes that may follow changes in moral values are not necessarily signs of disintegration. The egoist would probably be forced to decide the evidence is inconclusive that legalizing homosexual acts between consenting adults would materially contribute to social disintegration.

In addition, we have seen that the egoist favors laws that allow for maximum individual freedom, as long as conduct does not limit the equal freedom of others. The only way the egoist can obtain tolerance for his or her own conduct is to agree to a similar respect for the liberty of others. Suppressing homosexual conduct would be contrary to the principles of libertarianism and therefore contrary to the kind of social order the egoist prefers.

2. We must conclude that the egoist libertarian would probably find laws that suppress homosexual conduct between consenting adults to be indirectly contrary to his or her self-interest and therefore impermissible. This conclusion should not be taken to imply that egoist libertarians favor giving adults freedom to molest children, either homosexually or heterosexually. Even though libertarians are generally opposed to paternalism, protection of children by the state is perfectly compatible with the principles of libertarianism; in fact, it is simply an aspect of the state's protection of individual liberty. If we assume that children are not capable of making a free and informed decision about participation in sexual activity or that the relationship between a child and an adult in a sexual experience would be so one-sided as to exclude genuine freedom on the part of a child, we can easily justify paternalistic intervention on behalf of children by a libertarian state.

Case 3: A Lawyer's Dilemma

A youth, badly injured in an automobile wreck, sues the driver responsible for the injury.[4] The driver's defense lawyer has his doctor examine the youth; the doctor discovers an aortic aneurism, apparently caused by the accident, that the boy's doctor had not found. The aneurism is life-threatening unless operated on. But the defense lawyer realizes that, if the youth learns of the aneurism, he will demand a much higher settlement. Furthermore, the lawyer knows that, according to the code of ethics for lawyers, the lawyer's responsibilities are to keep secret the information gained in the professional relationship, the disclosure of which would likely be detrimental to the client. If the lawyer were an egoist, what should he do?

1. If the lawyer reveals the information to the youth's lawyer, his ability to defend his client will be substantially weakened, which will harm his reputation as a defense lawyer and perhaps result in fewer cases in the future. He also knows he has a basis for defending himself in the legal code of ethics. A consideration of these consequences suggests that he should

---

[4]Spaulding v. Zimmerman, 116 N.W.2d 704 (1962).

not reveal the information. However, if he does not reveal the information and the boy dies, his reputation will be hurt if it becomes public knowledge that he knew of the aneurism. He should also take into account the guilt that he would probably experience if the boy died; even if this guilt were unjustified from an egoistic standpoint, he might not be able to avoid it. He might also be subject to prosecution.

2. We cannot easily determine which alternative will produce the greatest long-range self-interest for the lawyer. The difficulty of knowing the consequences of various alternatives is a serious problem for egoism, as it is for any consequentialist theory. The limitations of factual knowledge pose a problem for this case, even though the moral principles are clear. The question the lawyer would have to ask himself is whether the information has much chance of becoming public. Since the physician as well as his client knew the information, it probably would eventually be made public. Therefore, the long-range self-interest of the lawyer probably requires that he reveal the information.

Evaluating Egoism as a Moral Theory

Now we are ready to evaluate egoism, using the four criteria established in Chapter 3. Keep in mind that some criticisms can be made of every moral theory; no theory is perfect. The final task will be to evaluate the relative strengths and weaknesses of the four moral theories. You should also keep in mind that a subjective element necessarily arises in evaluating moral theories. The following evaluations are my own, although they reflect widely held positions among moral philosophers. These evaluations are for your consideration rather than for uncritical acceptance.

It will be useful to display the ratings on scales like the one that follows, where the X indicates how, in my opinion, the moral theory should be rated for each particular criterion. Such a system is easy to read but is oversimplified. However, it is useful in stimulating thoughts about the relative merits of a moral theory. You may want to construct your own rating chart on each moral theory.[5]

---

[5]The suggestion for this rating chart comes from R. Murray Thomas, *Comparing Theories of Child Development* (Belmont, Calif.: Wadsworth, 1979), pp. 69–70.

The Ethics of Self-Interest

How well do I think the theory meets the criteria?

Criteria	Very Well	Moderately Well	Very Poorly
1. (Consistency)		X	
2. (Plausibility)		X	
3. (Usefulness)		X	
4. (Justification)	X		

Criterion 1: Consistency. I have given egoism a low mark for consistency. In fact, egoism has more difficulties with consistency than any other moral theory. Let's consider two types of inconsistency of which egoism is allegedly guilty.

The first type of inconsistency can be illustrated by the following example.[6] Suppose you and I are business partners and I stumble on what I think is an almost foolproof method for defrauding you of a half-million dollars in company funds. However, without my knowing it, you learn of my plan to defraud you. It would be in your interest but against my interest for you to prevent me from defrauding you. It would be in my interest for me to try to carry through with my scheme, from which it follows that I ought to try to defraud you, that it is wrong for me not to try, and that I have not behaved as I morally should until I have carried out my plan. Similarly, learning of my intentions, you ought to take steps to foil my plan. It would be wrong for you not to do so. You will not have acted as you morally should until you have done your best to protect yourself against my attempt to defraud you.

It follows that, if you prevent me from defrauding you, your act must be said to be both wrong and not wrong. It is wrong because it is the prevention of my doing what I ought to do and not wrong because it is what you ought to do. But one and the same act should not be said to be both morally wrong and not morally wrong from the standpoint of the same moral theory. A moral theory that generates these kinds of conflicting moral judgments must be said to be internally inconsistent.

[6]See Kurt Baier, *The Moral Point of View* (New York: Random House, 1966), pp. 95–96.

A second kind of inconsistency, external to the theory itself, is manifested in the conflict between one's being an egoist and advocating that others be egoists. We can illustrate this kind of inconsistency by means of the same example. As the example shows, it is often not in my self-interest for you to follow your self-interest, and it is often not in your self-interest for me to follow mine. In the light of this problem, why should an egoist ever advocate that others be egoists too? It is often not in the egoist's self-interest to advocate that others follow egoistic principles, and the egoist should do only what is in his or her self-interest. Let's consider the kinds of responses the egoist can make to this challenge.

One response is in terms of *personal egoism,* which holds that I should do what is in my self-interest and that everyone else should also do what is in my self-interest. Personal egoism requires only that I, not others, act in accordance with the principle of self-interest. An egoist who took this position could answer the problem we have posed. If I were such an egoist, I could maintain that everyone should do what is in my self-interest. No inconsistency exists in advocating this kind of egoism. Unfortunately, this form of egoism has little chance of being accepted by others. Why should everyone do what is in my self-interest? No reason has been given, and a plausible reason is difficult to imagine.

A more serious problem is that many moral philosophers believe that personal egoism is not a moral philosophy at all, but only a personal guide to action. We saw in Chapter 1 that one implication of any moral statement that an action is right (or wrong) is that others should (or should not) perform the same action in similar circumstances. Thus, if I make a moral claim that fraud is wrong, I mean that it is wrong for me as well as you. If I intend to say that it is wrong only for you, I am not making a genuine moral claim. Personal egoism is incompatible with this interpretation of the nature of moral statements, for according to personal egoism fraud might be right for me and wrong for you in a similar situation. Therefore, if our interpretation of the nature of a moral claim is correct, the personal egoist cannot claim to be adopting a moral point of view.

A second response is in terms of *impersonal egoism,* which holds that each individual should do what is in his or her self-interest. Impersonal egoism has the advantage of being more consistent with the moral point of view, and it is the kind of egoism formulated in the moral standard. Egoists have sometimes attempted to show that impersonal egoism is not inconsistent. One way to show consistency is by refusing to advocate that others be egoists. As an impersonal egoist, I may *judge* that others should be egoists, but I could refuse to *advocate* publicly that they be egoists; that is, I might recognize that others should follow their own self-interest, just as I should follow mine, but I would do nothing to encourage them to do so.

After all, an inconsistency exists between egoism and its public advocacy only if I publicly advocate egoism.

But this view makes it impossible to give sincere moral advice. Just as taking the moral point of view requires that we be willing for others to follow the same moral principles we adopt, so it requires that we should be able to give sincere moral advice to someone who asks for it. But suppose someone were to ask an impersonal egoist for advice as to how she should behave in a certain situation. If an egoist refused to advocate publicly his moral principles, he would have to advise the person to act from moral principles other than egoistic ones. Perhaps the egoist would advise the inquirer to do what leads to the general welfare or would give her some other counsel that does not reflect his true moral views. The impersonal egoist who refuses to advocate publicly his moral principles will not advise the inquirer to adopt egoistic principles, even though he may judge that he should do so.

Another tactic that the impersonal egoist might adopt is to claim that he will be better off in the long run if other people adopt an egoistic point of view, even if in doing so they sometimes pursue policies contrary to his own self-interest. In other words, it is in his self-interest that others pursue their self-interest. A society in which all members vigorously and rationally pursued their own self-interest might well be richer, more dynamic and interesting, and perhaps even more culturally creative than one composed of non-egoists. This enrichment would benefit the egoist himself.

Is this claim true? The evidence of common sense is against it. People's self-interest often conflicts. Therefore, in the absence of a strong argument to the contrary, we must conclude that this approach is an unsatisfactory resolution of the problem of inconsistency in egoism.

Another possible way to solve the problem of inconsistency is to introduce side constraints on the egoistic moral standard. In the case of an egoistic moral standard, a side constraint restricts the actions that may be taken in the name of self-interest. Thus the egoist might adopt a moral standard that reads as follows:

> MS: Actions are right if and only if they produce consequences that are at least as good for the self-interest of the egoist as the consequences of any alternative action, as long as they do not violate the basic rights of others.

This moral standard says in effect that a person cannot do certain things even in pursuit of her own self-interest—namely, perform actions that conflict with others' basic rights. These basic rights must be stipulated, but they usually include the right not to be killed, the right to protection from physical violence, and the right to protection from theft and fraud.

Libertarians accept these same rights, and one might easily conclude that egoists would have no trouble with this side constraint. But this conclusion would be in error. Without the side constraint, the egoist agrees to respect the basic rights of others *only* because she has no other way to get others to respect her rights. Furthermore, she will attempt to avoid this restriction whenever it is advantageous to do so, and such attempts will not be immoral. But, if she accepts the side constraint, it becomes immoral for her to attempt to violate others' basic rights, even if she knows she can do so without losing others' respect for her basic rights. Therefore the addition of the side constraint makes for a fundamentally different type of egoism.

Unfortunately, the added side constraint does not solve the problem of inconsistency. Instead it simply builds the inconsistency into the moral standard itself. The side constraint represents a conception of rights that is incompatible with egoism, so the constrained version of impersonal egoism actually contains two mutually incompatible moral standards, one egoistic and the other not. Nor is it clear why a consistent egoist would want others to adopt even this constrained form of egoism, since others can still do many things contrary to the egoist's self-interest. They can still ruin her business, steal her boyfriend or husband, embarrass her before friends, spread gossip about her, and do a thousand other things that will cause her unhappiness.

We must conclude that we have no obvious way to avoid either of the two inconsistencies in the egoistic position while retaining the moral point of view. Although it is possible to accept an internally inconsistent moral philosophy, the problems we have discussed must be taken as a severe criticism.

Criterion 2: Plausibility. A second way of evaluating a moral philosophy is to compare the moral judgments it produces with our most strongly held moral beliefs. Here again I have given egoism a relatively low mark.

Most of us have certain things we would not be willing to do even to advance our own welfare. We probably would not be willing to kill, and many of us would not be willing to lie to advance our own interests against those of others. Many people are not satisfied with the libertarian view that benevolence on the part of the state is not morally permissible. Even when egoists can justify actions that we consider right, they seem to give the wrong reasons. For example, self-interest seems to be an inappropriate reason to give for caring for members of one's family.

We must conclude that for many people egoism is incompatible with prior moral beliefs. In itself, this conclusion does not constitute a refutation of egoism, because these strongly held beliefs may be in error, but holding this incompatibility as a mark against egoism seems reasonable unless strong reasons are found for accepting it. So far we have not found such reasons.

Criterion 3: Usefulness. I have also given egoism a low rating on its ability to resolve moral conflicts. The following example will show why. After the Second World War, the British press published a story regarding two female counterspies. After years of work, the Nazi code was broken and the British War Office became aware that the Nazis knew the true loyalties of the two women. The War Office also knew that, if the women returned to Nazi Europe, they would almost certainly be caught, tortured, and killed. Yet, if they did not return, the Nazis would probably realize their code had been broken and would change it. The British and their Allies then would lose their major source of intelligence about Nazi war plans for at least two more years. As a result, the two counterspies were sent back to Europe and were never heard from again.

What was the right thing to do? How does one resolve such a clear conflict of interests? The personal egoist can only advise everyone to do whatever is in his (the egoist's) self-interest. The impersonal egoist can only advise each person in the dispute to follow his or her own self-interest: The officials in the War Office should have ordered the counterspies back to Europe and should not have informed them of the danger. The counterspies, if they had known their fate, should have resisted this order in every possible way. If one believes that a primary function of morality is to resolve disputes arising from a conflict of interests, egoism seems particularly ill-suited to accomplishing this aim. Egoism cannot rise to a higher level—such as considering the general welfare—to resolve conflicts of interest.

A second limitation to the usefulness of egoism in resolving moral dilemmas is that we sometimes cannot easily determine which alternative is in a person's long-range self-interest. Like utilitarianism, egoism judges the morality of an action by its consequences. Insofar as he does not know the consequences of various alternatives with any degree of certainty or precision, the egoist cannot determine what he ought to do. Case 3, "A Lawyer's Dilemma," illustrates this limitation of egoism.

Criterion 4: Justification. I have given egoism a slightly higher rating for its justification of the egoistic moral standard. Even though the justification is not as convincing as some egoists maintain, it does give a certain strength to the egoistic position in the minds of many people.

The most common justification of the egoistic moral standard is an appeal to psychological egoism. The ethical egoist points out that a person has no obligation to pick up 10,000 pounds of steel, because it is physically impossible to do so. She then advances the claim of psychological egoism—namely, that in fact people can and do act only out of motives of self-interest. The egoist then maintains that we do have moral obligations. Because the only valid moral obligations are to pursue our own self-interest, egoism must be the only correct moral philosophy.

Two kinds of criticisms can be made of the argument from psychological egoism to ethical egoism. One criticism attacks the logic of the argument itself and tries to show that the ethical egoist cannot fully support her case on the basis of psychological egoism, even if psychological egoism is true. The second argument is that psychological egoism is not true, at least insofar as it claims that all human behavior is motivated by self-interest. We shall consider each of these criticisms in turn.

Notice carefully what follows from the fact that people can act from self-interest and that a person has an obligation only if he or she can meet the obligation: The only legitimate conclusion is that no one is morally required to meet an obligation that is not based on self-interest. For example, I would not be obligated to make a contribution to charity if it were not in my self-interest to do so. But this conclusion is not equivalent to ethical egoism's claim that it is the only correct moral theory. Perhaps, though this argument is implausible, other moral principles exist that never require us to act contrary to our self-interest. Or perhaps, contrary to the original argument, we have no moral obligations at all, since the egoist has not proven the truth of her claim that we have moral obligations. Attempts to make a stronger claim—namely, that one is obligated to live by egoistic principles—have not been successful.[7] Nevertheless, if psychological egoism is true, ethical egoism is given strong support even if it is not strictly proven. So we must look at the other criticism.

The second kind of attack on the argument from psychological egoism to ethical egoism questions the validity of the claim that we always act out of motives of self-interest. Most of us would probably say that the psychological egoist has a great deal of truth on her side. Many apparently altruistic acts really are done out of self-interest. But some human actions do appear to be motivated by considerations other than self-interest. Parents often make sacrifices for their children in a way that is difficult to explain in terms

---

[7]See Terrance C. McConnell, "The Argument from Psychological Egoism to Ethical Egoism," *Australasian Journal of Philosophy,* 56 (1978), pp. 41–47. As McConnell points out, the ethical egoist actually claims that we always act according to what we believe is in our self-interest but people are often mistaken in these beliefs. However, we can afford to ignore this refinement here.

of selfishness. Heroic actions on the battlefield and in civilian life also seem to involve more than considerations of one's own well-being.

Morally praiseworthy actions are not the only actions that have motivations other than self-interest. Malice and hatred are often no more selfish than actions we admire. People often attempt to harm their enemies at great cost to themselves. They may try to kill or injure the enemy even when doing so will cost them large sums of money, loss of reputation and social status, or even the loss of their own lives.

Here the convinced psychological egoist will reply that whatever a person does he does because he gets satisfaction from it. If a mother sacrifices for her children it is because she gets more satisfaction from seeing them have a happy childhood or a good education than from anything else. If a person spends his life's savings to get revenge on his enemy, it is because he finds more satisfaction in revenge than in having his money.

Perhaps an example will show the limitations of this argument. A story (perhaps apocryphal) is told that Abraham Lincoln was once trying to convince a friend that all men were prompted by selfishness in doing good. As the coach in which they were riding crossed over a bridge, they saw an old razor-backed sow on the bank making a terrible noise because her pigs had fallen into the water and were in danger of drowning. Mr. Lincoln asked the driver to stop, lifted the pigs out of the water, and placed them on the bank.

> When he returned, his companion remarked: "Now Abe, where does selfishness come in on this little episode?" "Why, bless your soul Ed, that was the very essence of selfishness. I should have had no peace of mind all day had I gone on and left that suffering old sow worrying over those pigs. I did it to get peace of mind, don't you see?"[8]

Mr. Lincoln's argument is based on a misconception. If he had not cared for the pigs' welfare, he could not have derived pleasure from helping them. Had he not had a prior desire for something other than his own happiness, he would not have experienced satisfaction from helping them. His own satisfaction was not the *object* of his action, but rather the *consequence* of his preexisting desire for the animals' welfare. This example illustrates the fact that all actions cannot be egoistically motivated. If my welfare consists of the satisfaction of desires, some desires must exist prior to the desire for my own welfare.

---

[8]Quoted from the *Springfield* (Illinois) *Monitor,* by Joel Feinberg in "Psychological Egoism," in his *Reason and Responsibility,* 6th ed. (Belmont, Calif.: Wadsworth, 1985). Feinberg's article is a valuable discussion of psychological egoism, and the argument based on this example is derived from it.

Nevertheless, most of us would probably say that the psychological egoist has a great deal of truth on her side. Many apparently altruistic acts really are done out of self-interest. Even if not all human actions are motivated by self-interest, it still may be true that most actions are. So perhaps a weaker argument for ethical egoism can be made on the basis of psychological egoism—namely, that ethical egoism agrees at least as much with the facts of human psychology as any other moral philosophy, and perhaps more so. The ethical egoist could still conclude that, because moral philosophy should be based as solidly as possible on human nature, egoism has a strong justification.

As long as human beings are capable of non-egoistic behavior, and we have reason to believe they are, other moral positions are not eliminated. Considering the problems egoism has with the other criteria of evaluation, we must conclude that even its weaker defense should not lead us to accept egoism until we have looked at alternative moral philosophies.

CONCEPT SUMMARY

Egoistic moral theory faces a major problem of internal coherence following from the fact that, according to egoism, the same act can be both wrong and not wrong. Another inconsistency is that a potential conflict exists between the egoist's own self-interest and the requirement that a moral standard be stated impersonally. My self-interest is often not served by your following your self-interest, but the egoistic moral standard states that everyone should follow his or her own self-interest. The egoist has no satisfactory way of overcoming either type of inconsistency. Egoism generates many moral judgments that are at odds with our ordinary moral beliefs. It also encounters problems in attempting to resolve conflicts of interest, since it can only advocate that individuals follow their own self-interest. The egoist finds it difficult to make moral decisions when one alternative is not clearly the most conducive to his or her own self-interest. Finally, the justification of the egoistic moral standard by an appeal to psychological egoism is weakened by the logical problems with the argument and by the fact that the claim that we always act from self-interest seems false.

V

THE ETHICS OF NATURAL LAW

David and Martha are both conservative Roman Catholics. They have not practiced "artificial" contraception and as a result now have five children. They love their children and would enjoy having more, but they agree that David's income cannot adequately support a larger family. In fact, they are not sure how they will manage to put their children through college. They both shudder at the thought of Martha's becoming pregnant again, and this fear is beginning to interfere with their sex life. Their priest has told them that taking the contraceptive pill is against natural law and is immoral.

Consider another example. Sam Black is a Roman Catholic physician. One of his female patients wants him, as her family physician, to perform a tubal ligation (sterilization) on her. But his church teaches that sterilizations are contrary to natural law and hence immoral. Because of his close relationship to this patient, Dr. Black finds her request difficult to deny. Besides, he has been wondering about the validity of the moral objection to sterilization on the basis that it is contrary to natural law. How does a person determine what is and is not contrary to natural law? Even if one could make such a determination, would it be a good way to settle moral questions?

Finally, consider a third example. Gay liberation groups, liberal churches, and certain political organizations are sponsoring a statewide campaign to decriminalize homosexual acts between consenting adults. Several conservative religious groups and other organizations devoted to the defense of "family values" oppose this campaign. They argue that homosexuality will destroy the family, is a threat to young children, and is repugnant and unnatural. John prides himself on being a thoughtful citizen. He views many of the statements from both sides as rather empty rhetoric and hears few careful arguments in the debate. He tends to be suspicious of the claims that homosexuality will destroy the family and that homosexuals are more of a threat to young boys than heterosexuals are to young girls, but the charge that homosexuality is unnatural is more disturbing. He does believe the homosexual lifestyle has a repugnant and even perverse quality. Does this objection have any rational basis? Can a sexual act between two consenting adults be considered immoral because it is supposedly unnatural, even if each person is considerate of the other and no one is hurt?

All of these moral issues, and many others, reflect the continuing influence of the tradition of natural-law moral philosophy. This tradition is especially associated with the Roman Catholic Church, but its influence is not confined to that institution, as the third example illustrates. Most of us have the deep-seated feeling, especially with regard to sexual conduct, that if something is "unnatural" it is also immoral. Even the law sometimes makes reference to "unnatural acts" with the obvious intent of condemning them as wrong. The words *unnatural* and *immoral* are closely connected in popular thought. On the other hand, the connotation of the word *natural* is strongly positive. We tend to think that if something is "natural" it must also be right.

We shall see that much of this talk of what is and isn't "natural" has little to do with the more sophisticated versions of natural law. Nevertheless natural-law moralists do teach that human nature and the good life are connected. Our primary life goal is to realize as fully as we can our potential as a human being. This statement resembles egoism but has an important difference. Whereas the egoist strives to realize his own individual preferences, whatever they may be, the advocate of natural law believes in realizing those goods specified by a nature that he has in common with his fellow human beings. Thus the moral standard in natural law has an objective quality that egoism lacks.

We can easily see why the natural-law tradition provides an attractive approach to the problem of determining a moral standard. If ethics is supposed to regulate human conduct, the purpose of this regulation must surely be for the good of human beings themselves. And surely this good must be determined by the requirements of human nature. What more reasonable foundation could any ethical system have than human nature itself? Nevertheless all the examples given show that the appeal to human nature as a basis for making moral judgments has some trouble. Does this appeal imply that "doing whatever comes naturally" is right? Can a person who has a natural tendency to lie justify her lying behavior by an appeal to natural law? How do we determine what standards of conduct our human nature entails? In this chapter we shall look at the tradition in moral philosophy that raises such difficult questions and yet continues to influence our moral thinking.

The Moral Standard

What Is Natural Law?   The name *natural law* can be misleading. It implies that ethical laws are like "laws of nature" or scientific laws. An example of a scientific law is Boyle's law in physics, which states that the product of the pressure and the specific volume of a gas at constant temperature is constant. But scientific laws are *descriptive;* they state how phenomena in nature do in fact always behave. Ethical laws, on the other hand, are *prescriptive;* they stipulate how people *should* behave, whether or not they do so. Natural-law theorists assume that human beings have free will and that they can decide whether to act as they ought to act. This discussion implies that the word *law* has more in common with civil laws than with natural laws, because both civil and ethical laws can be disobeyed. Natural phenomena presumably always act according to the laws of nature, whereas people are not necessarily compelled to behave legally or morally.

But the analogy with civil laws can also be misleading, for the point of the term *natural* is to contrast ethical laws with the laws of governments. When the Roman jurists were looking for legal concepts that could apply throughout the Roman empire, they turned to the philosophy of natural law precisely because it proposed that certain ethical laws are "natural" rather than "conventional"; that is, they apply equally to all human beings, regardless of the conventions, customs, or beliefs of their particular society. These natural laws for all human behavior thus could serve as a basis for judging the actions of people throughout the Roman empire. Therefore we can say that *natural law* refers to ethical guidelines or rules that stipulate what people ought to do rather than what they in fact do and that apply equally to all humanity because they are rooted in human nature itself.

The term *natural law* can be misleading because it inevitably brings to mind some kind of ethical legalism—the belief that hard-and-fast guidelines cover every possible detail of conduct. This characterization, however, is unfair to the natural-law tradition. The greatest exponent of natural law, Thomas Aquinas (1224–1274), believed that the basic outlines of proper human behavior are relatively clear. But he also taught that, the closer we come to particular moral judgments, the more prone we are to error and the more room we make for differences of opinion. Some contemporary natural-law theorists even believe that natural law has a historical dimension, so that what is right in one epoch may not be right in another. Whether or not this view is accepted, the lively discussions of ethical issues in the Roman Catholic Church, where natural-law thinking is especially prominent, show that natural-law theorists by no means believe that all ethical problems have already been solved. The word *law* merely refers to the prescriptive character of the rules that should govern human behavior.

The natural-law theorist does, however, believe in an objective standard for morality: Moral truth exists just as scientific truth exists. The natural-law theorist cannot be a radical ethical relativist or an ethical sceptic. He generally believes we know the basic outlines of this standard, but this belief does not mean we have interpreted the implications of this standard correctly in every case. In ethics, as in science, human beings continually search for truth. The belief in objective truth should be no more stifling of human freedom and creativity in ethics than it is in science.

Human Nature and Natural Inclinations. What is the standard of truth in ethics? As an approximation we can say that the standard is human nature. People should do whatever promotes the fulfillment of human nature. Here again we can point out the similarity between natural law and egoism. But natural-law theorists have always believed that the individual alone cannot determine what counts as human nature. How then do we determine what human nature is?

Let us consider some analogous situations that illustrate the difficulty in describing human nature. It is often useful to describe something's nature in terms of its function—that is, in terms of the purpose it serves. For example, we can describe the nature of a pencil in terms of its function or purpose of enabling humans to make marks on paper. A "good" pencil is one that performs this function well—without smudging or scratching or breaking, for example. Similarly, if an automobile's function is to provide transportation, a good automobile is one that provides comfortable and reliable transportation. The function of a tomato plant is to produce tomatoes, and a good tomato plant is one that produces an abundance of tomatoes of high quality.

We can also determine the function of human beings if we confine a person to one particular social role. The function of a farmer is to grow food, and a good farmer produces food efficiently and with proper care for the animals and the land for which he has responsibility. By similar reasoning we can say that a good father is one who attends diligently to the welfare of his children. But now let us take human beings out of their social roles and ask simply "What is the function of a human being?" Here we see the problem faced by those who attempt to base ethics on human nature. Generally speaking, the more complex the animal, the more varied its behavior and presumably the less clearly defined is its "nature." The freedom of action possessed by human beings makes it plausible to argue, as some philosophers have, that human beings are characterized precisely by the fact that they have no set nature or function. How can we make sense out of natural law in the face of these problems?

Fortunately we can take another, more promising approach to discovering what human nature is like. One way to determine the characteristics of a thing is to observe its behavior. In chemistry we learn about the nature of iron by observing how it reacts with other elements. Perhaps we can find out what human nature is like by ascertaining those "natural inclinations," as Aquinas put it, that human beings have in common. To put it another way, perhaps we can discover what human nature is by identifying those goals that human beings generally tend to seek. These values would presumably reflect the structure of our human nature, which natural law directs us to follow. Therefore we shall propose the following statement as the moral standard of natural law:

> MS: Those actions are right that promote the values specified by the natural inclinations of human beings.

How do we find out what these natural inclinations are? We might first consult psychologists, sociologists, or anthropologists. Some contemporary natural-law theorists use studies from the social sciences to defend their conclusions. However, the natural-law tradition developed before the rise of the social sciences, and a more informal method of observation was used to discover the basic human inclinations. Most natural-law theorists would maintain that these observations are still valid. We can divide the values specified by natural human inclinations into two basic groups: (1) biological values, which are strongly linked with our bodies and which we share with other animals, and (2) characteristically human values, which are closely connected with our more specifically human aspects. (We will not call this second group uniquely human values because some of the inclinations that point to these values, such as the tendency to live in societies, are not unique to human beings.) We can summarize the values and the natural inclinations that point to them as follows:

1. *Biological Values*

   a. Life. From the natural inclinations that we and all other animals have to preserve our own existence, we can infer that life is good, that we have an obligation to promote our own health, and that we have the right of self-defense. Negatively, this inclination implies that murder and suicide are wrong.

   b. Procreation. From the natural inclination that we and all animals have to engage in sexual intercourse and to rear offspring, we

can infer that procreation is a value and that we have an obligation to produce and rear children. Negatively, this inclination
implies that such practices as sterilization, homosexuality, and
artificial contraception are wrong.

2. *Characteristically Human Values*

   a. Knowledge. From the natural tendency we have to know, includ-
      ing the tendency to seek knowledge of God, we can infer that
      knowledge is a value and that we have an obligation to pursue
      knowledge of the world and of God. Negatively, this inclination
      implies that the stifling of intellectual curiosity and the pursuit of
      knowledge is wrong. It also implies that a lack of religion is
      wrong.

   b. Sociability. From the natural tendency we have to form bonds of
      affection and love with other human beings and to associate with
      others in societies, we can infer that friendship and love are good
      and that the state is a natural institution and therefore good. We
      thus have an obligation to pursue close relationships with other
      human beings and to submit to the legitimate authority of the
      state. We can also infer that war can be justified under certain
      conditions if it is necessary to defend the state. Negatively, this
      inclination implies that activities that interfere with proper
      human relationships, such as spreading slander and lies, are
      wrong. Actions that destroy the power of the state are also wrong,
      so natural law finds a basis for argument against revolution and
      treason, except when the state is radically unjust.

These natural inclinations are reflections of human nature, and the
pursuit of the goods they specify is the way to individual fulfillment. Aquinas
himself makes it clear that the list of values, which in most respects follows
his account, is incomplete; other natural-law theorists have expanded the
list to include such things as play and aesthetic experience. However the
list given here has had the greatest historical influence, and we shall assume
it is basically complete.

The more important issue raised by this list is the potential for conflict
between the various values. What should we do when our need to defend
ourselves requires that we kill someone else? What should we do when
sterilization is necessary to prevent a life-threatening pregnancy? What should
be done when contraception seems necessary in order to limit family size
so that families can properly educate the children they already have? In
each of these examples, one aspect of natural law seems to conflict with
another, and the question arises whether these values have a hierarchy on

which a decision can be based. The answer to this question brings into focus one of the most important and controversial aspects of natural law—moral absolutism.

Moral Absolutism and Its Qualifying Principles

Moral Absolutism. Suppose you were on a military convoy from the United States to England during World War II. Your ship was attacked and sunk. Your life raft was carrying 24 persons, although it was designed to carry only 20. You had good reason to believe that the raft would sink unless four people were eliminated, and four people on board were so seriously injured in the catastrophe that they were probably going to die anyhow. Because no one volunteered to jump overboard, you, as the ranking officer on the boat, decided to have them pushed overboard. Were you morally justified in doing so? Many of us would say that under the circumstances you were, but natural-law theorists would say that you were not justified, even if everyone on the raft would have died otherwise.

Consider another wartime example. Suppose you know that some prisoners have information that will save a large number of lives. The only way to obtain the information is to threaten to kill the prisoners, but you know that they will not reveal what they know unless your threat is absolutely serious. To show them how serious you are, you have another prisoner shot before their eyes. As a result of your action, the information is revealed and many lives are saved. Is this action justified? Many people would say that under these extreme circumstances it is justified, but natural-law theorists would say that it is not.

Finally, recall the examples at the beginning of the chapter. The traditional natural-law position is that practicing "artificial" contraception, undergoing sterilization, or practicing homosexuality is wrong. For the natural-law theorist, these prohibitions are valid even if the consequences are that parents produce children they cannot afford to educate or that the life of the mother is endangered or if homosexual relationships are the only sexual relationships a person can have with any satisfaction. These examples point out one of the most significant aspects of natural-law theory—namely, its absolutism.

Moral absolutism can refer either to the belief that some objective standard of moral truth exists independently of us or that certain actions are right or wrong regardless of their consequences. Natural law is an absolutist moral theory in both senses, but the second meaning of absolutism is highlighted by the illustrations provided. Natural-law theorists believe that *none of the values specified by natural inclinations may be directly violated.* Innocent people may not be killed for any reason, even if other innocent people can thus be saved. The procreative function that is a part of our biological nature may not be violated by such practices as contraception and sterilization, even if these practices are necessary to preserve other values, such as a child's education or even the mother's life. Similarly, homosexuality violates the value of procreation and is prohibited, even if it is the only kind of sex a person can enjoy.

Natural-law theorists have two reasons to hold that basic values specified by natural inclinations cannot be violated whatever the consequences. First, *basic values cannot be measured or compared;* that is, basic values cannot be quantified or measured by some common unit, so they cannot be traded off for one another. For example, we cannot divide the good of knowledge into units of value and the good of procreation into units of value so that the two can be compared on a common scale. Nor can the good of a single life be compared with the good of a number of lives; thus we cannot say that a single life may be sacrificed to preserve a number of other lives. This idea is sometimes called the "absolute value" or "infinite value" of a human life, suggesting that a human life cannot be weighed against anything else, including another human life. Natural-law theorists also make this point by saying that basic values are *incommensurable.* Because we cannot measure values, we cannot calculate which consequences of an action are more important. Therefore consequences cannot be used to determine the moral status of actions.

Second, consequences cannot be used to determine moral judgments because *we must make moral judgments by evaluating the motives of the person performing the action.* The *motive* of an action is what a person wants to accomplish by performing the action. For example, a person can give money to charity because he wants a good reputation in the community. The consequences of the action are good, but the motive is not morally praiseworthy. Some moral philosophers distinguish between a moral evaluation of the consequences of an action and a moral evaluation of the motives of the person performing the action; with this distinction we can say the action of giving money to charity was praiseworthy but the person giving the money was not praiseworthy, because the motives were bad. Natural-law theorists always place primary emphasis on motives.

Qualifying Principles. Because values are incommensurable and may not ever be directly violated, we may find ourselves in a situation in which any action we could perform violates some value and hence is apparently immoral. For example, self-defense may sometimes require that we override the natural inclination of another human being to self-preservation. If we do nothing, we allow ourselves to be killed; if we defend ourselves, we kill someone else. To avoid this paralysis of action and to gain deeper insight into the dynamics of situations of moral choice, natural-law theorists have developed two ideas that are absolutely crucial in making moral judgments: the principle of forfeiture and the principle of double effect.

According to the *principle of forfeiture,* a person who threatens the life of an innocent person forfeits his or her own right to life. (An *innocent* person is one who has not threatened anyone's life.) Suppose you are a pioneer who is tilling his land. Your wife and small child are in a log cabin on the hill. Two men approach you and express an intent to kill you and your family in order to take the land. Is it morally permissible for you to defend yourself, even to the point of killing them? Natural-law theorists answer the question in the affirmative. Even though you might have to violate the lives of your would-be assailants, they have forfeited their innocence by unjustifiably threatening your life. Therefore they have forfeited their claim to have their lives respected. We can make this point by distinguishing between killing and murder. *Killing* is taking the life of a non-innocent person, whereas *murder* is taking the life of an innocent person. When you take the life of a person who is attempting to kill you, you are killing him but you are not committing murder.

The principle of forfeiture can be used to justify not only acts of individual self-defense, but also war and capital punishment. A defensive war may be justified under certain conditions, even though it involves killing other people, because the aggressors have forfeited their right to life. Similarly, murderers may justly be put to death because they have forfeited their right to life by killing others.

According to the *principle of double effect,* it is morally permissible to perform an action that has two effects, one good and the other bad, if (1) the bad effect is unavoidable if the good effect is to be achieved, (2) the bad effect is unintended—that is, not a direct means to the good effect, and (3) a proportionally serious reason exists for performing the action.

The best way to explain this principle is by example. A pregnant woman who has tuberculosis wants to take a drug that will cure her disease, but the drug has the side effect of aborting the pregnancy. Is taking the drug morally permissible? The principle of double effect justifies taking the drug in this case, because all three of its conditions are met.

First, the bad effect is unavoidable in that the good effect cannot be achieved without also producing the bad effect. Presumably no other drug will cure the woman's tuberculosis and the abortion cannot be prevented once the drug is taken.

Second, the bad effect is unintended in that it is not a direct means to achieving the good effect. We must clarify here what natural-law theorists mean. The bad effect is certainly foreseen; the woman knows the drug will produce an abortion. However, the bad effect is not intended as a direct means to the good effect: An abortion is not a necessary step in curing the tuberculosis; rather, it is an unfortunate and unintended side effect. Evidence that the abortion is unintended even though it is foreseen is that the woman would presumably choose a different treatment that did not kill the fetus if it were equally effective and readily available.

Third, a proportionally serious reason exists for performing the abortion. The death of the fetus is at least balanced by the saving of the mother's life. If the bad effect were serious (as in this case), but the good effect were relatively insignificant, the action would not be justifiable by the principle of double effect, even if the other conditions were met. Here, consequences do play a part in natural-law reasoning. But note that consequences can be considered *only* when the other two conditions have been met.

Two other examples will show more clearly how the principle of double effect works. Suppose I want to turn on a light so that I can read a book on ethics, but I know that turning on the light will electrocute a worker on the floor below. If I cannot get the reading done except by electrocuting the worker, we can say that the electrocution is unavoidable. The bad effect is unintended in that electrocuting a worker is not a direct means to reading philosophy, but rather only an unfortunate and unintended side effect. But the third condition of the principle of double effect is not satisfied. The killing of a human being, even if unintended and unavoidable in the circumstances, is not outweighed by the value of reading a book on ethics. Therefore, turning on the light is not justified by the principle of double effect. The existence of a proportionally serious reason is often difficult to determine, as are the questions of the action's ultimate intention and avoidability. But in this case the application of the principle is clear.

Consider another example. A woman's egg is fertilized in the fallopian tube; as the fertilized egg develops it will rupture the tube, killing both the mother and the fetus. Is an abortion justified by the principle of double effect? The bad effect (the abortion) is unavoidable; the mother's life cannot be saved without it. The bad effect is not unintended, though, since removing the fetus from the fallopian tube is the direct means of saving the mother's life. The principle of proportionality is satisfied, because we have a case of life against life. However, since the second condition is not met, the abortion in this case cannot be justified by the principle of double effect.

This case is, of course, tragic for natural-law theorists, and various attempts have been made to justify the abortion on other grounds. For example, some natural-law theorists argue that the principle of forfeiture can be invoked, since the fetus is actually an aggressor on the life of the mother. Even though the fetus is innocent of any conscious motive to harm its mother, the actual effect of its growth is to threaten the life of its mother. Natural-law theorists sometimes say that the fetus, having no malicious motive, is subjectively innocent but not objectively innocent, because it does threaten the mother's life. Whether this argument justifies an abortion is left to the reader to decide.

Checklist for Applying Natural-Law Ethics

_____ 1. Determine whether an action is in accord with or in violation of one of the four fundamental values specified by human inclinations.

_____ 2. Determine whether the qualifying principle of forfeiture applies to the action.

_____ 3. Determine whether the qualifying principle of double effect applies to the action. In order for the principle of double effect to apply, all three of the following conditions must be met:
    a. The bad effect must be unavoidable in that the good effect cannot be achieved without also producing the bad effect.
    b. The bad effect must be unintended—that is, not a direct means to the good effect.
    c. A proportionally serious reason must exist for performing the action.

_____ 4. Make a final decision on the morality of the action.
    a. If the action is in accord with the fundamental values, or if it is not in accord but is covered by one of the qualifying principles, the action is morally permissible.
    b. If the alternative to the action is a violation of a fundamental value, the action is morally obligatory.
    c. If the action is a violation of a fundamental value and the qualifying principles do not apply, the action is morally impermissible.

CONCEPT SUMMARY

The basic idea of natural law is that a person should promote those values that are the object of our fundamental human inclinations or tendencies. The realization of these values in a person's life will lead to a fulfillment of his or her human nature. As analyzed by natural-law theorists, these values include the biological values of life and procreation and the characteristically human values of knowledge and sociability.

Because natural law stipulates that no fundamental values may be indirectly violated, the question arises as to what action should be taken when situations seem to force a person to violate one of the values regardless of what is done. The qualifying principles of forfeiture and double effect are designed to remedy this problem. According to the principle of forfeiture, a person who threatens the life of an innocent person forfeits his or her own right to life. The principle of double effect distinguishes between direct and indirect action and classifies as morally permissible certain actions that only indirectly violate a fundamental value.

The Personal and Social Ethics of Natural Law

Duties to Self. In natural-law ethics, a person's primary duty to self is to promote the realization in his or her life of the four fundamental values of life, procreation, knowledge, and sociability. The duties to oneself have a positive and a negative dimension. I have a positive obligation to promote the values specified by natural law and a negative obligation not to act directly against those values.

Keep in mind that the negative obligations are more binding than the positive ones. Because of the absolutist orientation of natural law, we are never justified in directly violating a fundamental value, but we need not always actively promote these values. A certain amount of discretion is called for in determining when and how the fundamental values of natural law are to be promoted. For example, a person who decides not to marry and have a family in order to devote herself to the service of God does not violate the requirements of natural-law morality. She may be failing to use her procreative powers, but she is not directly violating them. It is generally easier to determine when a person has violated a negative obligation than when he or she has violated a positive obligation. It is not surprising, therefore, that some of the best-known moral judgments of natural law are negative.

The moral duties to self arising from the biological values of life and procreation have received more attention than the moral duties derivable from the characteristically human values of knowledge and sociability. As we have already seen, self-defense is a positive duty justified by the value of life. The value of life also requires us not to commit suicide, because suicide directly violates that value. Therefore suicide has been condemned in the natural-law tradition. However, some actions that appear to be suicide may not be, because the principle of double effect applies. When a soldier throws himself on a grenade in order to protect his buddies, he is acting directly to save the lives of his fellow soldiers; his own death is a tragic but unintended consequence. He may well foresee his own death but does not directly intend it, and, strictly speaking, his death is not a means to the good effect of saving other lives. Furthermore, the principle of proportionality applies, since his death saves the lives of other people.

The value of procreation leads to what is probably the most widely discussed conclusion of natural-law theory—namely, the prohibition of "artificial" contraception. Since the use of contraceptive devices could be considered a violation of a duty to oneself, we can appropriately discuss it here. To show that contraception is intrinsically immoral, we need only point out that it is indeed a direct violation of the value of procreation. We have seen that neglecting the value of procreation in order to pursue another value, such as knowledge of God, is permissible. But, when a person chooses to have intercourse with his or her spouse and does something to prevent conception, he or she is directly acting against the value of procreation. Therefore the action cannot be acceptable from the standpoint of natural law.

Attempts have been made to avoid this conclusion by appealing to the principle of double effect. For example, we might argue that, when parents use contraceptive devices, their direct intention is to promote the value of knowledge by limiting their family size in order to provide more effectively for the education of their children. Contraception, so the argument goes, is only indirectly intended as a side effect. Obviously, this argument will not work, because the second condition of the principle of double effect is not met. The prevention of conception is a direct means chosen by the parents to provide better for their children's education. Therefore contraception must be considered to be a direct violation of natural law and hence immoral. Even more obvious is that sterilization is morally wrong by natural law, since a person who has a tubal ligation or a vasectomy is also acting directly against the value of procreation.

The situation is quite different if an action that produces sterility is taken for a reason that is legitimate in itself. Suppose a woman with uterine cancer has her uterus removed in order to save her life. The woman will no longer be able to bear children, but her action is still morally justifiable because sterility is not a necessary means to the end of saving the woman's life, but merely an unintended and unavoidable side effect. Furthermore, since life is a fundamental value, the woman must do what she can to save her life, as long as her action is not directly contrary to another basic value. Even if the woman would prefer the resultant sterility, the operation is still morally justified. Her primary intention is still presumably to save her life.

Natural-law theorists have not devoted as much attention to the negative and positive duties to self derivable from the values of knowledge and sociability, but these duties should be just as binding. An interesting exercise would be to consider the duties arising from these values. Obviously a person has an obligation to develop her ability to pursue knowledge through education and to develop her capacities for relationships with other people. But what kinds of actions should be counted as a direct violation of these values? Do we directly violate the value of knowledge if we discontinue a promising education or if we stifle our scientific or philosophical curiosity? These questions are left to the reader to decide.

Finally, in thinking about duties to self, it is natural to think about such pursuits as pleasure. Many people seem to have a natural inclination to pursue pleasure, so why should it not be listed as a fundamental value? Natural-law theorists believe that, if we examine our motivations closely, we will find that we do not pursue pleasure in and for itself. To understand this claim, consider the following possibility. Suppose you could be connected to an "experience machine" that would produce any sensations you desired.[1] You could have the pleasures of sex, the pleasures of eating, the euphoria experienced after jogging ten miles, or any number of other delightful experiences. Suppose you could spend your entire lifetime connected to such a machine. Would you do it? Most of us would probably choose to spend very little if any time connected to such a machine. The reason is that we want more than experiences. We want to *do* things, to *be* a certain kind of person, and to interact genuinely with other human beings in specific ways. Pleasure in and of itself is not a fundamental pursuit. You may be interested in considering whether you agree with this claim and whether you accept the natural-law theorist's claim that fame, power, and wealth are also not fundamental human pursuits.

Duties to Others. The biological and characteristically human values provide the basis for many negative duties to others. Besides the duty not to kill another person, including a human fetus, directly, we also have a duty not to act directly against the values of knowledge and sociability. Deliberately discouraging a child's curiosity, for example, violates the value of knowledge. Lying is also an offense against another person's inclination to know the truth. Actions that destroy the ability of people to relate to one another, such as slander and malicious gossip, violate the value of sociability. You can probably think of many other negative duties that follow from the biological and characteristically human values.

The extent of one's obligation to help others is controversial. Our obligation to help others is clearly limited by the requirement not to directly

---

[1]For a modified version of this idea (used for different purposes), see Robert Nozick, *Anarchy, State and Utopia* (New York: Basic Books, 1974), pp. 42–45.

violate another basic value. I cannot donate my heart to save your life while I am still in good health, but consider the following case.[2] In 1956 Leon and Leonard Madsen, two 19-year-old brothers, presented themselves to the Peter Bent Brigham Hospital in Boston. Leon's only hope for life was a kidney transplant from Leonard. In 1954 the hospital had performed the first successful kidney transplant in two adult identical twins. Is Leonard's donation of one of his kidneys morally permissible by natural law?

The question hinges on whether, in giving one of his kidneys to his brother, Leonard is acting directly against the value of his own life. The loss of a kidney is not a serious danger to life, but many natural-law theorists have believed the donation is nevertheless impermissible. Natural-law theorists have generally taught that our obligation to help others falls short of this action. Could you set up any general guidelines for the limits of benevolence according to natural-law theory?

Social Ethics. Three principles characterize the natural-law approach to social ethics. First, the state has a right to defend itself against internal and external enemies, as long as it is fundamentally just. Sociability is a natural human inclination, and humans cannot find fulfillment apart from association with other human beings. Consequently the state is natural to human beings and is not an arbitrary and oppressive invention of tyrants. Thus war is justifiable in certain circumstances if it is necessary for the preservation of the social order. But a war must be just, and natural-law theorists have developed the "just-war theory" to define the legitimate conditions of war. First, the war must be declared by a lawful authority in the state and not by private individuals. Second, the war must have a just cause; that is, a violation, attempted or accomplished, of the nation's strict rights must be present. A just cause might be the carrying off of part of the population, the seizing of territory or resources or property, or a serious blow to the nation's honor such as to weaken its authority. Third, the cause must not only be just, but must also be known to be just by the rulers who declare the war. The rulers must have the right intention in starting the war. Fourth, the conduct of the war must include the right use of means. To seek a good through the direct violation of a basic value is morally wrong. The killing of innocents, for example, must be avoided.

A second principle of natural-law social ethics is that natural law is always more binding than the human laws of a particular state. As long as the laws of the state do not seriously violate the principles of natural law, citizens have an obligation to obey them. Nevertheless, when the moral

HOW ABOUT OTHER COUNTRIES?

[2]See Paul Ramsey, *The Patient as Person* (New Haven and London: Yale University Press, 1970), pp. 165–197.

wrongs perpetrated by the state are great and when it can be reasonably predicted that a rebellion would succeed, revolution may be justified. Natural-law theorists often distinguish between the question of whether a citizen's action is *objectively correct* (in accordance with natural law) or whether it is *subjectively correct* (done for the right reasons). For example, a conscientious objector's action in refusing military service may be objectively correct, because the war is actually unjust, but subjectively incorrect, because the objection is based not on moral grounds but perhaps on the fear of losing one's life. Or the objector's action can be objectively incorrect and subjectively correct, as when the war is just but the objector genuinely thinks it is not and so refuses to serve in the military. Of course, a citizen might believe a war is just when it is not, in which case his military service would also be objectively incorrect but subjectively correct. Natural-law theorists have always held that one's duty is to follow one's own conscience; that is, one's action should always be subjectively correct. At the same time, we also have an obligation to keep our conscience from being corrupted by factors like self-interest.

The third principle of natural-law social ethics is that the state should be organized for the common good. The state exists for the good of individuals; individuals do not exist for the benefit of the state. Therefore the common good is nothing more than the conditions necessary for the realization of the four values of life, procreation, knowledge, and sociability. Natural-law theorists have insisted, for example, that citizens should be accorded a "just wage" sufficient to allow them lives of dignity and productiveness and to realize the moral values of natural law in their lives. Exploitation by private business or the government is wrong. Many natural-law theorists have been sympathetic with socialism and welfare-state policies as the most appropriate means for realizing these goals. Whether or not natural law is compatible with an enlightened form of capitalism is a question worth considering.

If the state is obliged to give citizens the opportunity to realize the values prescribed by natural law, does it follow that the state should force the values of natural law on its citizens? This conclusion has often been drawn by moral theologians, as the following passage by Häring illustrates.

> The state has a duty to assume an unequivocal position in relation to natural and supernatural revelation. The Church was repeatedly forced to condemn the principle of the "liberal" state according to which every option, every doctrine, whether true or false, good or bad, has an equal right to be publicly expressed and defended through free speech and press. These so-called "liberal" principles, apart from dishonor to God, would ultimately lead the state to its own destruction. For its own survival, not to speak of progress, it must possess at least a minimum of

certain and unassailable principles regarding truth and error, good and evil. Only through the unconditional possession of such principles can the state avoid the dilemma of anarchy which forbids nothing 'or legislation which is utterly arbitrary in its sheer legal positivism.

To avoid very grave disunity in the public life of a nation, however, it is justifiable at times for the state to restrict its protection to the truths universally accepted by the major groups in its domain representing basic attitudes to life. And from a merely practical standpoint, it may go still further and grant the same freedom to any and every doctrine. However, such a situation is far from ideal.[3]

Häring's statement represents a completely different stand on the enforcement of morality from the libertarian position of the egoist. What is the basis of this extreme position on the obligation of the state to enforce the principles of natural law? Häring argues that actions contrary to natural law dishonor God and eventually result in the destruction of the state. However, he also admits that the conclusions of natural-law morality might not be accepted by a given population, in which case the generally accepted moral views should be allowed to prevail, even though the situation would be "far from ideal." (The ideal is the enforcement of moral precepts derived from natural law.)

Häring believes that the conclusions of natural law are objectively right, that they are matters of reason rather than revelation. Its conclusions are available to all those willing and able to use their faculty of reason. Thus, in asking the state to enforce natural-law morality, Häring does not believe he is calling for the enforcement of a uniquely Catholic, or even Christian, moral perspective. Like any natural-law moralist, Häring believes that he is advocating only what is in accord with human nature. From the standpoint of natural law, therefore, by allowing the advocacy and practice of actions contrary to true human inclinations, the state is promoting not self-realization, but rather the distortion of human nature.

Nevertheless, Häring's statements shock most people who have been raised in a democratic tradition. An interesting question is whether natural-law theorists can work out a political philosophy more genuinely supportive of individual freedom. Many sophisticated attempts have already been made in this direction, and Häring himself provides one possible avenue. Recalling the distinction between the objective and subjective morality of an action, we can see what is behind Häring's observation that some people may genuinely not be persuaded by the arguments of natural law. Because individuals should not do what they think is wrong and should do what

[3]Bernard Häring, *The Law of Christ*, trans. Edwin G. Kaiser (Paramus, N.J.: The Newman Press, 1966), Vol. 3, pp. 120–121. Used with permission.

they think is right, regardless of the objective morality of the actions, the state must be careful in forcing natural-law morality on its citizens. Even if natural-law moralists were to allow more freedom in behavior than Häring does, they may still believe the state is obliged to prevent immoral teachings and immoral behavior from unduly influencing other people. In any case, the criterion of the common good provides an instructive basis for a philosophy of the obligations of government to its citizens.

CONCEPT SUMMARY

The principle governing duties to self is that a person has an obligation to promote the realization in his or her life of the basic values specified by our natural inclinations and not to do anything that directly obstructs the realization of those values. Most of the duties to self discussed in traditional natural law have concerned the biological values of life and procreation. An interesting question to ask yourself is what positive and negative duties follow from the characteristically human values of knowledge and sociability.

Duties to others include the duty not to directly kill another person or to violate the values of knowledge (for example, by lying) or sociability (for example, by slander). Many other duties follow from the four fundamental values. The extent of one's positive obligations to others is limited by the duty not to violate obligations to oneself. The question of donating vital organs poses an interesting test case of the limits of duties to others.

Three principles characterize the natural-law approach to social ethics. First, the state has a right to defend itself against internal and external enemies, as long as the state is fundamentally just. Second, natural law takes priority over human laws, and it may sometimes be justifiable to engage in civil disobedience or even revolution. Third, the state should be organized for the common good; that is, the state should be ordered in a way that promotes the realization of the four values of natural law in the lives of its citizens.

Applying the Ethics of Natural Law

We can now apply natural law to some cases involving moral decision, following the methodology outlined in the checklist.

Case 1: A Case of Euthanasia

A 36-year-old accountant, married and the father of three young children, is diagnosed as having immunoblastic lymphadenopathy, a fatal malignant tumor of the lymph nodes. He has been receiving a variety of treatments, yet his condition has steadily worsened. He knows that all surgical and medical measures have been exhausted. He suffers daily from excruciating nerve-root pain; he must take addicting doses of narcotics but still is not free from pain. The expenses of his treatment are rapidly exhausting his family's financial resources. His wife and family are beginning to withdraw from him emotionally, in anticipation of his inevitable death. Having reconciled himself to his death, he asks the doctor for the means of killing himself in order to end his pain, the suffering of his family, and the depletion of the funds that are so important for his family's future well-being. Is it morally permissible for the physician to acquiesce in this request?[4]

1. Obviously, administering a drug to end the accountant's life is a direct action against one of the four fundamental values of natural law—namely, the value of life.

2. The only question is whether either of the two qualifying principles applies. The accountant is not guilty of any action that would cause him to forfeit his own right to life, so the principle of forfeiture does not apply.

3. The principle of double effect might be used to justify two kinds of actions the physician could perform to alleviate his patient's suffering. First, it could justify the use of a pain killer, even if the pain killer had the indirect effect of shortening the patient's life. (a) If no other drug could alleviate pain as effectively, the use of that particular drug could be considered unavoidable. (b) The direct intent of administering the pain killer would be to alleviate pain; the tendency of the pain killer to shorten life would be unintended because the shortening of life is not the direct means to eliminating pain. (c) Although some might argue that an action that shortens life is not justified by the desire to alleviate pain, most natural-law theorists would probably accept the use of the principle of proportionality in this case.

The principle of double effect could also justify the physician's decision not to use "heroic measures" to prolong the accountant's life. Natural-law theorists distinguish between "ordinary" and "extraordinary" means for preserving life. Father Gerald Kelly defines these two terms in the following way:

> *Ordinary* means of preserving life are all medicines, treatments, and operations [that] offer a reasonable hope of benefit for the patient and [that] can be obtained and used without excessive expense, pain, or other inconvenience . . . .

---

[4]This case was supplied by Harry S. Lipscomb, M.D. Used with permission.

Extraordinary means of preserving life [are] all medicines, treatments, and operations [that] cannot be obtained without excessive expense, pain, or other inconvenience, or [that], if used, would not offer a reasonable hope of benefit.[5]

The failure to use heroic or extraordinary means satisfies all three criteria of double effect. (a) The shortening of life is inevitable if extraordinary means are not used. (b) The shortening of life is unintended, because it is not a direct means to the use of ordinary means, and is simply an unfortunate side effect of the use of ordinary means. (c) The principle of proportionality is satisfied, since the use of extraordinary means would only prolong the accountant's dying process, not restore him to health. Therefore the decision not to use extraordinary means can be justified by the principle of double effect.

But the accountant's request goes far beyond the two measures described here. He is asking the physician to cooperate actively in directly ending his life. (a) The good effect of relieving the accountant's pain cannot be achieved without also producing the bad effect—namely, the accountant's death. So the first criterion is met. (b) However, the accountant's death is the direct means of achieving the release from pain, so the accountant's death is intended. The second criterion is not satisfied. (c) No proportionally serious reason exists for administering the lethal drug, since relief from pain cannot justify directly killing an innocent person, an act that is actually murder.

4. Because the physician's action in administering a lethal drug to the accountant is a violation of a fundamental value and because the qualifying principles of forfeiture and double effect do not apply, the action is morally impermissible.

Case 2: The Morality of Obliteration Bombing in World War II

During World War II, both the Germans and the Allied Forces bombed civilian residential areas, a practice called "obliteration bombing." Probably the two most famous examples of this practice, in which conventional explosives were used, were the German bombing of London and the Allied bombing of Dresden, Germany. Let us confine ourselves to the fire bombing of Dresden and ask whether this action was permissible by the principles of natural law.

1. The first question is whether the bombing of Dresden violated the value of life. The answer is that it did, so the action must be morally impermissible unless one of the two qualifying principles applies.

[5]Gerald Kelly, *Medico-Moral Problems* (St. Louis, Mo.: The Catholic Hospital Association, 1958), p. 120. Quoted in Paul Ramsey, *The Patient as Person*, p. 122.

2. The principle of forfeiture would apply if civilians in wartime can be considered non-innocent. If we assume that the criteria of just-war theory were met—that is, the Allied Forces were fighting a just war and the Germans were not fighting a just war—then the Germans in uniform were non-innocent and attacking them was morally justified. But most civilians in large cities were connected with the war effort in a very indirect way. Many had little direct knowledge of the reasons for war and certainly had no part in starting it. Therefore, the principle of forfeiture does not justify the bombing.

3. Some have argued that an appeal to the principle of double effect could justify the bombing. According to this argument, the intended effect of the bombing was to destroy war industries, communications, and military installations, whereas the damage to civilian life was unintentional and not a means to the production of the good effect. But a careful analysis of the conditions of the bombing will not sustain this argument. (a) Although killing of civilians truly is sometimes unavoidable when military targets are attacked, the massive civilian deaths in Dresden could have been avoided. (b) If the Allies were engaged in strategic bombing of war plants, with the direct intent to destroy the plants, and if the destruction of human life was unintended and unavoidable, the second condition of the principle of double effect would be satisfied. But, in this case, the maiming and death of hundreds of civilians was an immediate result of the bombing, and the undermining of civilian morale through terror was, on the testimony of military documents themselves, an object of the bombing. This goal of demoralization is impossible without a direct intent to injure and kill civilians. If one intends to create terror, one cannot escape intending the principle means of obtaining that end. Therefore the second condition of double effect is not met. (c) We can also question the allegation that the principle of proportionality was satisfied by the belief that obliteration bombing would shorten the war. That goal was speculative, futuristic, and problematic, whereas the evil effect was definite, immediate, and widespread. Thus we must conclude that the principle of double effect does not apply.

4. Because the Allied attack on Dresden involved the destruction of innocent human life and because the qualifying principles of forfeiture and double effect do not apply, we must conclude that the action was morally impermissible by natural-law theory.

Case 3: The Morality of Homosexuality

James has known since he was five years old that he was somehow different. Even then he enjoyed watching male athletes and seemed to "love" his older male playmates. In high school he was active in sports and his attraction to members of his own sex became obvious to him and to some of his friends. He has never been attracted to women sexually, although he likes some of them as friends, and the thought of sex with a woman has always repelled him. In college he began to associate with other homosexuals. He has talked to several counselors, and he now feels ready to admit to himself and to others, including his family, that he is a homosexual. However he still wonders about the morality of homosexuality, especially because he is a Roman Catholic. Is homosexuality wrong by natural law?

1. The determination of whether homosexuality violates natural law is more difficult than it might at first appear. The traditional natural-law argument against homosexuality was based on the view that homosexual relationships involve a perversion or misuse of the sexual organs. Because the sex organs are made for procreation, using them for purposes other than this "natural end" is immoral. This same argument also leads to the conclusion that masturbation is immoral, because it uses the sex organs for pleasure rather than procreation. By a similar argument, oral sex and anal sex, even between married partners, is immoral. Thus, it is also wrong for a woman to refuse to breast-feed her child. If female breasts have the natural function of lactation, a mother who decides not to breast-feed her child acts directly against this natural function and does something wrong. This so-called perverted-faculty argument leads to so many absurd conclusions that it is being increasingly rejected. It does not even seem to be in agreement with Thomas Aquinas' basic understanding of natural law. For homosexuality to be immoral by our version of natural law, it must involve a direct action against a fundamental value.

Of course, homosexuals who engage in sexual activity have no intention of producing children; they know that their sexual activity cannot be procreative. But a married heterosexual couple who engage in sex during a nonfertile period also know that they cannot produce children, yet their action is not immoral by natural law. Neither the homosexual nor the married couple has done anything directly to violate the procreative function. The same statement applies to masturbation, oral sex, and anal sex; they do not seem directly to violate the value of procreation.

Some, perhaps many, homosexual acts are immoral because they violate the value of sociability. If the acts are demeaning or destructive or if they involve trickery or deception, they are wrong because they violate the value of loving, supportive human relationships. But the same is true of some heterosexual relationships, even if they occur within marriage. So we must look elsewhere for an argument that homosexual acts are wrong simply because they are homosexual.

Although it seems mistaken to say that homosexuals act directly to violate the value of procreation in the same straightforward sense that the use of contraceptives does, either case involves sex that is closed to the possibility of procreation. In fact, an exclusively homosexual lifestyle is closed to the possibility of procreation in a more decisive way than contraceptive sex or other types of nonprocreative sex by a married couple, because a homosexual's nonprocreative sex lasts throughout a lifetime. Therefore we can say that, although homosexual acts do not constitute a direct violation of the value of procreation, the homosexual lifestyle is antiprocreative.

2. Since homosexuality is not a direct threat to life, the principle of forfeiture is inapplicable.

3. James might argue that choosing a homosexual lifestyle is justifiable by the principle of double effect. (a) He might believe that the criterion of unavoidability is met, because it is impossible for him to have a fulfilling sex life without also failing to produce children. (b) He could say that his direct intent is to promote a fulfilling relationship and that any violation of the value of procreation is an unintended side effect. The nonproduction of children is not, after all, a direct means to his end of having a fulfilling sex life; he might even want to have children. (c) He could argue that the principle of proportionality is satisfied because the value of a meaningful relationship outweighs the failure to have children.

The first argument is weak because a fulfilling sex life is not a fundamental value, but the second criterion presents the main problem with this argument. Although it is true that the absence of children is not, as such, a direct means to James's goal of a fulfilling lifestyle, nonprocreative sex is a part of the means to this end. Whether the principle of double effect is applicable depends on the conceptual issue of whether the absence of children or nonprocreative sex is considered the undesirable effect. The absence of children is arguably an unintended side effect, but nonprocreative sex is a means to the desired end.

4. We have found problems with the argument that homosexual acts violate the value of procreation and with the application of the principle of double effect. However, virtually all natural-law theorists have concluded that homosexual acts are morally impermissible. Ask yourself whether you agree with this conclusion.

Case 4: The Suppression of Galileo

Galileo Galilei (1564–1642) has a strong claim to the title of founder of modern science. At first he accepted the Ptolemaic theory that the sun and planets revolved around the earth. But his invention of the telescope and the discovery of the satellites of Jupiter led him to confess openly his adherence to the Copernican system in 1610. In 1616 the Office of the Holy Inquisition took the important step of entering the works of Copernicus on the list of forbidden books and declaring his teaching heretical. In 1632

Galileo published his *Dialogue on the Two Principal Systems of the World,* in which he contrasted the Ptolemaic and Copernican systems of astronomy. He thought that, if he merely gave an "objective" account of the differences between the two systems, he would not offend the Inquisition and would thereby avoid persecution.

Galileo's sympathies with the Copernican system were all too evident, however, and the Inquisition banned his book and summoned him to Rome for a hearing. After being threatened with torture, Galileo was forced, on June 22, 1633, to go down on his knees and renounce the doctrine that the earth revolves around the sun and to swear that he would cease any further promotion of Copernican astronomy. Galileo lived for several more years under conditions of virtual house arrest, but he was still able to produce his greatest scientific book. However, the spectacle of Galileo's persecution inhibited the advance of science. Can Galileo's suppression be justified by the principles of natural law?

1. The leaders of the Inquisition would no doubt have defended their action by arguing that they were defending the astronomical system that seemed to be in agreement with Holy Scripture. They were later shown to be defending false views, which raises the question of what kind of conduct is implied by the natural-law theorist's commitment to the value of knowledge. If we cannot always be sure what the truth is, acting in accordance with the natural human inclination to know would seem to imply supporting freedom of inquiry. The leaders of the Inquisition failed at this point. They attempted to suppress the free scientific search for truth and thereby violated the value of knowledge.

2. Since Galileo had not threatened anyone's life, he had done nothing to forfeit his own right to life.

3. The leaders of the Inquisition no doubt would have argued that they were defending truth according to their understanding and that any obstruction of truth was an indirect and unintended consequence of their action. Let's examine whether their action satisfies the three criteria of double effect. (a) The leaders of the Inquisition would probably have said that Galileo's persecution was unavoidable in that they had no other way to defend the truth as they knew it, that is, the only way to support truth is to suppress error. But we have already seen that this view is questionable, for it assumes that we always know what the truth is. Furthermore, even if the leaders of the Inquisition possessed an infallible knowledge of truth, it doesn't seem plausible that truth seeking is best encouraged by suppression of opinions that one believes (or knows) are false. Therefore we shall conclude that the action of the Inquisition does not satisfy the test of avoidability. (b) Because Galileo's suppression was a direct means of defending the truth (as the leaders of the Inquisition understood it), the test of inten-

tionality is also not met. (c) The leaders of the Inquisition probably would have said that their action passed the test of proportionality, since the negative consequences of Galileo's suppression were outweighed by the fact that truth was defended. But this claim is questionable, because the suppression of opinion (even if it is false) is probably not the best way to defend the truth. Besides, the test of proportionality is relevant only if the other tests are met.

4. Because the action of the Inquisition's leaders violates the value of knowledge by suppressing the right to dissent and because the two qualifying principles are inapplicable, we must conclude that the leaders' action was morally impermissible.

Evaluating Natural Law as a Moral Theory

We are now ready to evaluate natural law, using the four criteria set up in Chapter 3. I will give you my own evaluations and will try to defend them.

Natural Law

How well do I think the theory meets the criteria?

Criteria	Very Well	Moderately Well	Very Poorly
1. (Consistency)	X		
2. (Plausibility)		X	
3. (Usefulness)	X		
4. (Justification)			X

Criterion 1: Consistency. I have given natural law a rating slightly better than "moderately well" for consistency. Natural-law ethics is, for the most part, internally consistent, but some theorists have found a problem in the use of the principle of forfeiture to justify the direct taking of life. Traditional natural-law theorists take an absolutist position regarding the values of life, procreation, sociability, and knowledge and maintain that the values can never be directly violated for any reason. But the principle of forfeiture has seemed, even to some natural-law moralists, to be a violation

of the absolute value of life, for it allows the direct taking of life. Killing in war and in self-defense can be justified by the principle of double effect, because we can argue that the direct intent of these actions is to protect the country or to protect one's life. However, the principle of double effect cannot justify capital punishment, because it can only be counted as a direct taking of life. Here the principle of forfeiture is required if the taking of life by capital punishment is to be justified. Because capital punishment has been considered morally permissible by traditional natural-law moralists, a principle like the principle of forfeiture has been employed. It is interesting to consider whether the principle of forfeiture is a legitimate part of natural-law morality or whether its use in natural-law arguments is inconsistent with the theory.

Criterion 2: Plausibility. I have given natural law a relatively low rating for plausibility. As we have seen, a moral theory can be evaluated in part by comparing the moral judgments it produces with our own prior moral beliefs about these issues. Natural law certainly does produce some moral judgments that many of us find difficult to accept. Although our objection is inconclusive, because our moral judgments may be incorrect, the comparison is important. These seemingly irrational judgments produced by natural law fall into two primary categories.

First, in situations of "life against life," in which human life will be lost regardless of what decision is made, natural law teaches that innocent people must never be directly killed, even if the result is greater loss of life in the long run. For example, natural-law moralists hold that, when a choice must be made between pushing a person off a life raft or letting everyone drown, we must choose the second option. When the choice is between bombing civilians and shortening a war, thereby saving many lives, or not bombing civilians and thereby producing greater overall loss of life, we must again choose the second option. Finally, even when both the mother and the fetus will die if an abortion is not performed, natural law teaches that an abortion is immoral, unless the principle of double effect is applicable. These conclusions seem implausible—even cruel—to many people, yet they follow from the absolutist character of natural-law ethics—the view that a fundamental value must never be directly violated.

Second, natural law often seems to place excessive emphasis on the physical or biological values, giving them importance equal to or greater than the characteristically human values. The most widely known example of this tendency is the stress on procreation in marriage. Traditional natural law holds that the primary function of marriage is procreation and that the secondary function is companionship; that is, primary emphasis is placed on the biological function of reproduction, a function that human beings have in common with other animals. Characteristically human qualities, such as the capacity for love and commitment, are given secondary status. This view seems inconsistent with the form of natural law we have advocated, according to which the biological and characteristically human values are of equal importance. However, our proposed concept of natural law prohibits the use of contraception, because it is a direct violation of the value of procreation. Most people probably feel that the value of procreation should be violated in order to allow a couple more fully to enjoy a love relationship or more adequately to care for the children they already have. Why should procreation be a value that can never be violated?

Many contemporary natural-law theorists have agreed that the characteristically human values should be given priority over the biological values. They criticize traditional natural-law theory for being too "physicalistic" or for exhibiting the trait of *physicalism,* which is the understanding of human acts in terms of their physical or biological function.[6] Some natural-law theorists would regard as excessively physicalistic any version of natural-law theory that gives greater or even equal importance to the physical or biological values of life and procreation. For example, they might argue that, in marriage, love (sociability) and the proper rearing of children (knowledge) should have priority over any obligation to produce more children. Similarly, a concern for the quality of life as exhibited in the capacity for meaningful relationships (sociability) might justify euthanasia in situations like the one presented in Case 1, in which the accountant is dying of a malignancy of the lymph nodes. By the same kind of reasoning, the traditional natural-law prohibitions of sterilization, homosexuality, masturbation, and many other practices could also be reversed. It is left to the reader to decide whether this restructuring is compatible with natural-law morality.

Criterion 3: Usefulness. I have rated natural law better than "moderately well" on usefulness. In order to help people think clearly about moral issues and reach conclusions in difficult cases, a moral theory must provide a clear and plausible method for resolving moral controversies. Natural law has been reasonably successful in this regard. Natural-law moralists generally agree on many important ethical issues. However, the determination of whether a fundamental value has been violated is sometimes difficult, which impairs the usefulness of natural-law moral theory. Recall that a basic value may never be directly violated, but it may be indirectly violated when the principle of double effect applies. Examining the morality

[6] See Charles E. Curran, "Natural Law and Contemporary Moral Theology" in his *Contemporary Problems in Moral Theology* (Notre Dame, Ind.: Fides, 1970), pp. 97–158.

of homosexuality, however, points up the difficulty of deciding in some instances whether a fundamental value has been directly or only indirectly violated. We saw how homosexuality and some other sexual "deviations" could be regarded as only indirect violations of natural law, although many natural-law philosophers would disagree with this view.

Criterion 4: Justification. I have given natural law a very low rating for this criterion. Natural-law morality has been associated with religion since the advent of Christianity, so we might suppose that its advocates would attempt to justify the moral standard of natural law by an appeal to the will of God or divine revelation. But we have seen that both the Jewish and Catholic traditions have held that ethical truth is available to all human beings through the natural use of their reason, whether or not they accept a particular religious revelation. Certain religious injunctions, such as observing the Sabbath in Judaism or partaking of the Lord's Supper in Christianity, are derived exclusively from revelation. But, apart from such special commands, revelation is not necessary in order for us to know how we ought to live. While God's wisdom may be the ultimate foundation of ethical truths, these truths can be known independently of any specifically religious source.

What, then, is the basis of our knowledge of ethical truth that is equally available to all people? We have seen that it is human nature or, more specifically, the natural inclinations of human beings; but we still have not explained how these natural inclinations are known or how they establish ethical truth. Let's consider one account of the foundations of natural law.[7]

We can begin by considering some of the principles or norms that underlie our thinking in areas not necessarily related to ethics. For example, in science we assume that all occurrences in nature have an adequate reason, even if we do not know what this reason is. In logic, we assume that a self-refuting thesis is to be abandoned. In sense perception, we assume that the things we see are real unless we have reason to believe we are experiencing an illusion. Such principles cannot be proven, for they would be presupposed in any possible proof. But, although they cannot be proven, they are obviously valid to anyone who has any experience with scientific inquiry or even practical living. To deny them is to disqualify oneself from the pursuit of knowledge. In this sense these principles are self-evident.

Some natural-law theorists believe that certain ethical theses underlie

---

[7]See John Finnis, *Natural Law and Natural Rights* (Oxford: Clarendon, 1980), pp. 59–75.

our action in the same way. In particular, we assume in our action that value exists in life, procreation and child rearing, sociability, and knowledge. One way to see the self-evident nature of these values is to observe that anyone who denies them finds that he has refuted himself. We can illustrate this claim by showing self-refutation in the sceptical assertion that knowledge is not a good. One natural-law theorist states the contradiction in the sceptic's assertion in this manner:

> One who makes such an assertion, intending it as a serious contribution to rational discussion, is implicitly committed to the proposition that he believes his assertion is worth making, and worth making *qua* true; he thus is committed to the proposition that he believes that truth is a good worth pursuing or knowing. But the sense of his original assertion was precisely that truth is not a good worth pursuing or knowing. Thus he is implicitly committed to contradictory beliefs.[8]

Some natural-law theorists believe that similar demonstrations can be given for the other basic values, although the arguments have not been worked out in detail.

An important point is that, according to this version of natural-law theory, something is not good because we have a natural inclination to pursue it. Rather, we have a natural inclination to pursue it because it is good. Natural inclinations are indicators of those goods that we tend to pursue. Yet it is also true that, if our human nature or the general human condition were different, we might pursue different goods.

Even if we accept the argument that knowledge is a good, similar arguments for the other three values of natural-law morality are not readily available. Nor does this argument establish that these values can never be violated—that, for example, the good of procreation could not be violated in order to care better for the children we already have. In other words, the natural-law theorist finds it difficult to establish the absolutism that characterizes his position, in both of the senses in which this term is used. He encounters difficulties in identifying natural inclinations and in establishing that the values specified by these inclinations are objectively valid. He also encounters difficulties in establishing that the values of natural law can never be violated. Thus the claim of the natural-law theorist that the values of natural law are clear and objectively valid for all people has not been demonstrated.

---

[8]John Finnis, *Natural Law and Natural Rights,* pp. 74–75.

CONCEPT SUMMARY

Some natural-law theorists believe that traditional natural-law theory is inconsistent in using the principle of forfeiture to justify the direct taking of life, as in capital punishment. Natural-law theory also does not agree with our prior moral beliefs in several important respects. First, it does not agree with our prior moral beliefs in its claims that life can never be taken. Most of us would probably agree, for example, that a mother should have an abortion when both she and the fetus will otherwise die. Second, natural law also disagrees with most people's moral convictions in its emphasis that the biological values have an importance equal to or greater than that of the characteristically human values. This tendency to understand human action in terms of its biological or physical function is called *physicalism*.

The usefulness of natural-law ethics is limited by the fact that we sometimes have difficulty determining when a fundamental value has been directly violated. Natural-law moralists also have difficulty justifying their fundamental values. They sometimes attempt to justify the basic values of natural-law morality by arguing that the values are necessarily assumed in all human activity; however, this demonstration has not been completely worked out. Furthermore, the arguments do not show that basic values may never be violated.

VI

THE ETHICS OF UTILITARIANISM

In 1958 and 1959 the *New England Journal of Medicine* reported a series of experiments performed on patients and new admittees to the Willowbrook State School, a home for retarded children in Staten Island, New York.[1] The experiments were designed to confirm the usefulness of gamma globulin as an immunization against hepatitis, to improve that serum, and to learn more about hepatitis. The school was already experiencing a low-grade hepatitis epidemic. Researchers obtained the consent of the parents, since the children were both underage and retarded. The children were divided into experimental groups and control groups that received hepatitis virus at various levels of infectiousness and gamma globulin inoculations at various strengths. Some of the gamma globulin was given below the strength known to be effective. Children who contracted the disease suffered the usual symptoms (enlargement of the liver, vomiting, and anorexia), but all of them recovered.

When these experiments became public knowledge, they produced a storm of controversy. Many people objected that the children had been "used" in a morally unacceptable way. But the experimenters pointed out that the children would have been exposed to the virus anyhow, that none of them had died, and that valuable medical knowledge was gained from the experiments. Judged in terms of overall human well-being, the experiments do seem to be a good thing.

If this line of argument appeals to you, you may be a utilitarian. The basic question a utilitarian asks in determining the moral status of an action

[1]Robert Ward, Saul Krugman, Joan P. Giles, A. Milton Jacobs, and Oscar Bodansky, "Infectious Hepatitis: Studies of Its Natural History and Prevention," *New England Journal of Medicine* 258, No. 9 (February 27, 1958): 407–416; Saul Krugman, Robert Ward, Joan P. Giles, Oscar Bodansky, and A. Milton Jacobs, "Infectious Hepatitis: Detection of the Virus during the Incubation Period and Clinically Inapparent Infection," *New England Journal of Medicine* 261, No. 15 (October 8, 1959): 729–734.

LONG TERM? SHORT TERM?

is: "Will this action produce greater overall human well-being?" For the utilitarian, human well-being is the only good, although some utilitarians also include the well-being of animals. At any rate, the utilitarian considers everyone's well-being equally. Utilitarianism is thus midway between egoism and altruism. The egoist is concerned only with her own happiness, and the altruist is concerned only with the happiness of others. For the utilitarian, her own well-being is neither more nor less important than the well-being of anyone else.

Utilitarianism has its roots in 18th-century England, but it flowered in 19th-century England, particularly in the writings of Jeremy Bentham and John Stuart Mill. It greatly influenced liberal legislation in England and America and is probably the basic moral philosophy of most non-Christian humanists today.

Utilitarianism is one of the most powerful and persuasive traditions of moral thought in our culture. In fact, many moral controversies, such as the debate over euthanasia, can best be understood as a conflict between utilitarianism and traditional Hebrew-Christian morality. Jewish and Christian theorists generally condemn active euthanasia (for example, taking an injection of poison), even though passive euthanasia (for example, termination of life-saving medication) may sometimes be allowed. Their reasoning is usually based on the belief that God created human life and only He has the prerogative of directly ending it. But what if one does not believe in God? What if one believes that human life is solely the product of nonconscious forces and that the only source of value in the universe is human existence? Then it seems natural to conclude that the only possible good is the well-being of humanity. If an individual who is dying of incurable cancer sees only suffering for himself and those he loves, with no discernible good to come out of that suffering, why should he not take his life? If this course of action will produce the most overall human good or well-being, what better way of determining the right thing to do? Even someone who takes a religious perspective might well ask whether a loving God would not be concerned primarily with human welfare. Some Christian utilitarians maintain that the sanctity of life makes no sense if it is not related to human welfare. Thus, for both religious and nonreligious people, utilitarianism is an attractive moral position.

The Utilitarian Moral Standard

In the Willowbrook State School case and in the consideration of euthanasia, we have seen that the utilitarian can make a convincing case that welfare or well-being is a good criterion for deciding what ought to be done. But how are we to define well-being—what utilitarian theorists call *utility*—and what about the welfare of nonhuman creatures?

Before we answer these questions and formulate a utilitarian standard, we need to mention a commonly accepted rule in utilitarian moral thinking—"each counts for one and none for more than one." Thus, in deciding what is morally right, I must take into account all those affected by my action. But, because the utility (welfare) of different people is sometimes incompatible, the best I can do is to seek the greatest total utility. Also, many (probably most) utilitarians now believe that the evaluation of particular actions should be based on the utility of the general moral rules underlying these actions, and not on the actions themselves. Taking both of these considerations into account, we can formulate the utilitarian moral standard in the following way:

> MS: Those actions (or moral rules) are right that produce the most utility, or at least as much utility as any other actions (or rules).

Now we are in a position to discuss several aspects of this moral standard in more detail.

The Definition of Utility. How shall we define *utility*? Some utilitarians have maintained that utility is synonymous with happiness or even pleasure. But, unfortunately, these terms are defined differently by different people. And if we specify a particular definition of happiness or pleasure, we seem to be forcing our own values on others.

For example, J. S. Mill, an important 19th-century utilitarian, argued that human beings have capacities animals do not have and that, when we are aware of those capacities, we cannot regard anything as happiness unless it includes them. In particular, we must give "pleasures of the intellect, of the feeling and imagination, and of the moral sentiments a much higher value as pleasures than those of mere sensation."[2] Mill believed we could confirm the judgment that these pleasures have a higher value than the pleasures of food and sex, for example, simply by asking those who had experienced both kinds of pleasure which kind they preferred. Would you really want to exchange places with a person who had all of his physical desires satisfied but who had no close personal relationships, no intellectual or artistic interests, and no goals other than pleasure? Most of us would conclude, Mill believed, that it is better to be a dissatisfied Socrates than a satisfied fool.

---

[2]John Stuart Mill, *Utilitarianism* (New York: Liberal Arts Press, 1957), p. 10.

However, not everyone who has experienced both the pleasures of the intellect and the pleasures of sex will always choose the former over the latter. The novelist D. H. Lawrence believed that we relate most meaningfully to other human beings and obtain our deepest communication with the nature of things through sexual acts. So, as Mill himself acknowledges, the most we can say is that a majority of people who have experienced the various kinds of pleasures usually prefer the pleasures of the intellect, feelings, and imagination. But even so, have we established that the majority is right? It seems that the utilitarian cannot really define utility in terms of the "higher" pleasures without being arbitrary.

Perhaps it would be better to define utility as the satisfaction of any preferences or desires a person might have. But this definition seems too broad and permissive. Jack the Ripper satisfied his preferences by killing people. Must the utilitarian promote the satisfaction of his preferences even though they conflict with the desire of his victims to live?

As we have seen, for the utilitarian the satisfaction of any preference must be considered a "good" in some sense, but it need not be a good toward which the utilitarian aims. The utilitarian's goal is the greatest total amount of satisfaction of preferences. Some desires, such as the desire to become a cancer researcher, contribute at least potentially to the satisfaction of the desires of others as well, such as those who have cancer. Most of our desires are relatively neutral with respect to the desire-satisfaction of others. Thus my desire to buy an ice-cream cone after class neither contributes to nor detracts from your desire to go back to your apartment. Still other desires, like those of Jack the Ripper, decrease the ability of others to satisfy their desires. These categories of preferences or desires can be classified according to their claim to satisfaction, beginning with those that have the highest claim:

1. Preference whose satisfaction contributes to the preference-satisfaction of others
2. Preference whose satisfaction is neutral to the preference-satisfaction of others
3. Preference whose satisfaction decreases the preference-satisfaction of others

When we arrange the categories of preference-satisfaction into such a hierarchy, we can see that the utilitarian should aim at the satisfaction of preferences in the top two categories if he wishes to achieve the greatest total amount of desire-satisfaction. Although this solution to the problem of defining utility is not without its difficulties, it does seem to avoid the problem of arbitrariness inherent in the first attempt. We shall therefore define *utility* as the greatest total amount of preference- or desire-satisfaction.

Quantity versus Distribution of Utility. A second question raised by the moral standard has to do with the amount of utility, which can refer either to the total *quantity* of utility or to the maximum *distribution* of utility. Consider a situation represented by the following table:

Action	Number of People Affected	Units of Utility Per Person	Total Quantity of Utility
Act 1	2	100	200
Act 2	50	2	100

Note that Act 1 affects only 2 people, but it gives each of them 100 units of utility and gives no one any disutility, so that the total quantity of utility is 200 units. The alternative act affects 50 people, but it produces only 2 units of utility each. The act producing the greatest quantity of utility would not provide for its widest distribution, and the act producing the widest distribution would not produce the greatest quantity. Which action should be performed? The only way to resolve this issue consistently with utilitarianism is to perform the act that produces the greatest quantity of utility. If we choose the other option, we are adding another moral standard, having to do with the distribution of utility, to the basic utilitarian moral standard. Most utilitarians have concluded that this addition would introduce serious inconsistencies to the utilitarian position and so must be avoided. Nevertheless, eliminating any direct consideration of the distribution of utility raises questions about the compatibility of utilitarianism with ordinary standards of justice. We shall return to this issue later.

The Place of Animals. The third and final question in this section concerns the types of beings whose preferences are to be considered. If utilitarianism takes the satisfaction of preferences as the only thing that is good in and of itself, why should only the preferences of human beings be considered? Don't all animals have preferences or, at least, wants or needs? Mill seems to admit the force of this observation when he says that happiness should be secured not only to human beings, but "so far as the nature of things admits, to the whole of sentient creation."[3] Even though we use the concept of preference-satisfaction, the point is the same.

One of the most eloquent and moving pleas for the consideration of animals was made by Jeremy Bentham, the founder of modern utilitarianism. In a passage written when black slaves in parts of the British Empire were treated the way we treat animals today, Bentham wrote:

> The day may come when the rest of the animal creation may acquire those rights which never could have been withholden from them but by the hand of tyranny. The French have already discovered that the blackness of the skin is no reason why a human being should be abandoned without redress to the caprice of a tormentor. It may one day come to be recognized that the number of legs, the villosity of the skin, or the termination of the *os saccum,* are reasons equally insufficient for abandoning a sensitive being to the same fate. What else is it that should trace the insuperable line? Is it the faculty of reason, or perhaps the faculty of discourse? But a full-grown horse or dog is beyond comparison more rational, as well as a more conversable animal, than an infant of a day, a week, or even a month old. But suppose it were otherwise, what would it avail? The question is not, Can they reason? nor Can they talk? but, Can they suffer?[4]

Here Bentham makes the capacity to suffer—and to enjoy—the characteristic that entitles a being to consideration from a utilitarian standpoint. The capacity for suffering and enjoyment is not just another characteristic like the capacity for language or for higher mathematics. It is a prerequisite for having any claim to ethical consideration at all. A stone doesn't have any such claim precisely because it cannot suffer or enjoy. Animals have such claims because they can suffer and enjoy. Therefore, we have little justification for considering only human beings in our utilitarian calculations.

The human-centered ethical orientation has been called "speciesism" by Peter Singer, a utilitarian advocate of the rights of animals.[5] Just as the white racist fails to regard the interests of blacks as having the same importance as the interests of whites, so the speciesist excludes animals from having a claim to our consideration. Humans may suffer more intensely than animals, because of their greater self-consciousness and ability to anticipate the future. Therefore human interests can often outweigh the interests of animals. Nevertheless, equal suffering should count equally, according

---

[3]John Stuart Mill, *Utilitarianism,* p. 16.

[4]Jeremy Bentham, *Introduction to the Principles of Morals and Legislation,* Chapter 17, Sec. 1, note. Quoted in Peter Singer, *Practical Ethics* (Cambridge, Mass.: Cambridge University Press, 1979), pp. 49–50.

[5]Peter Singer, *Practical Ethics,* Chapter 3.

to the advocates of animal rights. So, in a utilitarian calculation, animal suffering or enjoyment should count equally to that of human beings in considering the morality of actions or rules, insofar as it is of the same degree or intensity. This position has some interesting implications for issues such as eating animal flesh, using animals in experimentation, wearing animal skins, hunting of all types, and keeping animals for circuses, zoos, and the pet business.

Act Utilitarianism and Rule Utilitarianism

One of the most frequently discussed issues in utilitarian theory is the distinction between act utilitarianism and rule utilitarianism. Because the differences in applying these two versions of utilitarianism can be difficult to understand, let us begin our discussion with an example.

John finds himself with an average score in a philosophy course that is ten points below passing. Without a passing grade he cannot graduate and take the coaching job he has been offered. He approaches his professor with the following argument:

> If you give me the ten points on my final average, I will not tell anyone. I know the information would hurt both of us. I'm married and have a small son. I will be out of school soon and my job is in another state. If I do not graduate I will lose the job offer, and my family and I will endure considerable hardship. In fact, I may have to drop out of school, since I am out of money. I studied as much as I could, but I find philosophy hard to understand and I work 40 hours a week. This has been a tough semester for me.

Suppose you are the professor and you know that John's story is true. Your concern is not simply to protect your own interests; rather, you want to do whatever produces the greatest total utility for those affected.

What you should do depends on whether you are an act utilitarian or a rule utilitarian:

> *Act utilitarianism* judges the morality of an action by whether or not the action itself produces the most utility, or at least as much utility as any other action.
>
> *Rule utilitarianism* judges the morality of an action by whether or not the moral rule presupposed by the action, if generally followed, would produce the most utility, or at least as much utility as any other rule.

What conclusions will these two versions of utilitarianism lead to in this particular case? Applying act utilitarianism, you would determine whether or not to give John the ten points on his final average by deciding which of the two alternatives would produce more utility in this particular situation. To make this determination, you must consider how everyone involved would be affected by the two alternatives.

A good argument can be made that, according to act utilitarianism, you should give John the ten points on his final average. Assuming the arrangement is kept secret, you would suffer no negative consequences, except perhaps a general feeling of uneasiness or guilt. If you are a confirmed act utilitarian, you may not feel any remorse, since by your own moral standards your action is justifiable. The other people who are directly affected by the action are John, his family, and the other students in the class. If John gets the ten points, his own desires will be met; he will graduate and get the job he has been promised. His family will then enjoy the benefits of a father and husband with a stable income. He may suffer some loss of pride, knowing that he has not fully earned his degree, but very likely this loss will be offset by the fact that he has a good job and can care for his family. He can also justify his action by remembering that he probably did the best he could under the circumstances. The welfare of the other students will not be adversely affected to any significant degree. Assuming that you do not allow the one higher grade to influence the grades you give to other students, their standing in the class will not be affected. So you will conclude that greater total utility will be produced by giving John the ten points than by refusing his request.

Rule utilitarianism leads to a different conclusion. In order to see the difference, you must compare the utilities of the two alternative rules involved in this case. If you give John the ten points, the rule underlying your action could be formulated as:

> Professors should assign grades according to the needs of students, not their merit.

If you decide not to give the ten points, the rule underlying your action could be formulated as:

> Professors should assign grades according to merit, not the needs of students.

As a rule utilitarian, you will ask: "Which of the two general rules will produce the greater overall utility?" You will be comparing not the utility of two specific actions, but the utility of two different policies. Would more utility be produced if professors generally graded according to need or if they graded according to merit?

Let us consider first the consequences of a general policy of grading according to need rather than merit. If this policy became widespread, grades would become relatively meaningless. Other teachers and prospective employers could not make any inference from grades to a student's true academic merit. They would have to spend a great deal of time asking questions like: "I know John received an A in your course, but was he really an A student?" Grades would no longer have the prestige they once had, which might possibly reduce many students' incentive to do well in school. Students could more easily deceive parents, teachers, fellow students, and prospective employers about their academic achievement.

Requiring that professors assign grades on the basis of merit seems not to have the same disadvantages. Although the present system of determining grades by merit is not without fault, it seems to produce more overall utility than the alternative system. Therefore, if the second rule is more justified by the utilitarian moral standard, it must be applied to John. He must be judged by merit rather than need, and his request must be denied.

As this example suggests, rule utilitarianism often leads to different, more plausible conclusions than act utilitarianism. Rule utilitarianism also does more justice to our belief that morality should be a matter of following rules; that is, it agrees with a widespread belief that a morally acceptable action is one we would willingly have others follow. Not surprisingly, then, many philosophers, especially since the Second World War, have favored rule utilitarianism over act utilitarianism. Following this tradition, we will use "utilitarianism" to mean "rule utilitarianism"; act utilitarianism, when discussed, will be indicated.

Act utilitarianism is an important adjunct to rule utilitarianism. It can be used, for example, when a rule and its most reasonable alternative produce approximately equal amounts of utility, in which case rule utilitarianism provides no basis for making a decision. If you cannot decide which of two alternatives is morally right by evaluating the utility of the rules underlying the two alternatives, look directly at the utility of the two actions themselves. If neither has appreciably greater utility, then rightness cannot be determined by the utilitarian moral standard. Some moral issues may well require that the utilitarian conclude that two or more alternatives are equally permissible.

Keep in mind that for the utilitarian nothing but utility is good in itself, and nothing but disutility is bad in itself. Particular actions and general rules must be evaluated by their consequences. Murder, rape, fraud, and theft are not somehow wrong in themselves; they are wrong only because they do not produce as much utility as alternative behaviors. If two or more actions or rules have the same utility, they are of equal moral worth.

Further Considerations in Applying Rule Utilitarianism

The basic idea of utilitarianism is simple: Rules or actions are right insofar as they promote utility and wrong insofar as they promote disutility. We have already seen some complications in applying this simple idea. Two additional issues, which we will encounter when we begin to apply utilitarianism, are (1) whether others will obey the rules that utilitarians find most desirable and (2) how we should go about formulating the rule presupposed by a particular action.

Will Others Obey the Rules? In the example of the student who asked for a higher grade, we assumed that professors could realistically be expected to follow either of the two rules we formulated. Our assumption was most likely valid; college teachers would probably be able to adopt either rule. But in some cases the rule that produces the most overall utility is unlikely to be generally adopted under any circumstances we can reasonably imagine. Is a rule utilitarian still morally obligated to follow the ideal rule?

Let us first consider a trivial example to illustrate the point and then proceed to a more serious example to show how important this issue can be. Suppose you are walking to your class and the most direct route is across the grass along a path that is well-worn by frequent use. A sign posted nearby reads "Please do not walk on the grass," but most people disregard it. Should you disregard the sign too? From a rule-utilitarian perspective, the rule that "Everyone should walk on the sidewalks rather than on the grass" will probably produce more utility than the rule "One may walk wherever one wishes." If everyone follows the first rule, we experience only minor inconvenience, the campus will have a neater appearance, and the maintenance crews will avoid the unnecessary expenses of filling the ruts and planting new grass, which will then be destroyed again. But you have good reason to believe that few people will follow this first rule. Moreover, from an act-utilitarian standpoint, you should probably take the path across the grass like everyone else. You will avoid a minor inconvenience, and the grass will not be any worse because one more student takes the easier way. Many utilitarians would say that you are not obligated to obey the sign "Please do not walk on the grass" until you have reason to believe that it will be generally followed, even though a rule requiring obedience to the sign would actually produce greater utility if generally followed.

Now let us consider a more serious example. Suppose you are a manager for a foreign operation of a multinational corporation. Your plant is in South Africa, where racial discrimination is still widely practiced. Ideally you would like to provide housing for your employees without regard to race or ethnic origin, but you know that such a policy would cause serious problems for your business. The plant might even be forced to close and your employees would lose their jobs. You feel confident that, if everyone were to adopt it, the rule that "Business should provide housing for employees without regard to race or ethnic origin" would produce greater utility in the long run than the alternative rule of following discriminatory policies; but you are just as confident that few companies would freely adopt the ideal rule. So the rule that could actually produce more utility, because it has a greater chance of being adopted, is "Business should adopt a policy of racially discriminatory housing in areas where this policy is the only practical one that can be followed." However, you do have to consider the example you are setting in following the traditional racist policies. If you have reason to think your example will cause others to rethink their practices, you should probably break precedent.

A general guideline for such circumstances might be: When you have reason to believe that the ideal utilitarian rule will not be generally followed and that a lesser rule, because it more likely would be generally adopted, would produce more utility, the non-ideal rule should be followed.

How Should the Rule Be Formulated?   So far we have discussed rule utilitarianism as if only one rule and one clear alternative can be presupposed by a course of action. However, many actions can be described by more than one rule. It is important to use a rule that (1) describes all of the features of the action that are relevant from a utilitarian standpoint, (2) does not describe features that are morally irrelevant, and (3) is as general as possible. Let's consider each of these three guidelines.

First, the rule should describe all relevant features of the action from a utilitarian standpoint. Suppose you are driving along a highway and see an orchard full of ripe apples. You are hungry and wonder whether it would be morally acceptable to stop and pick several apples. The rule presupposed by the action might be stated as:

A person should pick and eat fruit when he is hungry.

However, this rule does not adequately describe the situation and is therefore not an appropriate rule on which to base a moral decision. Its most obvious deficiency is its failure to mention at least one morally relevant fact: the apples belong to someone else, and they would be taken without the owner's permission. Since this fact is relevant to the utility that would be produced by the general adoption of the rule, you should restate the rule to include it:

> A person should pick apples that do not belong to him when he is hungry.

This rule is a better description of the circumstances of the case and is superior to the first rule. A utilitarian would most likely find this rule more acceptable.

This rule still might not fully describe the situation under which you took the apples, however. Suppose you are experiencing severe dehydration and the apples are the only available source of water. You might formulate the rule to take this need into account.

> A person should pick apples that do not belong to him if the apples are the only means of avoiding serious dehydration.

This rule would apply only to a small number of people, and its general adoption would probably produce more utility than the alternative rule requiring that the apples not be picked even under these extreme circumstances.

Second, the rules should not describe features that are morally irrelevant. If your name is Susan Brown and you are driving home after your first year in college, you might formulate the moral rule underlying your action as:

> Everyone whose name is Susan Brown and who is returning from her first year in college should pick apples that do not belong to her if the apples are the only means of avoiding serious dehydration.

This rule incorporates morally irrelevant features. It violates a criterion discussed in Chapter 1—namely, that moral statements have an impersonal character. Thus names, dates, and places should not be included in moral rules.

Third, the rules should be as general as possible. For example, as a utilitarian, you might well conclude that a rule covering many other types of actions would be acceptable. Rather than limit the rule to picking apples, and the possible harm to dehydration, it would be better to say:

Everyone should engage in petty theft if it is necessary to avoid serious harm.

Remember that the rules you are evaluating are supposed to be ones that could be adopted in a society. This rule is more likely to be a part of a moral code of a society than a rule limited to the particular case of eating apples.

Some utilitarians argue that the standard of utility should be applied not to particular rules, one at a time, but to a whole set of rules, even an entire moral code; that is, we must ask of a moral code whether its general acceptance by most people in a given society would produce more or less utility than the general acceptance of an alternative moral code. We have not used this version of rule utilitarianism because it is difficult to apply. Evaluating the utility of an entire moral code is no easy task, and it would take us far afield from our consideration of particular moral issues. Furthermore, it is still possible to modify a particular rule within a moral code by testing the rules much as we have been doing. So our method of testing particular rules would seem to be a part of any more elaborate version of rule utilitarianism.

The following two checklists cover both rule and act utilitarianism. The first checklist covers rule utilitarianism, the form favored by many utilitarians. However, we must appeal to act utilitarianism in situations in which two rules produce equal utility. Also, it is often important to see the different conclusions reached by act and rule utilitarianism on the same issue. Therefore a checklist for applying act utilitarianism is also included.

Checklist for Applying Rule Utilitarianism

_____ 1. State the rule that is presupposed by the action you are evaluating. The rule should be specific enough to describe those features of the situation that would produce positive or negative utility, but not so specific or impractical that it could not realistically be adopted by a society.

_____ 2. State the most reasonable alternative rule or rules, keeping in mind the precautions stated above.

_____ 3. Determine what people or animals would be affected by the rules and how they would be affected.

_____ 4. Identify the rule that would produce the greatest total utility, assuming that it could realistically be followed.
   a. The rule that produces the greatest utility or whose alternative produces the least utility is morally obligatory.

b. Rules that produce less utility overall are morally impermissible.

c. If two rules produce equal utility, or if for any reason a rule cannot be formulated, it is permissible to resort to act utilitarianism to decide the issue.

_____ 5. Apply the obligatory or permissible rule to the particular action. If no rule is justified, move to act utilitarianism.

Checklist for Applying Act Utilitarianism

_____ 1. Describe the action and the most reasonable alternatives to the action.

_____ 2. Determine what people or animals would be affected by the action and how they would be affected.

_____ 3. Identify the action that would produce the greatest total amount of utility, assuming it could realistically be followed.

a. The action that produces the greatest total amount of utility is morally obligatory.

b. Actions that produce less overall utility are morally impermissible.

c. If two or more actions produce equal utility, they are equally morally permissible.

CONCEPT SUMMARY

Utilitarianism is a highly influential moral philosophy in contemporary society. One of the most widely accepted forms of utilitarianism defines *utility* as the greatest total preference-satisfaction. The most consistent form of utilitarianism is one that disregards the distribution of utility (that is, whose preferences are satisfied) and aims simply for the greatest total utility or preference-satisfaction. A consistent utilitarianism must take account of the preferences of animals as well as humans, especially the natural tendency of all animals to avoid suffering. However, because humans have a greater self-consciousness and the ability to anticipate the future, they have greater capacity to suffer and enjoy. This capacity justifies giving human preferences special consideration.

Act utilitarianism focuses on the utility produced by a particular action, whereas rule utilitarianism focuses on the utility produced by the general acceptance of the rule presupposed by an action. These two forms of utilitarianism can sometimes lead to difficult moral conclusions, and many utilitarians favor rule utilitarianism as the more adequate version of utilitarian theory. However act utilitarianism is still useful in determining what to do when two rules seem equally acceptable from a utilitarian standpoint.

In applying rule utilitarianism, it is important to ask yourself whether the rule that would produce the greatest utility is one that others would be likely to follow. If others are not likely to follow it, the best procedure is to adopt a rule that does have a chance of being generally accepted. The rule should describe all of the features of the action that are relevant from a utilitarian standpoint, should not include features that are morally irrelevant, and should be as general as possible.

Utilitarian Personal and Social Ethics

In applying utilitarianism thus far, we have resolved moral problems by referring to the utilitarian moral standard; that is, we have analyzed the rule presupposed by an action and then tested the action by the standard of utility. But analysis is aided by knowing generally what the implications of utilitarianism are—that is, what kind of personal and social ethics the utilitarian moral standard supports. This section is devoted to clarifying these issues.

We must first, though, enter a cautionary note. Utilitarianism, like egoism, judges the morality of actions by their consequences. In both moral theories, knowledge of the consequences of actions (or rules, in the case of rule utilitarianism) is of central importance. The egoist cannot know which form of economic organization is justified by egoism unless he knows which one produces consequences that are most compatible with his own self-interest. Similarly, the utilitarian cannot know what character traits or types of behavior or forms of social organization are justified by the utilitarian moral standard unless she knows what consequences they produce and which consequences are most conducive to utility.

Thus, any discussion of the general implications of utilitarian theory must presuppose the truth of certain factual assumptions. If these assumptions are questioned, the implications drawn from them must also be questioned. It is important, therefore, that you try to identify the factual assumptions made in the following discussion and decide whether you agree with them.

Duties to Self. In the personal ethics of utilitarianism, a person's actions must be governed by those rules that in general lead to the greatest total utility. But this statement does not mean that I will make my maximum contribution to the well-being of others if I am doing something that I am unsuited for or that I detest. If I find my greatest satisfaction in being an engineer or a gardener, a physician or a plumber, this occupation is probably what I should do. Self-realization has a legitimate place in utilitarian ethics, although it should not be the ultimate justification of my actions. In this way I will not only satisfy my own interests but most likely make my most effective contribution to the satisfaction of the interests of others. Of course, if my greatest talent is robbing banks, I should not realize this talent, because it will not contribute to the general welfare. Nevertheless, utilitarianism clearly takes account of the psychological egoist's observation that all of us are powerfully motivated by considerations of self-interest. The utilitarian can argue that, in large measure, utilizing these motivations for utilitarian ends is possible.

In some important areas of duties to self, utilitarianism leads to different conclusions than traditional Hebrew-Christian morality. We have seen that natural-law ethics condemns suicide and euthanasia as violations of the sanctity of human life. A moment's consideration of this issue shows that the utilitarian will take a very different stance from a natural-law theorist. Just as we must count a desire to go on living as a reason against killing, so we must count a desire to die as a reason for killing. One can have a preference for dying as well as a preference for living.

Utilitarianism can even justify "active" as well as "passive" euthanasia. The Hebrew-Christian tradition has placed great emphasis on the distinction between acts and omissions. But utilitarians judge the morality of an action by its consequences—in particular, those consequences that affect the satisfaction of preferences. If two actions, one a commission and the other an omission, both have the same consequences in terms of preference-satisfaction, they do not have different moral evaluations from the utilitarian standpoint. Suppose a terminal cancer patient is receiving life-sustaining medication. The patient asks the physician to help him end his life. In one version of the story, the physician administers a lethal injection; in the other, she omits administering the life-sustaining medication. If the death is equally swift and painless in both cases, the utilitarian would have to evaluate both acts the same way. In this situation the physician would probably omit the life-sustaining medication, but, if the lethal injection produced a faster and less painful death, the utilitarian would find this "active" method to be the more morally desirable. In any event, the active–passive distinction would not be the deciding factor.

You can probably think of other issues within the category of duties to oneself for which the utilitarian would reach conclusions different from traditional Hebrew-Christian beliefs, especially the beliefs of natural-law theorists. What would utilitarians say about the morality of sterilization, masturbation, or the self-giving of vital organs, for example? A measure of the influence of utilitarianism is that ordinary morality already appears to be undergoing a change in the direction of the utilitarian approach to these issues.

Duties to Others. Utilitarianism can easily justify the common rules of morality relating to other people. Prohibitions against murder, theft, and fraud follow from the observations that such activities, if generally practiced, would not promote the general welfare. A more interesting case to consider from the utilitarian standpoint is the controversial issue of abortion.[6] The utilitarian believes that human beings do not deserve special consideration simply because they supposedly possess a soul. Rather, consideration must be based on possession of traits that allow a being to have interests or preferences, such as rationality and self-consciousness, and the ability to experience pain or enjoyment. Killing is wrong when it conflicts with the interest of living beings in staying alive, and the degree of interest a being can have depends on the extent to which it possesses these traits. The fertilized egg immediately after conception cannot possibly feel pain or be aware of anything. It cannot, therefore, have interests that deserve to be considered in a utilitarian calculus. As the fetus grows, it develops the capacity to feel pain and perhaps even to experience a degree of consciousness, but a calf, a pig, or a chicken has more developed interests than a fetus. By the utilitarian moral standard, we should accord the life of a fetus no greater value than the life of a nonhuman animal at a similar stage of self-consciousness and capacity to feel pain.

What specific conclusions should we arrive at regarding the morality of abortion from the utilitarian standpoint? Peter Singer has proposed that fetuses of less than 18 weeks are very unlikely to be capable of feeling anything at all, since their nervous systems are insufficiently developed. Therefore, we cannot say they have any interests to protect. Abortions during this period, Singer believes, should pose no moral problems. Between 18 weeks and birth, when the fetus certainly has a capacity to feel and may even be conscious, abortion should not be taken lightly. But even here the serious interests of the mother would ordinarily override the rudimentary interests of the fetus.

These same arguments apply to a newborn baby. A week-old baby is not a rational and self-conscious being. In fact, by the standards we have developed, the life of a newborn baby is of less value than the life of an adult pig, dog, or chimpanzee, and killing a newborn baby cannot be regarded as having the same degree of moral seriousness. Again, these views contrast sharply with Hebrew-Christian morality. But the utilitarian argues that we should modify our views to bring them into line with what he believes to be the more plausible, utilitarian standard.

---

[6]See Peter Singer, *Practical Ethics,* Chapter 6, for the basic argument in this section.

Social Ethics. The general principle governing utilitarian social ethics is that equal consideration should be given to the preferences of everyone affected by social policies, with a view to achieving the greatest total satisfaction of those preferences. Three implications of this guideline are especially interesting.

First, most utilitarians have argued for democratic government as a means of achieving the utilitarian ideal. The best way to ensure that the maximum number of preferences is satisfied is for each individual to exercise control over the government by means of the vote. Democracy also tends to encourage the development of an active and responsible character. When citizens have the responsibility of deciding the policies of government, however indirectly, they tend also to develop capacities of self-determination that are more conducive to self-realization than the more docile and passive character traits fostered by nondemocratic political orders.

Second, utilitarians have favored the maximum degree of individual freedom, especially in the realm of ideas. In his important essay *On Liberty,* John Stuart Mill observes that one can easily assume that, when democratic government has been established, the battle for individual liberty has been won. However, Mill argues, the majority can still restrict the rights of dissenting minorities, especially when the ideas of minorities are highly unpopular. Mill believes that the rights of dissenting minorities can be defended on utilitarian grounds. He first maintains that allowing individuals to pursue their own ideas and beliefs leads to the discovery of truth. In what some have called the "free marketplace of ideas," the best ideas will survive in the competition with other ideas. For example, science requires intellectual freedom so that ideas may be openly advanced and criticized in order to discover the truth. The same freedom is required in other areas, such as politics. The best way to conduct a society can be discovered only by allowing citizens the freedom to advance ideas and then to expose the ideas' flaws. Mill assumes that the discovery of truth leads to utility. Although he does not make any extended argument for this claim, we may assume his argument to be that knowledge of the consequences of actions provides the basis for a more effective pursuit of the utilitarian ideal. Thus a utilitarian will be a supporter of individual freedom, since individual liberty leads to the discovery of truth and the discovery of truth promotes the greatest satisfaction of people's preferences.

Third, 20th-century utilitarians have often argued for extensive welfare measures and at least a partial redistribution of wealth. Democracy and freedom for individual dissent are not enough to ensure maximum preference-satisfaction. Equal opportunity does not account for the influence of the home and social environment into which one is born. Perhaps even more important, it neglects the importance of genetic endowment. We know that early training has a great deal to do with emotional stability and how much effort individuals will expend to achieve their goals. We also know that IQ, physical health, and stamina, and probably many other traits, are primarily genetic. Therefore even if equal opportunity is provided, those with more fortunate family and social backgrounds and more desirable genetic endowments will be in a better position to satisfy their interests. They will be able to pursue more interesting and lucrative careers, achieve greater social prestige, and otherwise enjoy a more comfortable and rewarding life. This state of affairs will probably not produce the greatest total satisfaction of interests.

Some utilitarians, including Peter Singer, have proposed that the utilitarian ideal would be realized more completely if society could adopt the famous Marxist slogan: "From each according to his ability, to each according to his needs."[7] But Singer and most other utilitarians realize the practical difficulties in fully implementing this ideal. In this situation the ideal utilitarian rule will not in fact produce the greatest utility, because it has little chance of being generally adopted due to the natural selfishness of most human beings. If we don't pay a person more for being a computer programmer than for cleaning offices, she may not make the effort to get the advanced training needed for computer programming. And won't the failure to utilize fully the talents of many of the most gifted people result in less total preference-satisfaction? Most of the advances in society are produced by the more talented members. If they have no incentive to utilize their talents, it can be argued that we shall all be worse off. These considerations have convinced many utilitarians that social policy must reward individuals for utilizing their inherited abilities, rather than reward them strictly according to their needs. Therefore, we should, within certain limits, reward the more talented members of society for their special achievements. Nevertheless, many utilitarians still feel that providing the basic necessities for all citizens, as the welfare state attempts to do, is required by their philosophy.

Applying Utilitarian Ethics

We can now apply utilitarianism to some problems that require moral decision, using the methodology developed in the checklist.

---

[7]Peter Singer, *Practical Ethics,* p. 36.

Case 1: The Rules of Legal Ethics

In July 1973, Robert Garrow, a 38-year-old mechanic from Syracuse, New York, killed four persons, apparently at random.[8] The four were camping in the Adirondack Mountains. In early August, following a vigorous manhunt, he was captured by state police and indicted for the murder of a student from Schenectady. At the time of the arrest, no evidence connected Garrow to the other deaths; in fact, two of the people were not even known to be dead. One was a young Illinois woman, the other a Syracuse high school girl listed as a runaway. The body of the third, a camping companion of the Illinois woman, was found on July 20, before Garrow's capture. The court appointed two Syracuse lawyers, Francis R. Belge and Frank H. Armani, to defend Garrow.

Some weeks later, during discussions with his two lawyers, Garrow told them that he had raped and killed a woman in a mine shaft. Belge and Armani located the mine shaft and the body of the Illinois woman but did not take their discovery to the police. The body was finally discovered four months later by two children playing in the mine. In September, the lawyers found the second body by following Garrow's directions. This discovery, too, went unreported; the girl's body was uncovered by a student in December.

The Illinois woman's father read that Belge and Armani were defending a man accused of killing a camper in the Adirondacks. Knowing that his daughter's companion had also been found dead there, he journeyed to Syracuse to talk to the lawyers. He asked whether they knew anything about his daughter, but they denied having any knowledge that would help him. Belge and Armani maintained their silence until the following June. Then, to try to show that he was insane, Garrow made statements from the witness stand that implicated him in the other three murders. At a press conference the next day, Belge and Armani outlined for the first time the sequence of events.

The local community was outraged. The lawyers, however, believed they had honored the letter and spirit of their professional duty in a tough case. "We both, knowing how the parents feel, wanted to advise them where the bodies were," Belge said, "but since it was a privileged communication, we could not reveal any information that was given to us in confidence."

Their silence was based on the legal code that admonishes the lawyer to "preserve the confidence and secrets of a client." The lawyer–client "privilege" against disclosure of confidences is one of the oldest and most iron-clad in the law. If the defendant has no duty to confess his guilt or complicity in a crime, it can make no sense to assert that his lawyer has such a

---

[8]Reported in several sources, including the *New York Times,* June 20, 1974.

duty. Otherwise, the argument goes, the accused will tell his lawyer at best a deficient version of the facts, and the lawyer cannot as effectively defend the client. This argument frequently seems unconvincing; it certainly did to the people of Syracuse. Should the lawyer have revealed the whereabouts of the Illinois woman's body to her father? What was right from the utilitarian perspective?

1. This case illustrates the difficulty of formulating the rule presupposed by an action. Several rules can be seen as presupposed by the lawyer's action, each giving significantly different direction for action. For example, the rule underlying the lawyers' action can be stated in a way that requires lawyers never to reveal information gained in the confidential lawyer–client relationship. But this rule is stronger than most legal codes of ethics, which allow the breaking of confidentiality if the client clearly intends to commit a crime. Moreover, this exception has strong support in utilitarian theory, for a crime is a serious violation of the interests of others and the prevention of crime has positive utilitarian value.

Utilitarians will probably make at least one other exception to the lawyer–client confidentiality rule. Recalling the case presented earlier, suppose a youth is injured in an automobile accident and sues the driver responsible for the injury. The driver's defense lawyer has his own doctor examine the youth, and the doctor discovers an aortic aneurism, apparently caused by the accident, that the boy's doctor had not found. The aneurism is life threatening without an operation, but, if the youth learns of the aneurism, he will demand a much higher settlement. The loss of life is a much more serious violation of preferences than being forced to make a higher settlement, so the utilitarian rule should probably require the defense lawyer to reveal the information. Yet the information is included in what lawyers call the "secrets" of the client, a concept closely related to confidentiality. Therefore perhaps we can formulate the first rule as:

> Lawyers should never reveal information gained in the confidential lawyer–client relationship, unless the information is necessary to prevent a crime or to save a life.

We cannot be sure that this rule makes all of the exceptions a utilitarian would want to make, but it seems reasonably acceptable.

2. The alternative rule is also not easy to formulate. We want a rule that will justify revealing the location of the girl's body to her father, yet we do not want to destroy confidentiality altogether, because its utilitarian value certainly has good arguments. If lawyers were generally known to break the confidence of their clients, their ability to serve their clients would be impaired, since clients might hesitate to reveal sensitive information to their

lawyers. Suppose we stipulate that lawyers should maintain confidentiality unless the information is requested by a third party whose vital interests are affected or unless it is necessary to prevent a crime or save a life, provided the information will not be used against the lawyer's client. But this information seems to allow the defense lawyer to withhold the information about the aneurism from the youth, since the information will certainly be used against his client. Therefore, to make it clearer that the final clause is subordinate to the exceptions having to do with crimes and loss of life, we shall formulate the alternative rule as follows:

> Lawyers should not ordinarily reveal information gained in the confidential lawyer–client relationship. Confidential information should be revealed even if it does injure the lawyer's client, when the information is necessary to prevent a crime or to save a life or when it is vital to the interests of others.

This rule allows the lawyers to reveal the information requested by the father while avoiding the other problems our discussion has revealed.

3. The major groups affected by the two rules are lawyers, their clients, third parties (such as the father of the Illinois girl), and the general public. Lawyers would probably find the first rule to their advantage. Although on many occasions lawyers might sincerely want to help people by divulging confidential information, probably even more occasions arise in which they would not. In general the rule of confidentiality protects lawyers from having to make difficult decisions on their own; they can merely cite the relevant rules of professional conduct. The first rule would also protect the reputation of lawyers and their ability to get needed information from their clients. Clients would also benefit more from general acceptance of the first rule, for clients can be more confident that sensitive information given to their lawyers will not be revealed to others.

The harm and benefit to the general public and to third parties is more difficult to calculate: They could be denied knowledge important to their well-being, as the father of the Illinois girl was. But, on the other hand, anyone who might ever need a lawyer—which includes virtually everyone—would be reassured that lawyers would not reveal confidential information except under the most extreme conditions. Therefore even the public and third parties benefit approximately as much from the first rule as from the second.

4. Assuming that we have evaluated the consequences of the alternatives accurately, we can conclude that the first rule, requiring lawyers never to reveal information gained in the confidential lawyer–client relationship, unless the information is necessary to prevent a crime or save a life, will

most likely produce the greatest total utility. It is, then, morally obligatory that lawyers follow this rule.

5. Applying the rule to this case, we conclude that the two lawyers did the right thing, from a utilitarian standpoint, in concealing the information from the father of the Illinois girl.

Case 2: The Morality of Whaling

Whales are mammals. Whale calves are fed and cared for by their mothers, and the bond between mother and child appears to persist beyond the period of lactation. Their nervous systems and the parts of the brain relating to the perception of pain are essentially similar to our own. Although some authorities say that the killing of a whale takes only five minutes, others say that it often takes much longer. Whales are social animals; they live in groups and relate to each other as individuals. Some species are monogamous and, when one member of a family has been harpooned, other family members have been observed to wait offshore for days or even weeks for its return. Good scientific evidence backs up the ascription of a sophisticated emotional life to whales.

On the other hand, whalers in Japan and the Soviet Union (the two primary whaling countries) and in the other countries where whaling is permitted depend on whaling for their livelihood. Some whale products are quite useful to people. Whale oil is used to make soap and margarine, and whale meat is consumed by humans, livestock, and pets. Whales are also used for various commercial products, especially cosmetics.

So the question for the utilitarian is: If whaling can be controlled, to remove the threat of extinction, is it morally wrong to kill whales on a commercial basis?

1. The rule presupposed by the decision to kill whales on a commercial basis might be stated as:

Whales should be killed for commercial use, as long as they are not threatened by extinction.

2. The rule presupposed by the decision not to kill whales on a commercial basis might be stated as:

Whales should not be killed for commercial use, regardless of whether they are threatened by extinction.

3. The three groups affected are those engaged in the whaling industry, those who use whaling products, and whales. If the second rule is

generally followed, people in the whaling industry will lose their jobs. In countries such as Japan and the Soviet Union, this unemployment might involve a considerable hardship for a time, but the government could easily retrain the affected workers so their loss is not permanent. Since those who use whaling products can find substitutes, they stand to suffer no significant loss. Even if the price of certain products increases somewhat, monetary loss is relatively trivial in comparison with the whales' loss of life. The whales, of course, stand to suffer more serious harm if the first rule is followed. Although human beings probably outnumber whales, only the human beings affected by these two rules need to be considered. Furthermore, even whales who do not lose their lives may suffer the pain of separation from family members who have been harpooned.

4. It seems that a rule-utilitarian analysis must conclude that the second rule would produce the greatest total utility, so it is morally obligatory. We have no reason to believe that such a rule could not realistically be followed, since a number of nations have already discontinued whaling with no serious adverse consequences.

5. In this case the rule is applied not to a particular situation, but to a general practice. As the rule itself indicates, the conclusion must be that whales should not be killed for commercial use, even if they are not threatened by extinction.

Case 3: Reverse Discrimination

Allen Bakke, a white male, applied to the medical school at the University of California at Davis in both 1973 and 1974.[9] In both years Bakke's application was considered by the general admissions program and he received an interview. His 1973 interview was with Dr. Theodore H. West, who described Bakke as "a very desirable applicant to [the] medical school." Despite a strong composite evaluation score of 468 out of 500, Bakke was rejected. His application had come late in the year, and no applicants with scores below 470 were accepted in the general admissions process after Bakke's application was completed. After his 1973 rejection, Bakke wrote to Dr. George H. Lowrey, Associate Dean and Chairman of the Admissions Committee, protesting that the special admissions program operated as a racial and ethnic quota.

At the time Bakke was rejected, four slots were unfilled in the special admissions program for economically and educationally disadvantaged students. A total of 16 slots in the freshman class of 100 were reserved for

---

[9] 483 U.S. 265. Reprinted in James Sterba, *Morality in Practice* (Belmont, Calif.: Wadsworth, 1984), pp. 229–238.

students in the special admissions program. The students in the special admissions program did not have to meet the minimum 2.5 grade point average applied to regular students, and different standards were used in their general evaluation.

Bakke's 1974 application was completed early in the year. His composite score was 549 out of 600. Again Bakke's application was rejected. This year, as in the year before, applicants were admitted under the special admissions program with significantly lower composite evaluation scores as well as lower grade point averages and lower Medical College Admission Test scores. After the second rejection, Bakke filed a suit in the Superior Court of California. The case eventually reached the United States Supreme Court, which rendered its decision on June 28, 1978. The justices were divided 4–4 on the principal issues in the case, with Justice Powell deciding with one group on one issue and with the other group on the second issue. On the one hand, the Court found that the special admissions program under which Allen Bakke was denied admission was unlawful and directed that Bakke be admitted. On the other hand, it found that institutions of higher learning could consider race as one factor in the admissions process.

From the standpoint of utilitarianism, are admissions policies like that of the University of California at Davis morally permissible, morally obligatory, or morally impermissible?

1. Any formulation of the rule under which the University of California at Davis was operating when it reserved 16 slots for disadvantaged students will be controversial, because the concept of a *quota* produces legal and moral problems. However, we shall formulate the rule as:

A medical school may reserve a small percentage (less than 20%) of its openings for disadvantaged students.

2. The alternative rule would be:

A medical school may not reserve even a small percentage (less than 20%) of its openings for disadvantaged students.

3. Four groups are affected by the rule and its alternative: the disadvantaged students who are candidates for the special admissions program; the students who are applying through the regular admissions program; the minority population in the country, consisting primarily of blacks, Chicanos, Asians, and Native Americans; and the general population.

The disadvantaged students stand to benefit the most from the first rule, which gives them a greater chance of being admitted to medical schools. Not only are the admissions standards lower, but the students are competing for one slot out of 100, whereas the regular students are competing for one slot out of 84. The first rule has some negative effect on their interests, since their fellow students may regard them as inferiors who could not make it under normal competitive conditions. Their future patients might also have less confidence in them than in physicians who were admitted in the regular admissions program.

The regular students would suffer the most direct harm to their interests, because they would have less chance of admission into medical school. They would also find it more difficult to predict whether they would be admitted, because factors other than merit would be considered. This uncertainty could affect their ability to plan their lives. However, regular students would perhaps receive some benefit from a more diverse student population, composed in part of disadvantaged students.

The minority population would benefit if the disadvantaged students decided to serve in their communities. However this outcome is not guaranteed. A more effective means of supplying physicians to serve in minority communities would be to select students who had demonstrated a prior commitment to this kind of work, regardless of their social or ethnic background. If the disadvantaged students did decide to serve in their own communities, the minority youth would benefit from the role models the physicians would provide.

We have difficulty determining how the interests of the general public would be affected by either the first or second rule. The general public might benefit from the decreased social unrest if minorities became convinced that the effects of past discrimination were being vigorously attacked. But this effect could well be counterbalanced by the feeling among the general population that many applicants were being unfairly treated.

4. We have extreme difficulty totalling up the harms and benefits to various interests and reaching a conclusion about which rule produces the greatest total utility. However, if the effects of past discrimination could be more quickly eliminated by policies of reverse discrimination, a good case can be made that the first rule is superior from a utilitarian standpoint. The bad effects of reverse discrimination would be only temporary, and the good effects of eliminating the legacy of discrimination would be permanent. Keep in mind that, in making the utilitarian calculation, no abstract considerations of justice can be brought into the picture. Justice is important for the utilitarian only insofar as policies that are perceived to be just or unjust affect the interests of individuals.

5. Assuming that the first rule does produce greater total utility, we shall apply it to the Bakke case. We could then include that, from the utilitarian standpoint, the preferential admissions policy is obligatory.

Evaluating Utilitarianism as a Moral Theory

Now we are ready to evaluate utilitarianism according to our four criteria. Remember that every moral theory has points of vulnerability; no perfect moral theory exists. This lack of a perfect theory is a major reason why several influential moral philosophies have evolved rather than one. As with the other theories, the following evaluations are my own, although they reflect the opinions of many moral philosophers.

Utilitarianism

How well do I think the theory meets the criteria?

Criteria	Very Well	Moderately Well	Very Poorly
1. (Consistency)	X		
2. (Plausibility)		X	
3. (Usefulness)	X		
4. (Justification)		X	

Criterion 1: Consistency. I have given utilitarianism a high mark for consistency. The form of utilitarianism we have described does not suffer from obvious inconsistencies. If the utilitarian is willing to define right actions as those that produce the greatest total utility or interest-satisfaction, without arguing that some interests are inherently better than others, he cannot be charged with inconsistency. The temptation to be inconsistent arises when the utilitarian moral standard generates conclusions about conduct that conflict with our ordinary moral ideas.

Criterion 2: Plausibility. I have given utilitarianism a rating of "moderately well" for plausibility. One of the major problems with utilitarianism is that it appears to generate moral judgments that are at variance with our ordinary moral beliefs. We have already seen several moral issues in which this discrepancy arose. Another area in which these counterintuitive conclusions are generated is supererogatory acts—that is, acts that are "above and beyond the call of duty." We ordinarily distinguish between obligatory and supererogatory actions, but this distinction is difficult to make from the utilitarian standpoint, because any action that produces more total utility than an alternative action is obligatory. Since actions that we ordinarily consider supererogatory often produce more utility than any alternative, the utilitarian is forced to reclassify them as obligatory.

Consider the following example.[10] Suppose your foolish neighbor confides that he is mortgaging everything he can to make a speculative investment that you are convinced will be disastrous for him and his family. If you expend enough time and effort, you believe, you can dissuade him from making the investment, whereas no one else can do so. The disaster you anticipate for him would be far greater than any inconvenience and embarrassment you would suffer in dissuading him. Now, a utilitarian would argue that, on the whole, greater preference-satisfaction would result if we adopt the rule that "Everybody who has adequate reason to believe that the course of action a neighbor proposes will be disastrous to that neighbor has the duty to dissuade that neighbor if he can do so without grave inconvenience or embarrassment." But are you morally obligated to follow such a rule? The question is not simply whether you ought to express your opinion to him; you should surely do so. But is it your duty to embark on a lengthy attempt to change his mind? The rule utilitarian must answer this question in the affirmative, but most of us would not.

Our moral intuitions may also seem to conflict with utilitarianism in the area of justice. When Jesus of Nazareth was killed, Caiphas, the Jewish high priest, justified the killing with the claim that Jesus' crucifixion, however unjust, would avert a greater disaster—possibly a rebellion against the Jewish authorities or a Roman persecution of the Jewish people. Consider the rule "Judges may not depart from the law, except if, by doing so, they can avert a major calamity to their nation or to the world." A rule utilitarian might object that such a rule would so discredit the judiciary that public life would be gravely injured, but such might not be the case. Some might even sleep better knowing that their judges would not be overscrupulous in applying the law during a national emergency. Thus a rule utilitarian might be forced to admit that a miscarriage of justice is morally justified.

In the face of such objections, the utilitarian has two options: to reject ordinary beliefs as invalid because they conflict with utilitarian theory or to argue that utilitarian moral theory does not really conflict with ordinary beliefs. If she wants to argue that utilitarian theory can make a place for supererogatory actions, her argument might include the following: Praising

---

[10] For this example and a discussion of utilitarianism and problems with supererogation and justice, see Alan Donagan, "Is There a Credible Utilitarianism?" in Michael D. Bayles, ed., *Contemporary Utilitarianism* (New York: Doubleday, 1968), 194–198.

those who perform supererogatory acts is in accordance with utility, but condemning those who fail to do so is not. The distinction between obligatory and supererogatory acts could be based on the differing abilities of people to perform unusual acts of bravery and self-sacrifice. The interest of morality is not served by requiring people to perform too far beyond their ability, since this overtaxing would only inspire contempt for morality in general. Moreover, people who attempt risky acts are likely to fail, thus creating negative utility. On the other hand, when supererogatory actions are performed, they should receive praise, because they do contribute to the well-being of others. Whether this response is adequate is left to the reader to decide.

The problem of justice requires more sophisticated treatment. The utilitarian can certainly argue that, in general, rules requiring justice have greater utility; they inspire confidence in the judicial system and a sense of safety and well-being among the citizenry. However, if two rules have a serious conflict between them, a different approach may be required. For example, the utilitarian might argue that a conflict exists between the rule "Administer justice fairly" and the rule "Do what is necessary to save the nation from disaster." In such a case, the utilitarian would maintain, doing what leads to the greatest overall interest-satisfaction in the particular situation is justifiable, so that in the case of Jesus, Caiphas was right to imply that one man's dying for the people was expedient. We must appeal, in other words, to act utilitarianism to resolve a conflict between two rules, when both are justified by utility. As before, the reader is left to decide whether this reply is adequate.

Criterion 3: Usefulness. I have given utilitarianism a rating slightly better than "moderately well" here. A moral theory must provide a clear and workable method for resolving moral disputes, including disputes about which moral rule to adopt. The utilitarian decides on moral rules by determining their consequences for utility. But do we have the knowledge to trace the consequences of even a single action, much less the consequences of a general rule? Consider how a utilitarian would investigate the morality of premarital sexual relations. She would use the best available scientific data to determine the extent of possible negative consequences of the widespread practice of premarital sex, such as an increase in the number of pregnancies outside of marriage, an increase in the incidence of venereal disease, greater psychological disturbances, and the long-range effect on the stability of marriage. She would also have to investigate the advantages from a utilitarian standpoint of the widespread acceptance of the practice, such as the increased enjoyment of sex and a decrease in sexual frustration during the years when the sex drive is especially strong. She would also have to consider the possibility that people would have a healthier and more relaxed attitude toward sex and that sexual adjustment in marriage might be improved.

How adequately can we determine these consequences, especially the long-range consequences, such as the effect on sexual adjustment and the stability of marriage? Without knowing these effects, the utilitarian cannot pass judgment on the morality of premarital sexual relationships from the utilitarian standpoint. She must either recommend that present practices be continued or that we experiment in new directions without fully knowing whether the results will be good or bad. Neither alternative is wholly satisfactory from the utilitarian standpoint. You will encounter problems like this one when you evaluate many practices from the utilitarian perspective.

In dealing with the problem of consequences, some utilitarians have admitted that they must assume what has been called the ripples-in-the-pond postulate; that is, they must assume that the important consequences of an action occur in relative proximity in time and place to the action itself. Just as the ripples produced by dropping a pebble in a pond are strongest near the point of impact, so the consequences of an action must be assumed to be most significant relatively near the action. But what if an action, such as adding minute amounts of a pollutant to the atmosphere, produces insignificant effects for centuries and then suddenly results in a catastrophe? It might be that the widespread practice of premarital sex would have few negative consequences for a while but, after a few generations, would produce serious social consequences. What reason do we have for believing that the ripples-in-the-pond postulate is valid? And even if it is, can we calculate even the near-at-hand consequences of an action or rule?

The utilitarian's response is that we can at least have a rational opinion about the general consequences of many actions, and, if we have no opinion, perhaps we should hold to traditional moral rules. The standard of utility at least provides a method for evaluating some moral rules. The utilitarian may also argue that, if we do not know the consequences of adopting a given rule, we *should not* be able to pronounce on its morality. Furthermore, the problem of knowledge of consequences emphasizes again the importance of the social and physical sciences in utilitarian morality. Lack of knowledge about consequences is not so much a fault of utilitarian theory as it is a problem of the human condition, the utilitarian argues. Do you think this response is adequate?

Criterion 4: Justification. I have rated utilitarianism as "moderately well" for the criterion of justification. For a moral philosophy to be acceptable, it must give some reason to accept the moral standard. We have also seen that the moral standard is not susceptible to strict proof, because the moral standard cannot be derived from a higher moral standard, nor can it be derived in any direct or conclusive way from factual observation. What kind of justification, then, can be offered for the principle of utility? In a famous passage from Chapter 4 of *Utilitarianism,* John Stuart Mill presents some considerations that he hopes will convince his readers to accept the utilitarian doctrine. Mill starts by drawing an analogy between visibility and desirability, arguing that, just as the only proof that an object is visible is that people see it, so the only proof that anything is desirable is that people actually desire it. Then he points out that people do in fact desire happiness, so happiness must be desirable or good. Since each person's happiness is good for that person, the general happiness is a good to the aggregate of people.

If Mill intended his argument to be a "proof" of the utilitarian moral standard, he was certainly mistaken. Saying that something is "desirable" in the sense that it *is desired* by people has an entirely different meaning than saying that something is "desirable" in the sense that it *should be desired;* people may certainly desire what they should not desire. Another problem with Mill's argument, when taken as a proof, is that the fact that each person's happiness is a good for that person does not lead to the conclusion that promoting the general happiness is a moral obligation. People might be content to pursue their own happiness rather than the well-being of the majority. But these criticisms apply only if Mill was attempting to construct a strict proof, and his writings indicate that Mill was aware that the moral standard cannot be proven.

The most we can do, Mill may have believed, is show that the moral standard is a plausible one and that it commends itself to a rational person. Interpreted in this way, Mill's argument might be the following: People do desire their own happiness. This desire does not make happiness the right moral goal, but it does show that a morality based on happiness is solidly grounded in human nature. Such a morality is thus at least a possible candidate for a moral standard. Now if we combine this observation with the belief that a moral person has some obligation to others rather than merely to himself, we have some evidence to conclude that the happiness (or interest-satisfaction) of others is a legitimate moral goal. Mill also believed that further evidence for the plausibility of the principle of utility could be derived from the fact that most of the moral beliefs we hold can be justified by the principle of utility.

Although these observations contain claims that can be questioned and certainly do not constitute a proof, they do lend plausibility to the standard of utility. If we believe that the institution of morality must be related to the human good, what more intrinsically plausible standard could we propose?

CONCEPT SUMMARY

Since the utilitarian judges a rule by its consequences, any rules derived from the utilitarian moral standard must make assumptions about the consequences that will result from following the rules. If these assumptions are not accepted, different rules may be justified. Utilitarian personal ethics should be governed by the principle that the most effective way to contribute to the general welfare is usually to develop one's own abilities. While utilitarianism may condone traditional moral views in some areas of personal ethics, it does not support the traditional prohibitions of suicide and euthanasia. Utilitarianism can also justify many of the common duties to others, such as the duties not to commit murder, theft, or fraud, but it does not support the prohibition of abortion.

In the area of social ethics, utilitarianism has been taken by its classical advocates to justify democracy and individual liberty. More recent exponents of utilitarianism have sometimes argued that greater utility will be produced if the state attempts to provide for the basic needs of all citizens, regardless of their financial resources. Special rewards, however, must still be given to the more talented members of society in order to induce them to make their maximum contribution.

Utilitarianism is an internally consistent moral philosophy, but it does lead to some counterintuitive moral judgments, especially regarding supererogation and justice. The utilitarian's ability to resolve moral problems is limited, due to our ignorance of the full consequences of the general adoption of many moral rules. Mill's "proof" of utilitarianism fails as a proof, but it does given reason to believe that utilitarianism is a plausible moral philosophy.

VII

THE ETHICS OF RESPECT
FOR PERSONS

Dillard Johnson is a psychologist employed by the personnel department of a large corporation. One day his superior comes to him with a proposal: "Dillard, the company is worried about the possibility that some of our employees may try to form a union in the next year or two. We have always had good relationships with our employees, but we believe a union would change that. I want you to design a test for employees that will measure union sympathy. You should disguise the purpose of the test. Make it look like a test for new employment opportunities in the company. Can you do this for us?"[1]

Dillard knows he has a good chance to impress his boss with his value as a psychologist in the personnel department, but he has questions about the ethical acceptability of the assignment. What should he do? How would he feel if he knew someone were using deceit to ferret information out of him? Would he feel "used" or somehow that he was not being shown proper respect as a human being?

Most of us consider these questions fundamental to the nature of morality; they certainly have been central to the Hebrew-Christian tradition. According to the Talmud, the whole law can be summarized in the statement: "Do not do to your fellow what you hate to have done to you."[2] And, in Matthew 7:21, Jesus says that the whole law and the prophets can be summarized in the saying: "All things whatsoever ye would that men should do to you, do ye even so to them." The idea that everyone should be subject to the same moral rules is deeply embedded in our moral thought.

---

[1]This case is based on an example in American Psychological Association, *Casebook on Ethical Standards of Psychologists* (Washington, D.C.: American Psychological Association, 1967), p. 1. Used with permission.

[2]Rabbi Dr. I. Epstein, ed., *The Babylonian Talmud* (London: The Soncino Press, 1948–52), p. 31a. Quoted in Alan Donagan, *The Theory of Morality* (Chicago: University of Chicago Press, 1977), p. 57.

Sometimes we express a closely related moral insight by distinguishing between things and persons: persons should not be treated as mere things, nor manipulated in a way that disregards their states as moral beings. Slavery is wrong, for example, because it involves treating people as commodities, regardless of the purposes they might have set for themselves. A slave owner can work a human being like a machine, separate him from his family, and buy and sell him like an object. Slavery fails to give proper respect to the personhood of the slave, and it is certainly not a condition we would want for ourselves.

We shall refer to this ethical tradition, whose central theme is that equal respect must be paid to the personhood of all human beings, as the *ethics of respect for persons*. Like natural law, the ethics of respect for persons is an attempt to formulate the essence of the Hebrew-Christian religious tradition in a nonreligious vocabulary.

The ethics of respect for persons has been closely connected with Immanuel Kant (1724–1804), the greatest thinker of the German Enlightenment and one of the most important modern moral philosophers. Kant's terminology is too forbidding and his arguments are often too obscure to allow any straightforward exposition of his moral philosophy here. We shall use his philosophy in this text only as a general guide. Readers who are familiar with Kant will recognize his influence in many places, but keep in mind that this chapter is a discussion of the ethics of respect for persons, not of Kant's moral philosophy.

We shall use two of Kant's formulations of the moral standard as the basis for our discussion, even though our interpretation of these standards will often differ from Kant's. Kant himself believed that the two standards were equivalent, that they would always lead to the same conclusion regarding what is right or wrong. We have reasons to doubt this claim, thus we shall stipulate that, in order for an action to be morally permissible by the ethics of respect for persons, it must pass both versions of the moral standard.

The version of the moral standard we will look at first is the universalization principle. We shall discuss a test for its proper application, which we shall call the self-defeating test. The second version of the moral standard is the means-ends principle. We shall consider two tests for its proper application: the negative test and the positive test. Let us examine these principles and tests in turn.

The Principle of Universalization as a Version of the Moral Standard

The idea that equal respect is due to all human beings is the basis for the universalization principle. We can formulate this principle as a moral standard of the ethics of respect for persons in the following way:

> MS 1: An action is right if you can consent to everyone's adopting the moral rule presupposed by the action.

Like rule utilitarianism, this standard is based on the analysis of rules rather than individual actions. If we look only at actions, how can we determine whether our action is the same as the one we are willing to have others follow? Let us propose that we are willing to have others perform the same action if we are willing to have them adopt the moral rule that underlies our own action. This proposal assumes that every action involving moral choice does, in fact, presuppose a moral rule.[3]

To apply the universalization principle, we must first determine the moral rule presupposed by the action being evaluated. Suppose we are considering the possibility of obtaining some money by making a false promise to repay it. The rule presupposed by our action might be something like this:

> Everyone should obtain money by falsely promising to repay it.

Our second task is to decide whether we can consent to others' following the universalized rule. To do so, let's apply the self-defeating test.

The Self-Defeating Test.   The question posed by the *self-defeating test* is:

> Can I consent to others' acting simultaneously according to the same rule I use without undermining my own ability to act in accordance with it?

To determine whether I can consistently consent to others' acting according to the same rule I use, we must attempt to imagine realistically the *conditions* necessary for everyone to use this rule and the *consequences* that would normally follow if everyone did so *simultaneously*.[4] In the case of our current rule, the predictable result of everyone's performing the action in question would be that no one would lend money based on a promise

---

[3]My account of rules is in some ways like Kant's discussion of what he calls "maxims." But, again, we are not giving an exposition of Kant.

[4]See Onora Nell, *Acting on Principle: An Essay in Kantian Ethics* (New York: Columbia University Press, 1975), pp. 63–81. My version of the self-defeating test owes much to Nell's book, even though important differences exist. For an account of Kant's use of this same example that is probably closer to his intentions than either mine or Nell's, see Robert Paul Wolff, *The Autonomy of Reason: A Commentary on Kant's Groundwork of the Metaphysic of Morals* (New York: Harper & Row, 1973), pp. 165–169.

to repay, since everyone would assume (correctly) that such promises were lies. This result would undermine my ability to borrow money on the basis of a (false) promise to repay. Only if we postulated that people do not learn from experience could we consistently intend that others live by the same rule we adopted. So the rule is self-defeating.

Keep in mind that the self-defeating test assumes that we ask what would happen if I and others follow the rule simultaneously. Obviously if I adopt my policy of dishonesty now and others do not adopt the policy until a year from now, I could get away with a lot of false promises in the meantime. The case would be different if others adopt my policy at the same time I adopt it, and the policy would be self-defeating.

This conclusion about the morality of making false promises is not surprising; the self-defeating test would be weakened if it could not rule out false promising as immoral. Nevertheless, other examples seem to cause more trouble. It is sometimes argued that the universalization principle runs into difficulties with respect to an occupation such as farming, because it is no more desirable that everyone grow food than that no one grow food. Consider the following abbreviated but acceptable formulation of the rule:

Everyone should grow food.

I can certainly consistently intend that I and everyone else will grow food without fear of defeating my own rule. This state of affairs was once almost universal, and it still prevails in some parts of the world. But now consider the alternative rule:

Everyone should not grow food.

I can certainly consistently intend that I and all others will not grow food. This rule would lead to starvation, but starving people can refuse to do things as well as the best fed. So the rule is not self-defeating.

What shall we say, then, about the morality of growing food, since both the rule and its alternative can be universally followed? One scholar has proposed that, when both a rule and its alternative can be consistently universally adopted, acts in agreement with the rule or its alternative will both be classified as morally permissible; that is, they are neither required nor forbidden. In this case we are neither required to grow food (or to refrain from growing food) nor forbidden to grow food (or to refrain from growing it). This solution reflects the way we tend to think about such an issue and is generally consistent with the universalization principle.[5]

Another interesting class of examples is one in which neither the rules nor their alternatives can be consistently universalized. Consider the following rule:

> Everyone should buy shoes but not sell them.

Here, I clearly cannot consent to the universal adoption of this rule, since all purchases require simultaneous sales. But a similar conclusion follows when we consider the alternative rule:

> No one should buy shoes, but everyone should sell them.

In this case, and in similar cases, where both a rule and its alternative are self-defeating, actions in accordance with the rule or its alternative will both be classified as morally impermissible.

Let us take one final example, having to do with whether we have an obligation to obey the civil authorities. First, consider the following rule:

> Everyone should obey the civil authorities.

It seems clear that we can consistently and simultaneously consent to the universal adoption of this rule. We can without any problem accept the conditions required to carry out the intention, such as the general knowledge of and respect for law and authority. We can also accept the predictable results of successfully carrying out the rule, such as a safe, peaceful, and orderly society. This rule is not self-defeating. On the other hand, consider the alternative rule:

> No one should obey the civil authorities.

We can argue that we cannot consistently and simultaneously consent to this rule, for the results would be general chaos; pursuit of any goal with reasonable prospect of security and success would be impossible. Although, in a narrow sense, continuing to disobey the civil authorities under these chaotic conditions might be possible, the purpose a person most likely has in mind by this disobedience (namely, gaining an advantage over his or her law-abiding fellows) would, no doubt, be undermined. Thus, the rule is self-defeating.

[5]See Onora Nell, *Acting on Principle,* p. 79.

This example shows the importance of considering the fullest consequences of the general acceptance of a rule. It also shows that we have no completely mechanical way to determine whether a rule can be consistently and simultaneously adopted. Applying the universalization principle requires imagination and may sometimes be controversial. Remember, however, that you are not considering the consequences of the alternative actions in terms of their utility or their contribution to the general welfare of mankind. Rather, you are asking whether the universal adoption of a policy would undermine the possibility of your adopting it.

Formulating the Moral Rules. One problem in applying the self-defeating test may have already come to your attention. Recall that with the universalization principle we do not directly test the action, but rather a particular rule describing the action. We know that more than one rule can be used to describe a given action, and the particular rule we see as underlying an action can make an enormous difference in our evaluation of the action.

Suppose I am facing a major test for which I did not study adequately because I had to work overtime at my job. I decide to cheat on the exam by bringing into the classroom information that I am virtually certain will be on the test. I justify my action by formulating a rule that reads:

> All persons should cheat on tests when they have not had sufficient time to study due to conditions genuinely beyond their control and when the tests are vital to their academic career.

I might argue that this rule could be universalized. Cheating would be limited and would probably not be so widespread that it would undermine the grading system altogether. But you might conclude that the rule is nevertheless illegitimate. At the very least, you would probably find it morally troublesome.

Because different rules can describe the same action and because the rule we choose is so important in evaluating the action, what guidelines can be given for formulating the rules? We can only say that the rules should not be too specific or too broad.

A rule is too specific if it contains references to particular places, times, or persons. In formulating the rule to cover cheating on a test, it would be possible to make a rule that applies only to one situation:

> If my name is John Brown and I am taking a test in chemistry at Make-or-Break University on January 29, 1983, and if I am 21 years old and trying to get into medical school, I should cheat on the exam.

This rule is not genuinely universal, because it can apply only to one person in one situation. Such a rule subverts the purpose of universalization.

A rule that allows for no exceptions is often too broad. Few of us would be willing to accept the consequences of a rule that says "Never lie." If an obviously crazed man comes into the room with a bloody knife in his hand and asks for John Jones, I would probably think it morally justifiable to tell him a lie. We are much more likely to accept the consequences of a rule that allows lying in certain situations, such as "I can lie when it is necessary to save an innocent life." In other words, a rule must be specific enough to take into account the morally relevant facts.

Aside from these general guidelines, a person is alone in formulating the rule that seems most adequately to describe his or her own action or the action of another person. Because we know more about our own motivations and the circumstances of our own lives than about the motives and circumstances of another person, we are in a better position to formulate descriptions of our own actions than the actions of others. So we must always be cautious in evaluating the actions of others.

The Means-Ends Principle as a Version of the Moral Standard

A hypothetical person called John Whiteman is a racist of the old school: he believes that all blacks should be slaves. He would even be willing to be enslaved himself if he were found to have "black blood." Most of us would consider his view to be the very model of immorality, so we are more than a little disturbed to realize that Mr. Whiteman's position passes the test of the universalization principle. His viewpoint is not self-defeating, because everyone's holding this position and acting in accordance with it would not prohibit Mr. Whiteman from holding his views.

The fact that such a patently immoral action can pass the test of the universalization principle points out the inadequacy of this principle as a complete guide to morality. Relatively few actions are self-defeating, although the test is useful when it does apply. The universalization principle emphasizes the equality of all human beings, which is an important part of the ethics of respect for persons. It provides a minimal condition for morally acceptable rules. But the condition is not sufficient for a morally acceptable action, as this example shows. For this reason, we must consider another version of the moral standard of the ethics of respect for persons—the *means-ends principle*. The principle can be stated as follows:

MS 2: Those actions are right that treat human beings, whether you or another person, as an end and not simply as a means.

What does it mean to treat someone as an end rather than a means? The answer to this question goes to the heart of the distinction between things and persons. Persons or moral agents have a capacity to formulate and carry out their own goals, whereas things have their purposes determined from the outside. A pencil sharpener, for example, was manufactured to perform a specific function, as was a coffee mug. Human beings, on the other hand, can determine their own purposes. This capacity of persons or moral agents to determine their own purposes is the basis of the means-ends principle. We shall say that "treating a person as an end" means respecting the conditions necessary for his or her effective functioning as a moral agent.

Before examining the conditions for the effective exercise of one's moral agency, however, we should ask what is meant by the reference to treating someone "*simply* as a means." This phrase implies that in some sense it is legitimate to treat a person as a means. In relating to other people in our day-to-day lives, we often do treat them as a means in the sense of being relatively unconcerned with their status as persons. When I go to the post office, I have no special interest in the aspirations of the postal worker who sells me stamps, other than a general positive attitude toward her. In one sense, I do treat her as a means to my end of obtaining stamps. But I do not treat her *simply* or *merely* as a means, because I do nothing to negate her status as a moral being.

Many social relationships involve the element of treating others as a means, but not solely as a means. I may treat my doctor as a means to recover from my illness, but I do not treat him simply as a means, because I do not deny him his status as a person. Students treat their professors as a means to gaining knowledge and getting a degree, but they do not treat them simply as a means, because they do not obstruct the professors' humanity. Social relationships would be impossible if treating a person as a means were not permissible in this limited way.

Preliminary Concepts. The basic idea of the means-ends principle is simple, but its application is often difficult. In order to help you to apply the principle, we shall discuss three issues: (1) the conditions of moral agency, (2) the principle of forfeiture, and (3) the principle of equality.[6]

---

[6]The following discussion relies heavily on Alan Gewirth, *Reason and Morality* (Chicago: University of Chicago Press, 1978), especially pp. 199–271, 338–354.

1. The Conditions of Moral Agency. Two fundamental conditions are necessary in order for a person to act as a moral agent. The first of these conditions is *freedom* or *voluntariness*, whereby a person controls or initiates his behavior by his unforced choices. The second condition is *purposiveness* or *well-being*, whereby a person sets goals for herself and has the abilities necessary for achieving them. Let's consider both of these conditions.

The condition of freedom or voluntariness naturally brings to mind the right to protection from violence and coercion. In acts of violence, such as robbery or rape, a person's freedom is diminished. He or she is acted on with direct physical or psychological compulsion and has no opportunity for consent. In acts of coercion, such as forced prostitution, a person gives his or her consent but has no real free choice in doing so. Deception also limits the freedom of others; in deception the person gives unforced consent, but only as a result of falsehoods or misrepresentations intentionally presented to him or her.

A person's freedom may be interfered with in other ways as well. Physical or mental illness, willful ignorance or self-deception, and obsessive submission to some dominating passion like drugs or alcohol can limit a person's voluntary action. Lack of knowledge is also a major impediment to free decisions.

The other condition necessary for moral agency is what we have called well-being—namely, the goods necessary for carrying out one's freely chosen purposes. If a person can choose goals but has no ability to carry them out, his moral agency is worth very little.

Several categories of goods are necessary for effective moral agency. *Basic goods,* such as life, food, clothing, shelter, physical health, and emotional stability, are prerequisites of our purposive action. *Nonsubtractive goods* are abilities or conditions needed for maintaining undiminished one's level of purpose-fulfillment. These goods include not being lied to, cheated, defamed, or insulted. They also include not having one's promises broken or one's privacy invaded. We have already seen that breaking promises not only violates the self-defeating test, but also tends to lower a person's capacity for action. Finally, *additive goods* are abilities and conditions needed for raising the level of purpose-fulfillment. These goods include owning property, having a sense of well-being and self-respect, and being treated in a nondiscriminatory way. Additive goods also include the virtues of character, such as courage, temperance, and prudence, that enable people more effectively to pursue their goals. Other aspects of freedom and well-being also are important for one's being able to act as a moral agent. It is impossible to enumerate all aspects, but they will often be important in making moral decisions.

2. The Principle of Forfeiture. The means-ends principle requires that I treat everyone, myself and others alike, as ends and not mere means. The universalization principle also implies that everyone should live according to the same rules, which means that one loses the right to be treated as an end if he does not treat others this way. Therefore the ethics of respect for persons requires a principle of forfeiture, much as in natural law. The *principle of forfeiture* says that, if I treat others as mere means, I forfeit my rights to freedom and well-being. I do not necessarily forfeit all my rights, but in general my rights are forfeited in proportion to the rights of others that I trespass.

When the state punishes a criminal by putting him in prison or taking his life, he is deprived of some of the aspects of freedom and well-being necessary for his full functioning as a moral agent. Nevertheless the punishment is justified, because the criminal by his action has treated someone else as a mere means. Whether he has committed theft, fraud, rape, murder, or some other crime, he has done something to deprive others of their freedom or well-being. Punishment is a legitimate response to this action and is not a violation of the means-ends principle.

Criminal action is not the only way in which a person may forfeit some of his rights to be treated as an end and never as a mere means. If I slander or insult you, it might be appropriate for you to hit me or in some other way limit my freedom or well-being. When a businessperson or professional, through negligence, endangers the safety of her client or the general public, it may be appropriate to reprimand her or deprive her of her job, even if nothing worthy of legal action has been done.

A modified version of the principle of forfeiture is applicable when a person either voluntarily or by implication enters into certain kinds of relationships. If you and I are the proprietors of two different stores that are competing for the same business and I eventually run you out of business, I am certainly harming your freedom and well-being. Still, I may be justified in running you out of business, because one implicitly consents to this possibility when entering the competitive business environment.

3. The Principle of Equality. Another issue that you will frequently encounter in applying the means-ends principle is the problem of conflicting obligations. Recall the story of the two female counterspies who were in Britain during World War II. While they were there, the Allies learned that the Nazis knew their identity. If they were sent back, they would almost certainly be apprehended, tortured, and killed. What should have been done from the standpoint of the ethics of respect for persons?

The problem is that someone's freedom or well-being will be harmed regardless of which alternative is taken. If the counterspies are returned to the continent, they will suffer loss of freedom, physical violence, and death. If they are not returned, the Allied cause will lose a considerable advantage in the war, and probably many additional lives will be lost. Someone's freedom and well-being will be harmed with either alternative.

The idea of equal treatment implicit in the two moral standards again provides the fundamental guideline. The *principle of equality* says that, when someone's freedom or well-being must be violated, people should be treated equally unless reasons exist for them to be treated otherwise. Some additional criteria will be helpful in carrying out this principle: In treating everyone equally as an end, we must consider (1) how important the aspects of freedom and well-being are that are being threatened, (2) how severely these aspects will be limited, and (3) whether the aspects of freedom and well-being involved would be directly or indirectly violated.

If we applied these criteria to the case of the counterspies, we would probably come to the following conclusions: (1) The aspects of freedom and well-being involved are of the highest importance: ability to make a free decision and physical life itself. (2) The values of the women are seriously threatened; that is, they would suffer not simply harm to their freedom or well-being, but loss of life and freedom altogether. Those who would be killed or injured because of the prolongation of the war would also suffer loss of life and freedom. (3) The threat to the women is obviously more direct and immediate than the threat to the Allied soldiers and civilians who would be harmed by the loss of access to the Nazi code.

Applying the principle of equality, we would probably conclude that returning the counterspies to the continent was morally wrong, primarily because their rights are more directly and severely violated. They were being used as mere means. If we are to justify returning them to Germany, we must use utilitarian considerations rather than arguments derived from the ethics of respect for persons.

We can use two tests to determine whether we are treating a person as an end and not as a mere means. The negative test asks whether a person's freedom or well-being is threatened by our actions. (Have we treated the person as a mere means?) The positive test asks whether we have assisted others in achieving their freedom and well-being. (Have we treated them as an end?) The negative test is more stringent than the positive test. We shall consider each of them in turn.

The Negative Test. Our first inclination might be to argue that we should never override the rights of others, but the preceding considerations have shown us that sometimes we must. In situations that involve criminal activity or a conflict of obligations, someone's freedom or well-being must be overridden. Keeping this point in mind, we shall formulate the question that constitutes the *negative test* of the means-ends principle:

Does the action override my own or others' freedom or well-being?

As discussed in the previous section, this test is not always easy to apply. We must remember that the principle of forfeiture may apply. We must also remember that sometimes obligations can conflict such that someone's rights to freedom and well-being must be overridden or neglected to some degree.

Let us apply the negative test to the case of the 37-year-old accountant, discussed in Chapter 5. Elliott has been diagnosed as having a fatal cancer. He has only a few months to live, and he is experiencing excruciating nerve-root pain that drugs can no longer relieve. His illness is depleting his family's modest finances. Furthermore, he perceives that his wife and children have already begun withdrawing emotionally from him in preparation for his inevitable death. Would it be wrong for him to take his own life, according to the negative test of the means-ends principle?

We could formulate the rule Elliott would be using if he took his own life as the following:

A person may end his life when death is inevitable, he is in great pain, and he has no compelling reasons for staying alive.

The means-ends principle requires that Elliott treat both himself and others as an end and not merely as a means. The people affected in this case are the members of his immediate family. First let's consider the application of the negative test to Elliott. The negative test stipulates that Elliott must not override his own freedom or well-being. He is not overriding his own freedom if he genuinely wants to end his life. However he may feel unduly pressured by the fact that his illness is depleting the family resources. If he were actually ending his life to save his family's financial resources and acting against his own true desires, he would be treating his own life as a mere means and his suicide would be illegitimate. On the other hand, if he sincerely wishes to end his life as a gesture of self-sacrifice for his family, this act could be in accord with the negative test of the means-ends principle.

In Elliott's case, pursuit of freedom and well-being conflict. By committing suicide Elliott may be acting freely, but by doing so he eliminates his life and thereby all other goods as well. Is this decision to accord priority to freedom justifiable? In this case the pursuit of well-being beyond a minimal level is doomed to failure, and Elliott will soon lose his life in any case.

Therefore it seems legitimate for him to give freedom priority over well-being. We shall say that, if Elliott's decision to end his life is freely and knowledgeably made, it does not violate the negative test of the means-ends principle as far as he is concerned.

Now let us look at the effect of Elliott's suicide on his family. If his family has indeed begun to accept his inevitable death, then he probably is not overriding their freedom or well-being. However, they might be able to accept his natural death but not his voluntary death. Even if they could not accept his voluntary death, though, would Elliott's suicide indicate that he is using his family as a mere means? Two replies can be made here.

First, Elliott's and his family's wishes might conflict, in which case full freedom for both sides is not possible. If Elliott's family achieves the goal of keeping him alive as long as possible (assuming this choice is their goal), then he cannot achieve his goal of ending his own misery. Alternatively, if he achieves his goal of ending his misery, they cannot accomplish their goal. Given that full freedom is not possible, Elliott can argue plausibly that his freedom to control his life takes priority, using the guidelines developed from the principle of equality.

Second, Elliott could also maintain that ending his life does not interfere with the well-being of his family; in fact, he could argue that it enhances their well-being by preserving their economic independence. Therefore we can maintain that the negative test is not violated for Elliott's family. His suicide would then not be a violation of the means-ends principle.

The Positive Test. The positive test of the means-ends principle requires that we do more than simply refrain from interfering with our rights to freedom and well-being and those of others. In addition, we must positively contribute to others' status as moral agents, as well as our own. However this obligation does not require that we devote our lives slavishly to helping others achieve a fuller state of self-realization. We would then be treating ourselves as a mere means to the good of others, which is forbidden by the means-ends principle itself. Therefore, each individual must determine when, where, and how this moral obligation is to be fulfilled with respect to others. So we will state the question posed by the *positive test* as follows:

> Does the action assist oneself (or others, in certain circumstances) in achieving one's own (or others') freedom and well-being?

To see how this test might be applied, let us begin with an example.

Thirteen-year-old Jason Simmons has been diagnosed as having a ruptured appendix. His physician says he needs immediate surgery; however, Jason has been attending Christian Science services and has come to believe in healing through prayer. He does not want surgery, even though his parents do. Disregarding legal questions for the moment, should the physician defend the boy's right not to have surgery or should she go along with his parents' request?

Applying the ethics of respect for persons, the rule presupposed by the position Jason has taken might be formulated as follows:

> People should be allowed to follow their own convictions, even if the result is their death.

The self-defeating test is not violated by this rule, since Jason could pursue his course of action even if the rule presupposed by his action is universalized. His action would pass the negative test of the means-ends principle, because he is not interfering in an illegitimate way with others' freedom or well-being. Although he would be interfering with his parents' desires to keep him alive, his action does not deny them an equal freedom to determine their own lives. Must we conclude, then, that it is morally impermissible for the physician to oppose Jason's request?

This case involves *paternalism,* which we may define as using coercion to get another person to do or refrain from doing something for his or her own good. In the usual version of paternalism, which we shall call *strong paternalism,* another person determines what is for my own good. Strong paternalism is clearly incompatible with the means-ends principle, since it allows the freedom of other people to be overridden. Another kind of paternalism, called *weak paternalism,* says that paternalistic coercion can be used, but only to the extent necessary to preserve a person's freedom. Several circumstances—such as ignorance, intellectual immaturity, emotional disturbance, and social pressures—can decrease a person's ability to make a free and informed decision. Weak paternalism justifies the use of coercion to keep a person from making a decision under these circumstances or to enable someone else to make a decision for that person. The use of paternalistic coercion, the weak paternalist argues, actually protects the long-term freedom of the individual.

Does the positive test of the means-ends principle apply in any way to weak paternalism? I believe it does. We have already seen that the central idea in the means-ends principle is the preservation of people's ability to act as moral agents. The basic thrust of the positive test, then, must be that in certain situations we have an obligation to actively promote the status of others as moral agents. Weak paternalism is simply the use of coercion to preserve that status when it is threatened. Therefore weak paternalism can be justified by the positive test of the means-ends principle.

The key issue in this example for the ethics of respect for persons is whether Jason is making a genuinely free and informed decision. If he is, then living by the principles of Christian Science, even at the risk of losing his own life, represents his true goal. However, if Jason's decision is not genuinely free and informed, that choice does not represent his true goal. Several factors might prevent him from making a free and informed decision. For example, a 13-year-old boy may not be intellectually mature enough to evaluate the religious teachings on which he is basing his decision. Or he might be under undue emotional pressure from his peers or from Christian Scientists whom he has come to respect. Or he may be rebelling against his parents in his decision.

In order to justify disregarding Jason's wishes, the physician must believe that she is actually assisting him in achieving greater long-range freedom. She must also believe that her special relationship as the boy's physician provides the proper occasion for the application of the means-ends principle. Because we can plausibly argue that a boy of Jason's age is not in a position to make a free and informed decision about such a serious issue and that the special patient–physician relationship does justify the obligation to help Jason realize his true goals, paternalistic action by the physician seems permissible.

The positive test for the means-ends principle may be relevant in areas other than paternalism. Special relationships (for example, professional relationships and family relationships) are especially likely to require that we actively promote the opportunity of others to realize their goals. Being in a position to help another person in dire need also produces an obligation in accordance with the positive test of the means-ends principle. Suppose John is fishing in his boat and suddenly becomes aware that someone is struggling in the water several hundred feet away. The person is shouting for help and obviously is in immediate danger of drowning. John could easily rescue him but does not do so and the person drowns. Most people would agree that John ought to have tried to rescue him. But why? John's behavior passes the self-defeating test, so if John's action is immoral by the ethics of respect for persons, it is because it violates the means-ends principle. It does not violate the negative test, but it does violate the positive test. John is in a position to help a person in extreme danger with relatively little cost to himself. John's relationship to the person (his being in a position to help) therefore imposes an obligation to aid the person in distress.

Finally, merely living in a society creates an obligation to help less fortunate members of society, at least within certain limits. Just how far this obligation extends is a matter of considerable controversy, but it seems reasonable to hold that I have an obligation to pay taxes to help those who are unable to provide for themselves. This obligation must, however, have limits; otherwise I will be used as a mere means by the less fortunate. But we must keep in mind that the principle of equality requires that everyone should be treated equally as an end, insofar as is possible.

We are now ready to summarize the steps in applying the ethics of respect for persons in a checklist. However, one further problem in applying the ethics of respect for persons should be mentioned. If both the action and its alternative fail one or more of the tests, either action will ordinarily be considered morally permissible. However, an action that does not violate the tests as seriously as the alternative should be the chosen one. To settle this issue, do not use utilitarian considerations, but determine which tests are most seriously violated by the standards of the tests themselves. The principles of forfeiture and equality will often be useful.

Checklist for Applying the Ethics of Respect for Persons

_____ 1. Determine the most appropriate rule presupposed by the action whose morality you are evaluating.

_____ 2. Apply the self-defeating test of the universalization principle, which asks whether others could act by the rule without undermining the possibility of my acting by the rule. Remember to consider fully the consequences of acting according to the rule and the conditions necessary to act according to the rule. Remember also that the rule must be universalized at the same time as the action that is being tested.

_____ 3. Apply the negative test of the means-ends principle, which asks whether the action overrides the freedom or well-being of oneself or others.

_____ 4. If relevant, apply the positive test of the means-ends principle, which asks whether the action assists oneself (or others, in certain circumstances) in achieving one's own (or others') freedom and well-being.

_____ 5. Make a final decision on the morality of the action.
   a. If it passes the test of the universalization principle and the negative test of the means-ends principle (and the positive test where applicable), it is morally permissible.
   b. If it is morally permissible and its alternative violates the universalization principle or the negative test of the means-ends principle (or the positive test where applicable), it is morally obligatory.
   c. If it fails either the universalization principle or the negative test

of the means-ends principle (or the positive test where applicable), it is morally impermissible.

    d. If both the original action and its alternative fail one or more of the tests, either action will ordinarily be considered morally permissible. Sometimes one alternative should be chosen because it does not violate the three tests as seriously as the other alternative.

CONCEPT SUMMARY

The ethics of respect for persons takes as its central theme the equal dignity of all human beings. Our formulation of it is expressed in terms of two moral principles.

    The first principle, the universalization principle, states that an action is right if you can consent to everyone's adopting the moral rule presupposed by the action. The test for this principle involves asking whether the universalization of the rule would undermine the possibility of acting in accordance with the rule (the self-defeating test).

    The means-ends principle says that an action is right that treats human beings, whether you or someone else, as an end and not simply as a means. Two tests for the satisfaction of this principle are the negative test and the positive test. The negative test requires that an action must not override the freedom or well-being of people. The positive test requires that I promote my own freedom and well-being and help others, in certain circumstances, to achieve theirs. The positive test is applicable in a special relationship, such as the relationship of a professional to her client or of parents to their children. It is also applicable when others are in dire need or, to a lesser degree, when people are a part of a common social order.

    In applying the means-ends principle, we must remember these two points: First, a person may forfeit some of his or her freedom or well-being by violating the freedom or well-being of others or by voluntarily entering into relationships that subject the person to such a possible forfeiture. Second, where everyone's freedom and well-being cannot be satisfied, all persons should be respected equally, insofar as possible.

The Personal and Social Ethics of the Ethics of Respect for Persons

We are now ready to look at the implications of the ethics of respect for persons for personal and social ethics. You will usually find that the means-ends principle provides the most helpful guidance, but both principles are sometimes useful.

Duties to Self. The most useful guideline here is the means-ends principle. You may be inclined to ask "How can I treat myself as a mere means? Isn't the idea self-contradictory?" Yet a moment's reflection will show that one can indeed act in a way that diminishes or destroys the conditions one needs in order to exist as an effective goal-creating and goal-pursuing being. A review of these conditions will suggest some of the duties we owe to ourselves according to the ethics of respect for persons.

The first condition is physical life itself. I have a duty under normal conditions not to destroy or impair my health or the physical integrity of my body. The question of suicide, however, is an especially interesting issue in the category of duties to self. It might seem that I have a duty never to kill myself, because my death would destroy an essential condition for all further action. But perhaps my goals and values dictate that my life should end, in which case a conflict arises between my pursuit of my goals now and the conditions necessary for their pursuit in the future. As in Elliott's case, I may know that I am dying of cancer, that for a few months I will be enduring great pain, and that in this condition I will lose my personal dignity. I will no longer be able to pursue, let alone realize, my goals. In such circumstances, my freedom can take priority over my well-being. My wish to die should have priority over the fact that my death will nullify all possibilities of achieving any future goals.

This same obligation to preserve the condition of physical life also justifies self-defense in most circumstances. If someone threatens my life, I have the right and even the obligation to defend myself against this threat. The principle of forfeiture shows that I am not illegitimately overriding the goals of the one who attacks me.

I also have a duty under normal conditions to promote my physical and mental health. The positive test of the means-ends principle applies to duties to self, because I have a special obligation to my own freedom and well-being. In most instances, increasing my general knowledge and education will also promote my abilities to pursue my goals. An interesting exercise might be for you to decide which virtues or traits of character would enhance your abilities to act as a purposive agent.

Duties to Others. Ordinary moral prohibitions against harming others—prohibitions of such acts as murder, rape, theft, and physical assault—are easy to justify by the ethics of respect for persons. These acts directly override the freedom and well-being of others, so they violate the means-ends principle.

Our obligation to help others, especially when help can be given with relatively little cost to us, follows from the means-ends principle. We have already seen that failure to help others in distress violates the positive test of the means-ends principle, as long as giving the aid does not seriously jeopardize our own status as ends.

The means-ends principle provides especially useful and insightful tests in the area of sexual morality. Even our language about sexual relationships often sounds as though it was derived from the means-ends principle. Treating someone as a "mere sex object" is treating that individual as a thing rather than a person. If we treat a person as a mere means in a sexual relationship, we are not treating him or her as a goal-creating and goal-pursuing agent. In rape, for example, a person uses violence or coercion to override the freedom of another to choose her (or his) own sexual partner.

However, by far the most common way of treating another person as a mere means in a sexual relationship is by some form of deception. The boy who tells his girl friend "I love you" or "We'll get married if you get pregnant" without meaning it is depriving her of the ability to make an informed decision about a sexual relationship and is thereby treating her as a mere means. Seducing a person into a demeaning sexual relationship is also using him as a mere means, because it diminishes his self-esteem and reduces his ability to act effectively as a goal-pursuing agent.

Not all nonmarital sexual relationships are based on deception, nor are they all degrading. Suppose, for example, that two college students establish a sexual relationship based on mutual affection and pleasure, but not love. Each person knows the other's intentions, so no deception is present and the relationship is not demeaning. They take proper precautions against pregnancy but have agreed that, if a pregnancy results, they will get married or at least will properly care for the child. What can we say about the morality of this relationship? The universalization principle does not pose a problem, because the rule underlying the relationship can be universalized without being self-defeating. What, then, about the means-ends principle? Neither person is overriding the freedom of the other or diminishing the ability of the other to be an effective, goal-pursuing agent. However, some would want to point out the likelihood of mutual self-deception when sexual passion is involved. Whatever we conclude about the morality of such relationships, clearly the ethics of respect for persons provides the basis for a positive and insightful approach to sexual morality.

Social Ethics. The principle that governs the social ethics of respect for persons is that social institutions should respect the freedom and well-being of others by following rules that are universally applied; that is, the state should treat all individuals equally as ends and not mere means. How is this task accomplished? We have seen that the means-ends principle has both a positive and a negative test. Both of those tests have important implications.

Let's first consider the negative aspect of the state's responsibility to its citizens. This function is what libertarians call the minimal state. It involves the state's protection of citizens' rights not to have their rights to freedom and well-being overridden by other citizens or by the state itself. This protection is needed in several areas. First, the state must protect citizens against murder, theft, fraud, and physical violence. Without these protections, individuals do not have the conditions necessary to realize their purposes. Second, the liberty of individual conduct should extend to the economic sphere. Economic goals are central in the lives of many people, and the right to pursue these goals should be protected as long as the rights of others are not seriously impaired. Third, the individual should have as much freedom as possible in the area of beliefs and lifestyle, including freedoms of speech, the press, religion, and assembly. Laws regulating controversial activities like polygamy or homosexuality can be justified only when the activity regulated poses a clear threat to the liberty of others.

The state also has positive obligations to its citizens. This function is what we shall call the supportive state.[7] The relationship of the state to its citizens and of citizens to one another requires that the positive test of the means-ends principle be applied, which in turn requires the state to promote the freedom and well-being of its citizens. The state could not claim political authority without a commitment to the welfare of its citizens, and citizens have some obligation to one another by virtue of their living in the same society. Thus the state should make some provision for the health, education, and general welfare of its citizens and give special support for those who, through no fault of their own, are not able to provide for themselves.

The question inevitably arises whether the positive obligation of the state can be fulfilled without violating the goals of other citizens. In taxing productive citizens to provide for the disadvantaged, isn't the state using productive citizens as mere means? Isn't the state limiting the moral agency of the advantaged in order to provide for the disadvantaged? The answer is that we must adopt our usual policy of dealing with conflicts produced by the application of the means-end principle. We must remember that the final obligation is to treat everyone equally as ends insofar as possible; we must try to produce a situation in which the least serious violations of the principle are produced. Thus, the advantaged must be taxed to provide benefits for other members of society, but the gifted should be allowed to keep most of the wealth they have earned. This requirement is made not

---

[7]See Alan Gewirth, *Reason and Morality,* pp. 312–327.

to preserve incentive to productivity, as in utilitarian social ethics, but to avoid violating the status of the gifted as ends and not mere means to the good of others. The reader must determine just how these guidelines should be followed in practice.

CONCEPT SUMMARY

One can act in ways that destroy the conditions necessary for one's existence as an effective moral agent. Therefore one has a duty to preserve one's life and health, pursue an education, and develop whatever abilities and character traits are important for advancing one's status as a person.

The negative duties to others that are a part of most moral philosophies—such as the duties not to commit murder, theft, or fraud—are justified by the universalization and means-ends principles. A duty to help others in distress is mandated by both principles, if carrying out this duty does not require us to treat ourselves as mere means to the ends of others. Respect for persons also provides many useful insights into sexual morality.

The principle that governs the social ethics of respect for persons is that social institutions should be designed to help citizens function as effective goal-pursuing agents. Thus the state has an obligation to protect citizens from one another and to help the disadvantaged achieve their freedom and well-being.

Applying the Ethics of Respect for Persons

Now let's apply the ethics of respect for persons to some problems that require moral decision, using the methodology outlined in the checklist.

Case 1: Should the Truth Be Told to the Dying?

Mrs. Trinkmann has been admitted to the hospital with complaints of abdominal pains and persistent indigestion. She fears that she may have cancer, and she has given signals that she does not want to be told if cancer is found. Exploratory surgery reveals that she has cancer of the liver at such an advanced stage that her death is imminent. The physician, Dr. Alexander, is aware that Mrs. Trinkmann is emotionally vulnerable. Telling her the truth may cause her and her family a great deal of suffering, so he is tempted to abide by Mrs. Trinkmann's wishes. On the other hand, without knowing her true condition, she may not be able to prepare adequately for her death, and the doctor has no sufficient reason to believe that Mrs. Trinkmann would seriously deteriorate emotionally if he told her the truth. Should he tell her the truth?

1. First let us consider the rule for this situation:

> When patients make it clear that they do not want to know their true medical condition, physicians should conceal the truth from them, even when the patients are facing imminent death.

2. The self-defeating test encounters a problem in this case; if this rule were generally adopted, patients would have less confidence in their physicians. Thus Mrs. Trinkmann, knowing that Dr. Alexander would not tell her the truth if she had cancer, would not believe him or would at least doubt his assurances if he told her she was healthy. So the intended goal of reassuring Mrs. Trinkmann would be only partially accomplished, if at all. Perhaps the goal would not be totally frustrated by the adoption of the rule, because physicians would still tell the truth in many cases, but the goal would be seriously impaired.

3. The negative test of the means-ends principle requires that Mrs. Trinkmann's freedom and well-being not be overridden. One of the conditions for freedom is accurate knowledge, and Dr. Alexander would be violating this condition by keeping her in ignorance. The only extenuating consideration might be that, if she were told of her illness, she might lose all ability to act in a rational manner. In this way we could argue that the basic good of mental equilibrium is being protected, even if the method prevents the full operation of Mrs. Trinkmann's freedom of choice. Because we have insufficient reason to believe that Mrs. Trinkmann would seriously deteriorate emotionally if she were told the truth, we must conclude that this argument is unconvincing and that the means-ends principle is violated.

4. The positive test of the means-ends principle is relevant, since Dr. Alexander has a special obligation to his patient. Beyond not treating her as a mere means, he must treat her as an end, helping her to realize her freedom and well-being. This obligation requires that he give her the knowledge she needs in order to make responsible decisions regarding her impending death. Therefore this rule also violates the positive test.

5. It will be helpful in this case to examine the alternative rule, which can be stated as follows:

> When patients make it clear that they do not want to know their true medical condition, physicians should still tell them the truth even when the patients are facing imminent death.

This rule passes the self-defeating test. All physicians could consistently adopt the rule, and in fact they must if patients are to have full confidence in the word of their physicians.

The negative test of the means-ends principle is not violated by the alternative rule, because the freedom of individuals is not limited by telling them the truth. The positive test is also not violated, since telling patients the truth preserves and enhances their status as free moral agents.

Because the first rule violates all three tests and the alternative rule violates none, we must conclude that, according to the ethics of respect for persons, Dr. Alexander is morally obligated to tell Mrs. Trinkmann the truth.

Case 2: Should a Physician Violate His Conscience?

APPLY EQUALITY PRINCIPLE

Dr. Sanchez is the only physician in a small village in Mexico. Mrs. Rodriguez asks to be sterilized so that she will not have any more children, because she believes she could not raise them properly. Dr. Sanchez believes sterilizations are contrary to natural law and therefore immoral. However, Mrs. Rodriguez cannot afford to go to another town for the operation, so Dr. Sanchez wonders whether he should suppress his own moral scruples to comply with Mrs. Rodriguez's wishes. What should Dr. Sanchez do according to the ethics of respect for persons?

1. The moral rule presupposed by Dr. Sanchez's action, if he were to comply with his patient's wishes, is not easy to formulate. The rule must not be too broad. Physicians could not accept a rule that required them to follow their patient's wishes without exception. Such a rule would commit them to such actions as giving patients narcotics they do not need or even helping them commit murder. A realistic rule might be:

> Physicians should follow the wishes of their patients, even if these wishes involve violating the physician's strongly held moral beliefs, as long as the patient's request is within the bounds of ordinary morality.

This rule is still ambiguous, because the phrase "within the bounds of ordinary morality" has various interpretations. But this form is at least workable.

2. Application of the self-defeating test is also not easy. One can argue that, if physicians generally adopted this rule, the possibility of any individual physician's following the rule would not be undermined. For example, some physicians who do not believe in artificial contraceptives would prescribe them anyhow, but the general practice would not produce a problem for the self-defeating test. On the other hand, this rule might prove so

demoralizing to members of the medical profession that some highly negative consequences would result. But let us assume that even these consequences would not undermine the possibility of acting in accordance with the rule, so that the self-defeating test can be met.

3. The negative test of the means-ends principle is clearly violated, because a physician would be allowing violation of his freedom to live by his own values.

4. The positive test is relevant and is not violated by this rule, because the physician is helping the patient achieve her freedom and well-being. But, given the problems with the negative test of the means-ends principle, we must conclude that the rule fails the tests imposed by the ethics of respect for persons.

5. The alternative rule can be stated as follows:

> Physicians should not follow the wishes of their patients when they violate the physicians' own strongly held moral beliefs, even when the patient's request is within the bounds of ordinary moral beliefs.

This rule passes the self-defeating test. Even though some people may be severely inconvenienced or even unable to fulfill their purposes, as is the case with Mrs. Rodriguez, the rule can still be universalized without inconsistency.

The alternative rule passes the negative test of the means-ends principle with respect to the physician, because the major point of the rule is precisely to protect physicians like Dr. Sanchez from having their strongly held values overridden. But what about the patient? Does the physician's refusal to perform the sterilization override her moral agency? This question raises the distinction between nonaction and inaction. *Nonaction* is the simple absence of any action, whereas *inaction* is the refraining from a certain action in a voluntary and purposive way. Voluntarily and purposively refraining from doing something is a type of action and thus is subject to moral evaluation. A physician who is refraining from performing a procedure must be considered to be performing an action, so it seems most reasonable to look upon his action as overriding the patient's purposes. But, by performing the sterilization, the physician seriously violates his own freedom, and this violation is perhaps direct. The question is whether a violation of one's strongly held moral convictions is more serious than the violation of the request for the sterilization.

Both rules violate the negative test of the means-ends principle, and the second rule obviously violates the positive test. Therefore we shall conclude that it is permissible for Dr. Sanchez either to refuse to perform the abortion or to perform the abortion. Because the physician's freedom is directly violated, the physician should probably refuse to perform the abortion. But either action is permissible.

Case 3: Should the Lawyer Tell the Adversary?

This case, which we considered previously, produces some interesting problems when subjected to full analysis by the standards of the ethics of respect for persons.[8] Tommy Compton is a 15-year-old boy who was badly injured in an automobile accident. He sues the driver responsible for the injury. The driver's defense lawyer, Charles Johnson, has his own physician examine Tommy. The physician discovers an aortic aneurism, apparently caused by the accident, that Tommy's physician had not found. The aneurism is life-threatening unless operated on. Charles realizes that, if the youth learns of the aneurism, he will demand a much higher settlement. According to the American Bar Association code, a lawyer must keep the client's secrets unless the client is contemplating commission of a crime. *Secrets,* according to the code, are the "information gained in the professional relationship . . . the disclosure of which . . . would be likely to be detrimental to the client." From the standpoint of the ethics of respect for persons, is withholding the information ethically sound?

1. First let us formulate the rule that would apply if Johnson followed the ABA code:

> Lawyers should keep the secrets learned in their professional relationships, even when the practice deprives adversaries of information vital to their well-being.

2. This rule does not have problems with the self-defeating test. It can be generally followed—as it apparently is—without any obvious inconsistency.

3. The negative test of the means-ends principle asks whether the action in question overrides the individual's freedom or well-being. But to which individual does the question refer? The rule above would clearly override Tommy's freedom by depriving him of vital knowledge. It would not, on the other hand, override the freedom or well-being of the client whose interests are being protected. But, because the rule can result in dramatic cases of using people as mere means, as the present example illustrates, the most reasonable statement is that the rule fails the negative test.

---

[8]Spaulding v. Zimmerman, 116 N.W. 2d 704 (1962). The names are fictitious.

4. The positive test has different results. A lawyer is ordinarily thought to have a special obligation to clients, and the present ABA rules require a lawyer to protect and promote the purposes of the client. Therefore the lawyer's action does not fail the positive test of the means-ends principle.

5. The alternative rule might be stated in the following way:

Lawyers should not keep the secrets learned in their professional relationships when this practice deprives adversaries of information vital to their well-being.

This rule encounters problems with the self-defeating test, although their seriousness is difficult to determine. The advocate of traditional legal morality can argue that, if clients knew lawyers would reveal confidential information, they would not be honest with their lawyers nor would they allow those over whom they have control to be honest. This dishonesty might keep lawyers from learning secrets of the kind illustrated in the case, although this dire state of affairs is unlikely to transpire. Assuming it did, the legal profession would still not be totally undermined, although clients might be less candid with their lawyers.

The negative test of the means-ends principle as applied to the alternative rule encounters problems just the reverse of those encountered by the original rule. Whereas the original rule threatens to override the freedom of the third party (Tommy), the alternative rule threatens to override the well-being of the client by requiring that information important to the adversary be made public. This case presents a conflict of the rights to freedom and well-being. A preliminary conclusion would be that either action is morally permissible. Because the threat is to one of Tommy's most important basic goods—namely, life itself—and because the threat is direct and pressing, the principle of equality requires us to conclude that Tommy's rights are more seriously threatened. So we shall say that the principle of equal respect for persons requires that the information be revealed. Revealing the information is morally obligatory.

Evaluating the Ethics of Respect for Persons as a Moral Theory

Now we are ready to evaluate the ethics of respect for persons with our four criteria. Remember that a subjective element is always present in evaluating moral theories. The following evaluations are my own, although they reflect widely held positions among moral philosophers. These evaluations are for your own consideration rather than for uncritical acceptance.

The Ethics of Respect for Persons

How well do I think the theory meets the criteria?

Criteria	Very Well	Moderately Well	Very Poorly
1. (Consistency)	X		
2. (Plausibility)		X	
3. (Usefulness)		X	
4. (Justification)		X	

Criterion 1: Consistency. I have given the ethics of respect for persons a high mark for consistency. The fact that this moral philosophy has two moral standards rather than one might be considered a source of inconsistency, because the two standards sometimes yield different conclusions. But the stipulation that an action must pass the tests of both standards before it is considered morally acceptable rules out this problem. Besides, the two moral standards taken together express a common moral theme—namely, the equal respect due all persons.

Another possible source of inconsistency is the two principles used in applying the means-ends principle. These principles are (1) that a person can forfeit his rights to freedom and well-being by violating the rights of others and (2) that the rights of others should be respected equally. If they are not derivable from the theory itself, a problem of consistency arises. But because both of these principles can be derived from the idea of equality embodied in the universalization principle, they are not inconsistent with the theory.

Criterion 2: Plausibility. I have given the ethics of respect for persons a slightly lower rating for plausibility. Many people, especially those strongly influenced by traditional moral ideas, would maintain that the ethics of respect for persons is more compatible with their previously held moral beliefs than utilitarianism or egoism. They might well hold that it is closer to their moral beliefs than natural law, although the version of the theory presented here has not suggested traditional conclusions to such issues as premarital sex or suicide.

Perhaps the most general criticism of the ethics of respect for persons—from the standpoint of agreement or disagreement with our previously held moral beliefs—is that the theory does not sufficiently account for an action's consequences. In many issues of public policy, for example, utilitarian considerations seem relevant. Sometimes it seems justifiable to sacrifice some innocent lives to save the lives of a larger number of people. If killing some civilians is necessary to end a war and ultimately to save many more lives, is it wrong to do so? Is it wrong to adopt policies that increase unemployment somewhat but reduce the inflation rate? It sometimes seems morally permissible, if not obligatory, to engage in an action that involves wrongs to individuals because the overall consequences justify it. Many moral philosophers have trouble with the answers given to these questions by the ethics of respect for persons.

Criterion 3: Usefulness. I have rated the ethics of respect for persons as "moderately well" on this criterion for three reasons. First, the rule describing an action can be stated in many different ways, which means that different conclusions will be drawn depending on which rule is used. Usually this problem is not too severe, because the most adequate rule is reasonably obvious. However the rule sometimes must be stated in an ambiguous or open-ended way in order to be acceptable, as Case 2, involving Dr. Sanchez and Mrs. Rodriguez, demonstrates. At other times the proper rule may be difficult to determine, and the way in which the rule is stated may decisively influence the outcome of the ethical analysis. When these problems arise, they diminish the usefulness of the theory in providing a clear indication of what should be done.

A second difficulty is that we sometimes find it hard to determine whether an action passes the tests of the two moral standards. Sometimes the self-defeating test is hard to apply. If it were generally accepted that physicians will lie to their patients when their patients do not want to know the truth, would patients no longer trust physicians? If lawyers generally broke the confidentiality bond between them and their clients in order to reveal information necessary to protect the well-being of others, would this breach undermine lawyers' ability to do their jobs? We have also seen that the means-ends principle is difficult to apply in many ethical controversies. It is not always easy to determine how the negative test applies or whether the positive test is relevant.

A third problem with this theory is that we sometimes find that both an action and its alternative have difficulties with one or more of the tests. We are forced to make a judgment as to which violations are more serious, and this judgment makes the solution to the problem controversial. Any moral theory will yield ambiguous conclusions in some instances, so this state of affairs is not a refutation of a moral philosophy. Nevertheless, the limitation, which should be noted in any evaluation, is especially prominent in respect-for-persons morality. This criticism is illustrated in the cases of Dr. Sanchez and Tommy Compton.

Criterion 4: Justification. I have rated the ethics of respect for persons as "moderately well" for this criterion. Evaluating the justifications of the two moral standards of the ethics of respect for persons presents special difficulties. The arguments of Kant himself are too complex and controversial to be discussed here. We shall therefore evaluate arguments by contemporary writers who advocate principles at least analogous to the universalization principle and the means-ends principle, beginning with a consideration of the universalization principle.

The universalization principle is primarily a requirement of equality. It states that everyone must be able to adopt the rule underlying an action. The idea underlying this requirement is that rules applicable to me must be applicable to others in similar situations. If the rules cannot be universally applied without undermining my own ability to use them, then I must not act in accordance with them either. But in what sense must I be willing for others to adopt the same rules of behavior I adopt? In other words, how would I justify the universalization principle?

One answer to this question is that the force behind the universalization principle is derived from the nature of morality itself. Some philosophers have maintained that the plausibility of the principle is derived from the term *moral*. To see the force of this claim, consider the case of the lawyer Charles Johnson whose physician discovers an aneurism in his adversary's client. Suppose he refuses to reveal the information and the boy dies. Suppose, also, that a few months later his own daughter is in an accident and the attorney for the other side discovers information about his daughter's medical condition that could save her life if he revealed it. Instead, he conceals the information and Johnson's daughter dies. When Johnson discovers what the lawyer has done, he is enraged and tries in every way possible to have the attorney disbarred or otherwise punished. He calls the lawyer's conduct immoral, an outrage to society, and a disgrace to the legal profession. Now most of us would say that, by this reaction, Johnson has conceded that his own conduct in concealing similar information was immoral. But suppose Johnson insists that his conduct was not immoral, even though he admits that the only significant difference between the two cases is that in this case he is related to the deceased person.

At this point we would probably severely criticize Johnson's behavior. One way of stating our criticism would be to say that Johnson does not know how to use the words *moral* and *immoral*. If he is going to use moral language correctly, he must apply the same rules to himself that he applies to others. Johnson is violating the rules that govern the use of the words *moral* and *immoral*.

How could Johnson respond to this argument? On the one hand he could deny that he is violating the rule that governs the use of the words *moral* and *immoral*. He could say that he is just an ethical egoist who is unwilling to universalize his egoism. And surely one would want to call such egoism either moral or immoral, not amoral as one would have to do if egoism were outside the boundaries of morality altogether. On the other hand, Johnson could say that, although his position may not be "moral" in the proper sense of that term, he doesn't care. "Why should I be moral if it is contrary to my self-interest?" he might ask. Even if the defender of the universalization principle manages to show that a nonuniversalized egoism is not a genuine moral position at all, she must then show why a person should govern his actions by moral principles. This controversial issue has been discussed at length by moral philosophers, and its difficulties show that the justification of the universalization principle is not easy.

The justification of the means-ends principle is, if anything, more controversial.[9] However, one possible argument might be the following. The fundamental assertion of the means-ends principle is that human beings should be treated with the respect due to them as persons. Two questions arise: (1) What is this respect due individuals as persons? (2) Why should they be given this respect? The second question is the question of justification, but we must begin with the first question. Human beings are goal-creating and goal-pursuing agents. Therefore, in order to respect persons as purposive agents, we must respect the essential conditions necessary for the effective creation and pursuit of values and purposes. These essential conditions are freedom and well-being. Freedom includes the absence of coercion, violence, ignorance, self-deception, debilitating obsessions, and other similar factors. Well-being includes basic goods, such as life, health, food and shelter, and other goods necessary to maintain and raise one's level of purpose-fulfillment.

Now, how is the means-ends principle to be justified? One of the most plausible arguments is that refusal to respect the essential nature of per-

---

[9]One of the most interesting attempts to justify a principle like the means-ends principle is Alan Gewirth's *Reason and Morality*. I am indebted to his book for the basic ideas presented here, although this particular version is my own and differs in important aspects from Gewirth's. I am also indebted to Henry Veatch's review of Gewirth's book in *Ethics*, Vol. 89 (July 1979) for my presentation and criticism of these ideas. For a more recent discussion of this issue, see Marcus Singer, "On Gewirth's Derivation of the Principle of Generic Consistency," in *Ethics*, Vol. 95, No. 2 (January 1985), pp. 297–301; and Alan Gewirth, "From the Prudential to the Moral: Reply to Singer" in *Ethics*, Vol. 95, No. 2 (January 1985), pp. 302–304.

sonhood in oneself or others involves a contradiction. If we cannot be personal agents without having our freedom and well-being respected, we will necessarily claim the right to have these aspects of our person respected. But, if we must think of ourselves as having the right to respect of our purposes and the conditions necessary for the realization of those purposes, and *on no other ground than the fact that we are agents,* then we must acknowledge that any other person who is an agent like we are has exactly the same right. To deny this respect to other agents while claiming it for ourselves is inconsistent.

Even though this argument is impressive, we can still ask how the fact that we are agents presupposes that we have the moral right to respect for our purposes and the conditions necessary for their realization. Are we not then moving from a factual claim to a moral claim, which we have criticized before? The fact that I am an agent does not mean in and of itself that I have a right to anything. The fact that I claim a right doesn't mean the claim is valid. A successful justification of the means-ends principle must answer this objection.

CONCEPT SUMMARY

The ethics of respect for persons has no obvious inconsistencies. It is generally consistent with most people's prior moral beliefs, although its lack of emphasis on consequences leads to some conclusions that many people find implausible. However, respect-for-persons morality sometimes cannot produce a clear conclusion to moral dilemmas. Possible problems are that the rule describing an action can be stated in more than one way or that it is difficult to know whether an action passes the tests of the two moral standards or that it finds the action and its alternative equally justifiable or unjustifiable.

An argument for the universalization principle is that the principle is required by the meaning of the word *moral,* but this argument makes it impossible to criticize nonuniversalized forms of egoism as immoral. Even if we can show that such egoism is immoral, we still must show why a person should be moral. An argument for the means-ends principle can be made on the basis that as agents we necessarily claim that our purposes and the conditions necessary for their realization should be respected. If we make this claim because we are agents, we must respect an equal claim on the part of other agents. But the fact that we make a claim to certain rights does not necessarily mean the claim is valid.

VIII

APPLYING THE FOUR THEORIES

When the light from an atomic explosion flashed across the New Mexico desert on July 16, 1945, a new kind of warfare was introduced. The effects of that warfare were experienced a few weeks later in Hiroshima and Naga-saki. The accounts of the only experience the human race has had with nuclear war still fill us with nausea and horror. A report from a German Jesuit priest living in Hiroshima records his experience of walking through a park after the blast. He heard a voice from the underbrush asking "Have you anything to drink?"

> When he had penetrated the bushes, he saw there were about twenty men, and they were all in exactly the same nightmarish state: their eyesockets were hollow, the fluid from their melted eyes had run down their cheeks. (They must have had their faces upturned when the bomb went off; perhaps they were anti-aircraft personnel.) Their mouths were mere swollen, pus-covered wounds, which they could not bear to stretch enough to admit the spout of the teapot.[1]

Another report describes hundreds of people squirming in the streets, their faces swollen and gray, their hair standing on end. Others, their hands held high, were rushing to the river, groaning. Some accounts of the after-math of the blast mention that victims were so deformed that one couldn't tell whether one was looking at them from the front or the back. Other accounts include seeing a child with a blackened body running through the streets, an infant nursing its dead mother, and a human hand burning with a blue flame. One report described a naked man holding his eyeball in his hand.

People fleeing from the city often walked like automata. When asked where they were coming from they would point back toward the devastated

---

[1]John Hersey, *Hiroshima* (New York: Alfred A. Knopf, 1946), p. 68.

city and say "That way." When asked where they were going, they would point away from the city and say "That way." Some people busily pursued tasks that they were engaged in before the blast but that now made no sense at all. Some Catholic priests were determined to bring to safety a suitcase, containing diocesan accounts and a sum of money, that they had rescued from the fire and were carrying around with them through the burning city.

Nuclear war is by almost any measure one of the central moral problems of our time. Could it ever be morally justifiable to use nuclear weapons, even in retaliation against a first strike? Is it morally justifiable to engage in a policy of nuclear deterrence that is based on the threat to use nuclear weapons? Although it is impossible to deal adequately with this complex and momentous issue in a book on moral theory, we can show how some of the concepts and theories we have developed supply a useful basis for discussing it.

First we must take a closer look at the four theories, for we have not yet come to any conclusion about which theory is best or how we are to deal with the conflicting moral directives. On the one hand, you may have concluded that we cannot say that one theory is unquestionably superior or that one theory is equally appropriate for all types of moral problems. On the other hand, you may be uncomfortable with a "cafeteria-style" approach to moral theories that encourages you to pick a theory just because it seems more suited to a particular issue. It would be helpful, therefore, to determine whether the theories can be rated in any way and whether we can reach any conclusions about the limits of ethical theory.

Rating the Four Theories

A theory can be evaluated either negatively (from the standpoint of the criticisms that can be made of a theory) or positively (from the standpoint of the strengths of a theory). Recall the evaluations that we have already made of the four theories; an impartial evaluation is unlikely to identify any single theory as the only correct one. Every theory has strengths and weaknesses, and we cannot easily say that one theory is right and the others are wrong. But this conclusion does not answer the question of what to do when the theories lead to different conclusions. Can we rate the four theories, so that moral judgments derived from them can be assigned varying weights when they conflict? Let's consider both the negative and positive approaches to evaluating the theory to determine whether we can arrive at any differential evaluation of the theories, even if we cannot say that one theory is right and the others are wrong.

The Negative Approach to Evaluation.   One reason that no theory can be called right or wrong is that, every theory has weaknesses, although we might argue that some theories have more defects or more serious defects than others. We can determine the theories' relative weaknesses by reviewing each of the four criteria by which the theories have been evaluated.

Criterion 1: Consistency.   Egoism has the most serious problems with consistency, because egoism can lead to conflicting moral judgments. If the egoist advocates that others follow their self-interest, they may act in ways that are contrary to his own self-interest. Many critics believe that this inconsistency cannot be effectively eliminated. Natural law also appears inconsistent to some critics because it holds that a fundamental value can never be directly violated and then allows an exception in the case of the principle of forfeiture. However, the natural-law theorist can reply that the prohibition of direct action against a fundamental value applies only to action against *innocent* human beings, as required by the principle of forfeiture. Alternatively, the natural-law theorist can abandon the principle of forfeiture altogether without any serious harm to the system of natural-law morality. Therefore the problem of internal consistency is not as serious in natural law as in egoism.

Criterion 2: Plausibility.   All four moral theories generate some moral judgments that are at variance with our prior moral beliefs. The discussion of the Goodrich aircraft-brake scandal shows that the egoist can justify concealing the problems of the brake, even when concealing the problem could endanger human life. By holding that a fundamental value can never be directly violated except when the principle of forfeiture is involved, natural-law theorists can sometimes justify actions that seem to result in needless loss of human life. Natural law also seems to place excessive emphasis on the physical or biological values, giving secondary importance to the characteristically human values. Utilitarianism can also justify conclusions that are at variance with our prior moral beliefs, especially with regard to supererogatory acts and justice. Perhaps the most serious problem with the ethics of respect for persons, from the standpoint of the second criterion, is that it does not take sufficient account of the consequences of actions.

Criterion 3: Usefulness.   Egoism does not seem to be a particularly useful theory for resolving moral conflicts, because the egoist can only advocate that each person follow his or her own self-interest. Often the conflict of self-interest is the initial source of the problem, so the advice is not very useful. An impersonal moral standpoint is needed from which conflicts of interest can be arbitrated, and this standpoint is precisely what egoism does not provide. The egoist can agree to impersonal rules if others will agree to the same rules, but each egoist will continually attempt to circumvent the rules if he can do so successfully. Natural law is reasonably successful in providing a clear method for resolving moral controversies, but sometimes the determination of whether a fundamental value has been violated is difficult. Usually difficulties arise in applying the three criteria of the principle of double effect. The greatest hindrance to the usefulness of utilitarianism is the problems one often encounters in ascertaining the consequences of proposed courses of action. Utilitarians defend themselves by arguing that this difficulty is a limitation of human knowledge, not of utilitarian theory, but the end result is still that we often cannot determine what is right or wrong from a utilitarian standpoint. The morality of respect for persons is often not easy to apply because of problems in formulating the rules that are to be tested, the difficulties in determining whether an action passes one of the tests, and the fact that sometimes the alternative actions all fail to pass one or more of the tests.

Criterion 4: Justification. In attempting to justify the moral standard, the egoist encounters the fact that not all our actions appear to be motivated by self-interest. If only some of our actions are motivated by self-interest, the question of whether self-interest should be their motivation is left open. In arguing for the fundamental values, the natural-law theorist has not clearly shown how to identify them or why they can never be violated. We characterized natural-law moral theory as absolutist in the sense that it holds that moral values are objective (independent of human beings) and that they can never be directly violated. The problems in arguing for the fundamental values render both of these claims suspect. Mill's utilitarianism must answer the criticism that for something to be desired does not mean it is desirable. Furthermore, the fact that I desire (or even should desire) something for myself does not mean that I will desire (or should desire) it for others. Finally, both versions of the moral standard of the ethics of respect for persons are subject to criticism. The first version assumes that I want to act from the moral point of view and hence universalize my actions. This assumption may be false. The argument that I must always treat others as ends rather than means is weakened by the fact that my need for the conditions necessary for my achieving freedom and well-being does not automatically impose an obligation on others.

None of the four theories is free from criticism, but egoism seems to show more weaknesses than any other theory. Only egoism has serious problems with all four evaluational criteria. Natural law also has problems with all four criteria if we consider the principle of forfeiture to be raising a question of consistency, but this inconsistency could be eliminated by either of the two methods we have already suggested. The problem of inconsistency in egoism cannot be so easily eliminated. Not only does it have problems with all four criteria, but its problems are especially severe.

The conclusions to which egoism leads on the Goodrich case are strongly at odds with what most people would probably think, and egoism is especially inept at resolving conflicts of interest.

We cannot easily derive a ranking of the four theories from the negative approach to evaluation except to conclude that egoism is an inferior moral theory. Therefore we shall say that, as a result of the negative approach, egoism must be accorded a lower rating than the other three theories. Now let's turn to the positive approach to evaluating the theories.

The Positive Approach to Evaluation. One of the assumptions underlying several of the theories we have used is that each has a single right-making characteristic. For egoism it is self-interest, for utilitarianism it is interest-satisfaction, and for the ethics of respect for persons it is the value of the human person. Natural law is the only moral theory to propose several basic right-making characteristics, all related to our human nature. However, perhaps the basic right-making characteristics are more extensive than even natural law supposes. And possibly some of the right-making characteristics that are prominent in one theory are included in other theories as well. This might provide a way of rating the four theories from the standpoint of the right-making characteristics they espouse. The most adequate theory, by this criterion, would be the one that most fully encompasses the right-making characteristics of action. Let's examine the four theories by this criterion.

The right-making characteristic of egoism is self-interest. The appeal of this characteristic is that it is deeply rooted in human nature. Even if people do not always act out of self-interest, as some psychological egoists maintain, they do much of the time. But an unbridled egoism leads to moral judgments that most of us would reject. Furthermore, a limited place for self-interest can be found in each of the other moral theories. Natural law, utilitarianism and the ethics of respect for persons all justify duties to oneself. Therefore what is most valuable in egoism can be incorporated in a more plausible way in other moral theories.

There are four right-making characteristics in the version of natural law we have presented: life, procreation, sociability, and knowledge. From the standpoint of our positive analysis, there are two problems with natural law. First, the four values find a place in other moral theories. The value of life can be accounted for in all four theories. All four goods are necessary for the realization of the self-interest of most egoists or interest-satisfaction for most utilitarians. Life is a basic good in the ethics of respect for persons, and the other three values can find a legitimate place in the categories of nonsubtractive or additive goods. The second problem with natural law is that the fundamental goods are held to be absolute, and we have seen that this produces many problems. Therefore we can conclude that the right-making characteristics of natural law can be accounted for in a more adequate way by the other three theories.

The right-making characteristic of utilitarianism is welfare or interest-satisfaction. This characteristic is not directly accounted for by any of the other moral theories. Egoism, like utilitarianism, takes the consequences of an action to be decisive for its moral evaluation, but it considers only the consequences for one's own welfare rather than for the general welfare. The criterion of the general human welfare, which has great persuasiveness, is not emphasized by any of the other moral theories. Thus utilitarianism must be taken to have an important place in the moral analysis of actions.

The right-making characteristic of the ethics of respect for persons is that an action must meet the tests of the universalization principle and the means-ends principle. However the point of these two tests is to ensure that actions respect the equal value of all human beings. This important value is not adequately accounted for by utilitarianism because of utilitarianism's problem with justice. Therefore the ethics of respect for persons must be accorded a place of fundamental importance.

When we combine the positive and negative ratings, we arrive at these conclusions: Egoism is the weakest moral theory, all things considered. It has the most serious problems from the negative standpoint, and the right-making characteristic of regard for self can be more adequately accounted for by other theories. Natural law is the theory with the next lowest rating. The values it espouses can be accounted for by other theories without involving its implausible absolutism. Utilitarianism and the ethics of respect for persons seem to be the two most adequate theories, and each embodies right-making characteristics that cannot be incorporated into the other theory. Therefore we shall conclude that these two theories should be given special consideration in any complete ethical analysis.

This rating of the four theories would probably correspond with the evaluation of most moral philosophers. We have not said that only utilitarianism and the ethics of respect for persons should be used in a moral analysis; each of the four theories makes important contributions to a complete ethical discussion. But, when the evaluations given by the four theories disagree, the answers given by utilitarianism and the ethics of respect for persons should probably be given priority over the other theories.

Moral Scepticism and the Limits of Moral Theory. Our ranking of the four theories is not a complete answer to moral scepticism. We have not shown that a single correct set of moral principles exists. The ranking of moral theories does not allow us to say that one moral theory is right, to the exclusion of the others. We have only claimed that we have some basis for saying that some theories are more adequate than others, all things considered. Utilitarianism and the ethics of respect for persons have been ranked equally, and some suggestions have been provided for deciding which theory gives the right answers when the two disagree.

If moral scepticism can be answered only by showing that a single set of moral principles is unquestionably correct and is adequate to answer all moral problems clearly, then we have not provided an answer. But these considerations show that this fact is not as destructive to the integrity of moral theory as you might suppose.

First, it is important to note that the four moral theories tend to come to similar conclusions in many areas. With the possible exception of egoism, the theories would agree that murder, lying, theft, slavery, rape, assault, slander, fraud, and so on, are generally wrong. Even the egoist would find these actions not to his long-range self-interest in most cases. The theories converge on a core area of morality.

Second, moral scepticism is an abstract position that is not usually relevant to our moral life. Remember that whatever decision we make can be seen to follow from some moral principles. The real question, then, is whether these principles are the most rational ones we could adopt. In other words, the problem we face in practice is choosing among various moral principles and theories, not deciding whether we should adopt any moral principles at all. The realistic question is whether we are choosing the *best* principles, from a rational standpoint, not whether the principles we choose are ultimately the right ones. Whether one set of principles is in some ultimate sense the right one is not directly relevant to the choices we make. Although we have not shown that a single best set of moral principles exists, we have shown that some principles—namely, those of utilitarianism and respect for persons—are generally better than the others.

Third, we have shown that argument about moral principles and moral theories is possible. It makes no sense to say that ethics is an area in which we merely express our feelings. One cannot just say anything one pleases in morality, without rational analysis and argument. Ethics is, after all, a rational activity.

Fourth, moral philosophers have reached some consensus about what should be done when utilitarianism and the ethics of respect for persons disagree. In general, the ethics of respect for persons should prevail except when utilitarian considerations are very strong. Thus is would not be morally permissible to kill a person and use his organs to save the lives of several other people, even though greater overall utility would be produced. But suppose a small number of people are carriers of a plague that will kill 99% of the people who contract it. They became carriers of the plague through no fault of their own, and they will not themselves die of it. Due to unusual conditions, such as those that would prevail after a nuclear war, it is not possible to isolate the individuals from other humans. Would it be permissible to kill them in order to prevent massive deaths? Many people would say that it is permissible, even though the disease carriers have done nothing worthy of death and would not die of the plague themselves.

After making these points, however, we must still concede that morality has a place for personal judgment and even personal commitment. Moral theory can provide enormous insight into moral problems and their solutions, but it has limits. It cannot provide automatic answers in all cases, nor can it take the place of the morally sensitive and discerning individual. It is not a dictatorial master, but a helpful guide in the moral life.

With these considerations in mind, we are ready to look at a particular case involving nuclear retaliation and deterrence and then see what insight can be gained by applying the four theories.

CONCEPT SUMMARY

In rating the four theories by negative and positive criteria, we concluded that egoism has the lowest ranking. Negatively, it has problems with all four criteria; positively, its right-making characteristic of self-interest has been incorporated into the other theories, without the objectionable features found in egoism. Natural law has the next lowest rating, because the values it espouses can be incorporated into the other theories without the implausible absolutism with which it is associated. Utilitarianism and the ethics of respect for persons have the highest ratings and are approximately equal; some suggestions have been made for reconciling conflicts between them.

Even though a master theory in ethics has not yet been produced, certain considerations should be emphasized against radical moral scepticism. First, the four theories often lead to the same or similar conclusions. Second, in making ethical decisions, the practical decision is between one set of ethical principles or another, not between the "correct" principles and no principles at all. We have discovered that some principles are more rationally acceptable than others. Third, argument about moral principles is possible, so ethics is a rational activity. Fourth, there is some consensus as to what should be done when utilitarianism and the ethics of respect for persons disagree.

The Problem of Nuclear Retaliation and Deterrence

In order to simplify the complex issue of nuclear retaliation and deterrence, we shall begin by focusing on a particular scenario and then subject it to an ethical analysis in terms of all four moral theories. This analysis will show how each theory can contribute to the understanding of the moral problem. The proper method of analyzing a complex moral problem includes the use of all four theories.

The scenario we shall use is the following: Suppose the advance warning system of the United States gives notice that the Soviet Union has launched a massive nuclear attack against this country. Every attempt will be made to intercept the missiles, but at least 50% of them will reach their targets. A decision must be made within the next 15 minutes on whether to launch a full-scale counterattack. Only military targets will be directly attacked, but the result would still probably be more than 100 million civilian deaths in the Soviet Union, because many military targets are located near civilian population centers. For example, Moscow alone has over 60 military targets.

A full-scale attack on the Soviet Union might keep some missiles from being launched or some bombers from getting off the ground. Even if an attack on the Soviet Union did not decrease the magnitude of the attack on the United States, it might keep the Soviets from attacking other areas of the world, because their own country would be severely disabled. However, in addition to the enormous toll in human life such an attack would take, damage to the environment would be vastly increased by several hundred additional nuclear explosions. The attack on the Soviet Union would lower the chances for survival of the human race. Assuming that one has had sufficient time to consider a decision prior to such an occurrence, what should be done?

In discussing this problem, we shall use our earlier classification and divide the issues into factual issues, moral issues, and conceptual issues.

Factual Issues. The bombs that fell on the two Japanese cities were small compared to more modern weapons.[2] The uranium-fueled bomb that fell on Hiroshima was only 3 kilotons; the plutonium-fueled bomb that fell on Nagasaki was 22 kilotons. Yet in Hiroshima, at the point of explosion,

---

[2]See Harold Freeman, "The Effects of Nuclear War," in *This Is the Way the World Will End, This Is the Way You Will End Unless* (Cambridge, Mass.: Schenkman, 1983), pp. 9–25. Reprinted in James P. Sterba, ed., *The Ethics of Nuclear War* (Belmont, Calif.: Wadsworth, 1985), pp. 68–79.

the temperature reached several million degrees Fahrenheit in one-millionth of a second. The firestorm, which covered approximately $\frac{1}{5}$ square mile, raged for four hours at 9,000 degrees. Within that area almost all died instantly. Approximately 90% of the buildings were destroyed; 110,000 people were killed and 80,000 injured. Of the city's more than 1,780 nurses, 1,650 were killed, virtually eliminating medical services.

Each of the two bombs destroyed an area of approximately 3 square miles. Compare the areas of our current weaponry: One Minuteman II missile will destroy 72 square miles. One MX missile with 10 Mark 12-A weapons will be able to destroy 234 square miles. If a 1-megaton bomb were dropped on New York City, $2\frac{1}{4}$ million people could die, 1 million of them within 11 seconds. The fireball, hotter than the sun, would cover approximately $1\frac{3}{4}$ square miles. The resulting firestorm would cover about 100 square miles. Skyscrapers would topple. The city would be replaced by acres and acres of radioactive rubble.

Medical and psychological effects would also be devastating. Leukemia, many kinds of tumors, diffuse hemorrhage, and infection would be common. Children would be born with small heads. Concentration of plutonium in the testicles and ovaries could last for 50,000 years. Psychological trauma would be commonplace. Virtually all communication would be halted. Food would be contaminated, and medical services would be almost nonexistent.

In a full-scale nuclear war, an explosion such as the one we have described in New York would be only one of many. In thinking about a holocaust involving hundreds of nuclear explosions, we must consider not only the devastation of every major city in the United States, Europe, and the Soviet Union, but also the effects on the natural environment of the whole planet. One of the most widely discussed of these phenomena is the "nuclear winter." Some scientists believe that nuclear explosions could pump enormous amounts of soot and smoke into the atmosphere. The dark smoke would block sunlight. Something like this situation occurred on a smaller scale in 1816 when the Indonesian volcano Tambora erupted. It was a year without a summer; North America and Europe saw snow fall in July. Some scientists believe the nuclear winter that could result from a holocaust would last as long as five years, killing crops and endangering the survival of the human species as well as most other forms of life.

Nuclear attacks like the ones in the scenario we have described present many other potential sources of devastation. We have not considered the consequences of nuclear strikes at most of the nuclear power plants of the world, nor the effect of the damage to the ozone layer that protects the earth from harmful ultraviolet light, nor the effects of the destruction of oceanic life, especially those species at the base of the food chain in the oceans. Other possibilities are global epidemics due to the weakened condition of human beings, the likely increase in disease-carrying insects, and the destruction of most medical facilities and personnel. We can only conclude that a full-scale nuclear war could threaten the existence of the human race.

You can no doubt think of many other factual issues that are prominent in the debate over nuclear warfare and deterrence. Differences of opinion exist over how much the probability of Soviet attack would be increased if the United States were to divest itself of nuclear weapons. We do not know the extent to which the Soviet Union would try to dominate international politics if it were the primary nuclear power. We do not know whether a response to a Soviet first strike would deter further Soviet attacks and thereby save American lives or how extensive a Soviet first strike would be. Many of these factual issues, as well as others, will be brought up in the context of particular ethical analyses.

Conceptual Issues.   One of the important conceptual issues raised by this case is the proper object of moral evaluation. Should we focus on the decision of whether or not to retaliate, or should we focus on the general policy of deterrence, of which the decision of whether to retaliate is a part? The answer to this question could determine or at least strongly influence the outcome of the moral analysis. Let's look at each of these two options and some arguments in their favor, beginning with the arguments for focusing on the decision of whether or not to retaliate.

Focusing on the decision of whether or not to retaliate, as it is described in the scenario, has two arguments in its favor. First, the issue is so momentous that it is difficult to imagine that we would fail to consider a particular act of retaliation on its own merits. How could one fail to ask himself or herself about the morality of a decision that could result in 100 million deaths? We could evaluate the general policy of deterrence and then consider the decision of whether or not to retaliate as following from the general policy, but some would argue that the seriousness of the decision makes this approach inappropriate.

Second, focusing on some of the important moral issues without considering a particular case is difficult. Let's look again at the scenario we described earlier. In a few minutes the major population centers of the United States will be radioactive rubble. Officials of the United States are considering the possibility of retaliation. But what would be the purpose of retaliation? One justification would be revenge, but would this purpose justify killing 100 million people? The retaliation could probably not be justified as a part of the defense of the United States, because the United States might not exist any longer as an organized society. Some writers have suggested that we must retaliate to show that we keep our word, so that we or other nations will be believed in the future when retaliation is threatened. But, if retaliation is carried out, there might not be any future; and killing 100 million people does not seem to be a justifiable means of showing that a nation keeps its word. These problems might not be adequately faced by looking at the broader issue of deterrence.

Two arguments for taking the general policy of retaliation as the proper object of moral evaluation are the following: First, the earlier mode of analysis considers only a situation in which deterrence has failed, whereas an adequate evaluation would also take into account the possibility that deterrence will succeed. If the Soviet Union launches an attack, deterrence obviously has failed. But the policy of deterrence might also be successful. At any rate, the deterrence policy must be evaluated as a whole, weighing the benefits of success as well as the disadvantages of failure. Only from this perspective are we able to make an accurate assessment of the moral status of deterrence.

Second, the earlier mode of analysis does not consider that a particular action can sometimes seem irrational even though it is actually right because the general policy under which it falls is right. In such cases we should evaluate only the general policy and not the morality of particular actions falling under it. Recalling an example from Chapter 6, a professor might be justified in giving a student a failing grade he deserves, even though more utility would be produced in the particular case by giving him a passing grade. Similarly, if the general policy of deterrence is rationally and morally justified, retaliation as an implementation of the policy should perhaps be considered rational and moral, even though the action might seem otherwise if evaluated on its own merits.

Because we have no clear way of deciding which arguments are right, we shall look at the scenario from both perspectives. First we shall focus on the scenario from the standpoint of the morality of retaliation. Then we shall look at the more general policy of nuclear deterrence, viewing the issue of retaliation in the light of the answer to the more general question. Remember that the following analyses are not intended to be exhaustive treatments of this complex topic. Rather they are sketches designed to show how a difficult moral problem can be fruitfully analyzed from the standpoint of several moral theories and two different conceptual perspectives.

The Moral Issue. The heart of the moral problem raised by this case is that a nuclear attack would destroy the lives of millions of innocent people and perhaps even threaten the existence of the human race itself. This prospect raises one of the greatest moral issues of our time. Could circumstances ever arise in which the launching of attacks on Soviet cities would be morally justifiable, even in response to an attack on U.S. cities?

According to just-war theory, which is the standard way to conceptualize war in Western philosophy, the killing of innocent civilians is morally impermissible unless the principle of double effect can be invoked. Most proponents of just-war theory believe nuclear warfare fails this test, for reasons that we shall consider shortly. The doctrine of mutually assured destruction (MAD) was based on the assumption that the United States could eliminate one-fourth the population of the Soviet Union and one-half its industrial capacity. This policy involved a "countervalue" strategy of attacking civilian populations. President Carter, in his Presidential Directive 59, replaced this countervalue strategy with a "counterforce" strategy, according to which America would destroy Soviet military targets (missile sites, armaments factories, and so on) rather than civilian populations.

However, counterforce and countervalue strategies probably have little practical difference between them. Many factories and military installations are close to civilian population centers, and, given the destructiveness of nuclear weapons, large numbers of civilians would be killed anyway. Therefore enormous destruction of civilian life in nuclear war cannot be avoided. Many people who are not immediately killed would die from the devastating secondary effects of nuclear warfare—pollution of the environment, nuclear winters, and so on.

The question becomes particularly acute when the advantages of a nuclear attack are themselves questioned. In the scenario we have constructed, Soviet missiles have already been launched, and massive civilian casualties in the United States cannot be avoided. Would the possible prevention of a second strike or the other advantages of retaliation, such as protection of other countries from Soviet domination, justify the infliction of massive civilian deaths on Soviet society? Any analysis of retaliation must face this moral issue.

An Ethical Analysis of Nuclear Retaliation

An Egoistic Analysis. Since an egoistic analysis must take the standpoint of a particular egoist, we must assume that the egoist is an American citizen who will survive the initial Soviet attack. We must consider what she would want to have happen from the standpoint of her own self-interest. We shall assume that her interests are the conventional ones of pursuing an interesting and financially rewarding career, having a satisfying family life, and enjoying above-average social status. We shall further assume that she believes she can best enjoy the good life in a social order that conforms as closely as possible to the libertarian ideal. These goals would no longer be achievable in American society, because it would have been destroyed, so the question she must ask is what course of events would most contribute to her self-interest.

1. One interest she might have in these circumstances is to experience the satisfaction of taking revenge on those who have made her previous way of life no longer possible. She may well want to ensure that many Soviet citizens, including those who launched the attack, will also be prevented from living their lives in their accustomed way. They will also suffer by seeing their society in ruins and many of their loved ones dead. Revenge may be the most satisfying type of experience possible to her under the circumstances.

But the rational egoist who is concerned primarily with her long-range self-interest cannot allow herself to think only of revenge. She will want first and foremost to consider the options for continuing her life in a way that is compatible with her self-interest. If she believes the Soviets will emerge from the war victorious, she might become a collaborator with them. She might even try to move to the Soviet Union. But she might find the consequent loss of self-respect impossible to overcome, so this course of action may not be open to her. She could move to a country in the Southern Hemisphere where the damage to the environment might be less. Perhaps she could go to Australia or New Zealand, for example. She might even try living in some remote part of the United States that was less affected by the explosions.

If she moved to the Soviet Union or became a collaborator with the Soviets, she would not want the Soviet Union destroyed. Even if she stayed in the United States or moved to the Southern Hemisphere, she might not want any further attacks because of the enormous increase in environmental damage caused by hundreds of additional nuclear explosions and because of an increased chance that the human race would not survive at all.

On the other hand, if the Soviet Union were not attacked, she would almost certainly live under Soviet domination, regardless of where she went. If the Soviet Union were attacked, she might be able to live under a less oppressive political regime. An attack on the Soviet Union might also prevent a further attack on the United States or diminish the number of missiles launched or planes that got off the ground, which would increase her own chance of survival.

2. Given these complex considerations, what would be in the egoist's long-range self-interest? As with any form of consequentialism, the results of various courses of action are often difficult to predict with enough precision to determine the proper action with any degree of certainty. However the motive of revenge, the desire to decrease the intensity or even the

possibility of any further attack on the United States, and the desire not to live under Soviet domination would likely tip the scales in favor of retaliation. We would have to conclude that nuclear retaliation is at least morally permissible if not obligatory from the standpoint of egoism.

A Natural-Law Analysis. Natural law has a long history of concern with the morality of war. We must first show how war can be in agreement with human inclinations.

1. According to natural-law teaching, the state is a necessary part of man's well-being, because humans have a natural inclination to live in societies. Therefore war can be justified if it is necessary to preserve the state. In order to justify the particular act of retaliation in our scenario, we must determine whether it passes the four criteria for a just war. The retaliation would be authorized by a lawful authority, because only governmental action could launch nuclear weapons. Response to a nuclear attack would have a just cause, because it would be a response to aggression and might prevent a further attack. We can assume that retaliation is known to be just by those who launch it. The fourth criterion requires that there be a right use of means. In order to apply this fourth criterion, we must look at the two qualifying principles.

2. The two qualifying principles are the principle of forfeiture and the principle of double effect. The principle of forfeiture says that a person who threatens the life of an innocent person forfeits his or her own right to life. The Soviet Union has, to be sure, violated this principle by launching an aggressive war. But have Soviet civilians violated the principle? Soviet citizens have little to say about the conduct of their government, and those who are neither in uniform nor in any direct way connected with the military have not violated the principle of forfeiture by traditional interpretations of this principle. We must therefore conclude that most of the civilians in large cities should be considered innocent. They must not be directly attacked in a nuclear retaliation. So the large number of civilian deaths resulting from even a counterforce nuclear strike can be justified only if the principle of double effect can be invoked.

3. The principle of double effect states that, if an action has two effects, one morally desirable and the other not, the action can be justified only if the bad effect is unavoidable and unintended and the principle of proportionality is met. The bad effect of retaliation—namely, the death of civilians—is unavoidable in that a strike at military targets with nuclear weapons without killing innocent civilians is impossible. The second criterion is that civilian deaths must not be a means to achieving the good effect—namely, keeping the Soviet Union from making any further attacks on the United States or other nations. Assuming that only military targets are directly

aimed at and that only their destruction is necessary for a successful retaliation, we shall say that the second criterion has been met.

The principle of proportionality requires that a proper proportion exist between the good end and the means used to achieve it. In nuclear warfare the blast of the weapons and the radioactive fallout are much greater than what is necessary to eliminate the military targets themselves. In addition, the location of militarily significant targets within heavily populated areas leads to massive civilian casualties. There are over 40,000 "military" targets in the Soviet Union, many of them within heavily populated areas. The consequent civilian deaths mean that the principle of proportionality is not met. Therefore we must conclude that the use of nuclear weapons fails the principle of double effect.[3]

4. Because nuclear retaliation against military targets fails both of the two qualifying principles of natural law, we must conclude that it is morally impermissible.

A Utilitarian Analysis. Most utilitarian analyses should take the rule-utilitarian approach. But the rule-utilitarian analysis inevitably leads to a consideration of the policy of deterrence. Therefore we shall focus on an act-utilitarian analysis.

1. We shall first describe the action and the most reasonable alternative to the action. The action is launching a full-scale nuclear attack on the Soviet Union, and the most reasonable alternatives are launching a more limited attack or not attacking at all. A complete utilitarian analysis would encompass both of these alternatives, but for the sake of brevity we shall consider only the first.

2. We must now determine what people and animals would be affected by a full-scale nuclear attack on the Soviet Union and how they would be affected. The four principle groups that would be affected by the actions are: The human population of the Soviet Union, the human population of the United States, the human population of the other parts of the world that are not directly attacked, and the animal population throughout the world.

It seems fair to say that the overall effect on the citizens of the Soviet Union of a full-scale counterattack would be overwhelmingly negative. Perhaps 100 million would die and the Soviet Union would suffer massive destruction. The Soviet citizens who survived might have an opportunity for greater freedom than they enjoyed under a fully-functioning Soviet gov-

---

[3]The recent statement by the U.S. Catholic Bishops takes the position that the principle of proportionality would be violated by a nuclear attack, even if the attacker did not intend to attack civilians directly. See *The Challenge of Peace: God's Promise and Our Response.* Copyright 1982 by the United States Catholic Conference.

ernment, but this result would be far outweighed by the massive death and destruction.

The effect of a counterattack on the surviving residents of the United States and the other parts of the world would perhaps be positive overall. First, the survivors would have the knowledge that revenge had been taken, which must be counted as the satisfaction of an interest from a utilitarian standpoint. Second, the magnitude and possibly the likelihood of a second attack would be reduced, because many Soviet launching facilities would be destroyed. Western nations also would be less likely to fall under Soviet domination.

The effect on those parts of the world that were not directly attacked would be mixed. On the one hand, the residents of these areas would probably have a greater chance of political freedom if the Soviet Union were not the dominant power. On the other hand, they would suffer the deleterious effects of additional nuclear explosions. There would be greater damage to the environment and greater probability of catastrophic effects, such as the nuclear winter.

The effects of additional nuclear explosions on the animal population of the earth would be wholly negative.

3. We cannot easily identify the action that would produce the greatest amount of utility or the least amount of disutility. Because the probabilities of the various consequences must also be considered, the virtual certainty of the deaths of large numbers of Soviet citizens and animals must be given special weight. We must also consider the equally certain increase in environmental damage. Against these certain negative consequences of retaliation, we must balance the more nebulous positive consequences, such as revenge, the possibility of eliminating or reducing the size of a second attack, and the greater chance (though not certainty) of living in freedom and rebuilding a Western-oriented political order. Therefore we must conclude that an act-utilitarian analysis would find full-scale retaliation impermissible.

A Respect-for-Persons Analysis. The final type of ethical analysis that we shall use involves the two versions of the moral standard of the ethics of respect for persons.

1. We can formulate the moral rule presupposed by the attack on the Soviet Union in the following way:

> When a nation is attacked by nuclear weapons, it should retaliate with a similar attack, even when it has been (or will be) virtually destroyed itself.

2. This rule would pass the self-defeating test, because it would not prevent the United States from retaliating against a nuclear attack if other nations had the right to retaliate defensively in the same way.

3. The negative test of the means-end principle requires us to ask whether the action being evaluated harms the freedom or well-being of those affected by it. Certainly a full-scale nuclear attack on the Soviet Union would destroy or strongly negatively affect the freedom and well-being of Soviet citizens. Millions would be killed and many others would be deprived of the conditions of effective moral agency. But, before we conclude that the rule does not pass the negative test, we must investigate the relevance of the principles of forfeiture and equality.

The principle of forfeiture might be invoked to defend a full-scale nuclear response: By overriding the freedom and well-being of the citizens of the United States, the leaders of the Soviet Union have forfeited their right to freedom and well-being. However a problem does arise regarding innocent civilians in the Soviet Union, a problem similar to the one we found in the natural-law analysis. Individual Soviet citizens who have no effect on national policy and who have no connection with the military or with armaments industries have not forfeited their rights to freedom and well-being. It we attack them, we are using them as a mere means to achieve the retaliatory ends of the United States. Therefore the principle of forfeiture does not provide an escape from the conclusion that the rule fails the negative test.

The principle of equality stipulates that if the freedom and well-being of someone must be violated, people should be treated equally, unless good reasons exist for them to be treated otherwise. The freedom and well-being of American citizens would clearly be violated by a Soviet strike, and the probability of a second strike might be diminished by an American counterattack. But does the principle of equality justify killing millions of innocent Soviet citizens? Let's review some examples in order to answer this question.

First consider two examples in which the principle of equality clearly applies. A lifeboat has 12 passengers, but can hold only 10. If two people do not go overboard, everyone will drown. Nobody volunteers to jump, so the strongest person pushes two people over the side. The second example is of a woman who is 7 months pregnant. She is told that she has a medical condition that requires an operation. If she has the operation, she will live, but the fetus will die. If she does not have the operation, both she and the fetus will die. She decides to have the operation.

The principle of equality justifies the actions taken in both of these examples. In both examples, innocent people will die regardless of what is done. Because all human life deserves respect, it makes sense to save as many lives as possible. Even though some lives are used as a means to the safety of others, these lives would be lost anyhow.

Now consider a third example. A motorman has lost control of his trolley, and it is racing downhill at increasing speed. If the switchman ahead does nothing, the trolley will collide with the trolley ahead, and five people will die. If the switchman throws the switch, the trolley will go on a spur and collide with another trolley, killing two people. What should the switchman do? Most people would probably say that he should throw the switch and thereby save three lives. But is this belief justified by the principle of equality or, rather, by the more general principle stated earlier that, when utilitarian theory conflicts with the ethics of respect for persons, we can act in accordance with utility if the utilitarian considerations are sufficiently strong? Unlike the other two examples, the trolley example does not involve innocent lives that would be lost either way. The people in the trolley on the spur will not die if the switchman does not throw the switch.

The trolley example more closely parallels the problem at hand. Soviet citizens will not die if they are not attacked by American weapons. Even if the number of American deaths is reduced by the retaliation, millions of innocent Soviet citizens, including children, will die by the implementation of the first rule. It seems more reasonable to justify the switchman's decision to throw the switch by utilitarian considerations rather than by considerations appropriate to the ethics of respect for persons, if it can be justified at all. Thus the principle of equality is not applicable. Using similar reasoning, it seems more plausible to say that the principle of equality does not justify the policy of retaliation. Thus, we must conclude that the first rule does not pass the negative test of the means-ends principle.

4. We shall assume that we have no positive obligation to help Soviet citizens realize their goals and values. With respect to the citizens of the United States, the positive test is passed or at least not violated.

5. Because the first rule does not clearly pass the negative test of the means-ends principle, we shall consider the retaliation on the Soviet Union to be morally impermissible at this point in the analysis.

Now we shall look at the alternative rule, which can be formulated in this way:

> When a nation is attacked by nuclear weapons, it should not retaliate, even when it has been (or will be) virtually destroyed itself.

This rule would not violate the self-defeating test, because other nations' adopting this policy would not preclude its adoption by the United States.

The negative test of the means-ends principle is not violated by a refusal to retaliate, even if further attacks by the Soviet Union on the United

States could be prevented by retaliation. A policy of nonretaliation does not directly interfere with the freedom or well-being of American or Soviet citizens.

The positive test of the means-end principle is relevant if we apply it to the remaining citizens of the United States. Leaders of the United States have a positive obligation to promote the freedom and well-being of their citizens, especially when national survival is involved. If we assume that retaliation against the Soviet Union would provide protection from further Soviet attacks and decrease the chance that Americans would live under Soviet domination, we can conclude that the alternative rule violates the positive test.

Because the direct taking of large numbers of innocent lives is more serious than the violation of the alternative rule, we shall conclude that retaliation is impermissible.

An Ethical Analysis of the Policy of Nuclear Deterrence

Now we are ready to focus on the more general policy of nuclear deterrence, viewing our scenario as a special instance of this general policy. Keep in mind that the following brief analyses are only sketches of the kinds of considerations that are relevant. We shall shorten the discussion further by not repeating points made in the earlier analyses.

An Egoistic Analysis.   The policy of nuclear deterrence is a threat to retaliate with nuclear weapons against an attack by an enemy, the threat being intended to prevent the attack. Can this policy be justified from the standpoint of ethical egoism?

1. In order to answer this question, the egoist must examine the effects on his self-interest of a policy of nondeterrence and a policy of deterrence. If the United States elects a policy of nondeterrence, the chances of war will probably increase. The Soviet Union might be encouraged to attack the United States, knowing that it will not be attacked with nuclear weapons in return. Even if the United States were to retaliate with non-nuclear weapons, the destruction would not be as great and might be considered tolerable. The rewards of conquest might be considered worth the risk. If the United States elects a policy of nuclear deterrence, the chances of war will probably decrease, because the Soviet Union will be less likely to risk nuclear dev-

astation. On the other hand, if war does break out, it will probably be more destructive for both sides. The desire for revenge must also be considered here, just as it was in the earlier analysis.

2. Given these considerations, it is probably in the egoist's self-interest to advocate a policy of deterrence. Without a policy of deterrence, the egoist's homeland is more likely to be destroyed, and retaliation would primarily affect the well-being of the citizens of a country other than the egoist's. Therefore we shall assume that a policy of nuclear deterrence is justified from the egoistic standpoint.

A Natural-Law Analysis. Is a policy of threatening to use nuclear weapons in retaliation against a nuclear strike contrary to natural law? We have already seen that actual nuclear retaliation is impermissible by natural law because it violates the criterion of proportionality. But the policy of nuclear deterrence does not kill people; rather it is a threat to kill them if the other side attacks first. Many critics of deterrence argue, however, that, if an action is wrong, the threat of that action is also wrong. For example, they might claim that, if a man fully intends to kill someone but is prevented from doing so by circumstances beyond his control, we should regard him as being just as guilty—or at least almost as guilty—as a man who performs a murder. Accordingly, if engaging in nuclear war is never justifiable, threatening to use nuclear weapons would surely also be wrong.

Of course, important differences are noted between the intentions in the two cases. The intentions involved in nuclear deterrence are remarkably unlike the intentions of a man attempting or even contemplating murder. The intention to retaliate against an enemy is an intention a nation presumably does not want to carry out. In fact, the intention is adopted to prevent the circumstances in which it would have to be carried out. Nevertheless the threat to retaliate with nuclear weapons if attacked is a threat to do something that is immoral by natural-law morality. The only clear way to eliminate this problem is for the United States to make a threat that it has no intention of implementing. However, it seems doubtful that a bluff could be successfully carried out for an extended period of time in an open society, because the true policy of the country would become a matter of public discussion. We can only conclude that an effective policy of nuclear deterrence is probably impermissible from the standpoint of natural law.

A Utilitarian Analysis. Can a utilitarian justify a policy of nuclear deterrence? Before we can answer this question, we must decide whether to use act or rule utilitarianism. Because we are evaluating a general policy, rule utilitarianism is more appropriate.

1. The rule to be considered can be stated as:

A nation should threaten to engage in nuclear retaliation against an attack with nuclear weapons.

2. The alternative rule states a policy that does not allow either the threat or the actual use of nuclear retaliation. This alternative would be equivalent to a policy of nuclear disarmament, but not conventional disarmament. Although the second rule would not permit the United States to use nuclear weapons against the Soviet Union, for example, it would permit the use of conventional weapons. The rule could be stated as:

A nation should not threaten to engage in nuclear retaliation against an attack with nuclear weapons.

3. Both alternatives would potentially affect the general welfare or preference-satisfaction of the whole human race and all of the animal population. In addition to the direct effects of nuclear explosions, we must consider the possibilities of the global effects on ecology and climate. Furthermore, because the rule applies to any country possessing nuclear weapons, a complete analysis must consider the effect of other countries' adopting the two rules. However it is doubtful that a world-wide nuclear war would be started by nuclear attacks launched by nations other than the United States or the Soviet Union. In fact, the two major nuclear powers would probably join forces to stop the use of nuclear weapons by other nations; both countries have generally opposed the proliferation of nuclear weapons. Therefore, for the sake of convenience, we shall limit the utilitarian analysis to a consideration of the effects of the two rules on policies in the United States and the Soviet Union.

One way of determining which policy would lead to the greatest utility for human beings is to poll the preferences of all the people of the world. In the United States, Western Europe, Australia, Canada, South Korea, Taiwan, Israel, and perhaps a few other countries of the world, the majority vote would probably favor the first rule. But these countries account for less than 20% of the world's population. In the Soviet Union, China, Japan, Eastern Europe, Latin America, most of Africa, and most of Southeast Asia, the majority vote would probably favor the second rule.

But perhaps we have to look at more than simple majority preferences in order to determine where the greatest preference-satisfaction lies. Perhaps we need to consider the actual results that the majority prefers, rather than the policies the majority prefers. After all, the majority might be mistaken in judging the results of various policy alternatives. The question, then, is "Would the policy outlined in the first rule actually produce results that the majority would prefer?"

The calculation of the probable utilities of these two rules is extremely difficult. Nevertheless we shall consider a utilitarian argument favoring the second rule and a counterargument that supports the first rule. We cannot evaluate all the utilitarian considerations that are relevant to this difficult and complex issue, but we shall discuss four issues: The potential loss of human life, the damage to the environment, the chances of accidentally starting a war, and the possibilities for nuclear intimidation or blackmail. We shall begin with arguments for the second rule.

In order to consider the potential loss of human life, it will be useful to introduce the concept of expected death. An *expected death* is a death multiplied by the probability of its occurring within a given period of time.[4] Thus if 100 people experience a 10% risk of death within a given period, there are 10 expected deaths. The rule that produces the fewer expected deaths is the rule that produces more utility, all other things being equal. We shall consider other factors besides expected deaths in determining the overall utility of a rule, but this consideration is one of the most important in a utilitarian analysis.

The concept of expected death contains two elements: the number of deaths and the probability of the deaths. The estimates of the numbers of people that would die in a full-scale nuclear exchange are less controversial than the estimates of the probability of such an exchange. The reason for this difference is obvious. The damage estimates involve scientific issues, whereas the risk estimates involve judgments about human behavior. Let's begin by considering the estimates of the number of deaths.

If both sides adopted the policy stated in the first rule, an all-out war could result that would produce as many as 200 million deaths. If the United States adopted the alternative rule, and the Soviet Union believed it would not suffer nuclear retaliation, the number of deaths might be as low as 14 million. This argument assumes that the Soviet Union would employ weapons to destroy a strategic sector of American industry, such as oil refineries, or strike a few American cities in order to terrorize the population.

The probability of a Soviet first strike would no doubt be increased by a U.S. decision to adopt the second rule, but it would have to be 15 times as great in order to produce as many expected deaths as an all-out war that might result from the first rule. Several considerations make an increase in

---

[4]See Douglas P. Lackey, *Moral Principles and Nuclear Weapons* (Totowa, N.J.: Roman and Allenheld, 1984), p. 128. Several of the arguments in this section are taken from Lackey's work. See also his "Missiles and Morals: A Utilitarian Look at Nuclear Deterrence" in *Philosophy and Public Affairs*, Vol. 11, No. 3 (Summer, 1982), pp. 189–231.

probability of this magnitude unlikely, according to supporters of the second rule. One of these considerations is that the Soviet Union would not want to contaminate the farmlands of the United States, from which it would hope to benefit. Another is that the Soviet leaders would not want to risk the environmental damage to the Soviet Union that could result from large numbers of nuclear explosions in the United States. Therefore it is unlikely, according to this argument, that the expected deaths would be as high under the second rule as under the first.

Without question, if a nuclear war occurred, the damage to the environment and to human and nonhuman life not destroyed by the blasts would be greater under the first rule than the second. The mere fact of a larger number of nuclear explosions would increase the damage to the ozone layer, the destruction of oceanic life, and the possibility of the nuclear winter.

The advocate of the second rule believes that the chance of starting an accidental war would also be lower if the United States adopted the second rule rather than the first. The Soviet Union would have good reasons for believing the United States would not start a war, because, without nuclear weapons, it would run the risk of greater loss in a war. Therefore any attack on the Soviet Union by the United States would more than likely be considered a mistake and would be less likely to initiate nuclear retaliation by the Soviet Union.

Finally, the advocate of the second rule could maintain that the likelihood of the Soviet Union's being able to manipulate a non-nuclear United States would be minimal. The United States was not able to manipulate the policies of the Soviet Union from 1945 to 1949, when the United States possessed nuclear capabilities and the Soviet Union did not. Some strategists cite the swift fall of Japan after Hiroshima as evidence of the power of nuclear threats to influence national policies, but there is strong evidence that the Emperor of Japan had decided in favor of surrender by January 1945, well before the nuclear attacks on Japan in August of that same year. There is good reason to believe that it was the Russian declaration of war on Japan on August 8, 1945, that finally tipped the scales in favor of peace. The Japanese military command had already concluded that the United States had a small supply of atomic bombs, that bombs of this type could not be used to support a ground invasion, and that improved antiaircraft measures could prevent any further bombs from being delivered.

A response to these arguments might take the following form. Regarding the first argument, the most likely criticism is the estimation of the likelihood of Soviet attack. The chance of a nuclear strike, given that the United States had unilaterally dismantled its nuclear forces, could easily be 20 times greater than the chance of either an American or Soviet first strike under present conditions.[5] This increased probability would make the expected deaths from the second rule greater than the expected deaths from the first rule.

Most strategists believe that, without nuclear weapons, we would already have had a disastrous war with the Soviet Union. That the era since World War II is one of the longest periods of peace in European history is probably due to the presence of nuclear weapons. The fundamental element of nuclear deterrence is the threat of unacceptable punishment. Conventional deterrence signals to the enemy "If you attack us, you will not get what you want, because we will repulse you." Nuclear deterrence signals "If you attack us, you and your society may be totally destroyed." The first might be more credible, because it would be less likely to initiate nuclear reprisal. But the second threat is far more intimidating, because the potential for loss is much greater. After surveying 12 cases of conventional deterrence between 1938 and 1979, one scholar has concluded that it worked in 2 cases and failed in 10 cases; so far nuclear deterrence has a zero failure rate. Contrary to the earlier argument, there is reason to believe that nuclear deterrence has greater utility in preserving human life.[6]

The estimates of casualties in a war in which only the Soviets possessed nuclear weapons are also probably too low. Unless the United States had already decided on a policy of surrender if attacked by the Soviet Union, it would probably counterattack with conventional weapons. Even if the attacks were confined to military targets, the number of deaths would be far higher, because many Soviet military targets are located in or near civilian population centers. Furthermore, the Soviets could never be sure that we had destroyed all our nuclear weapons, and they might launch a massive attack on possible nuclear targets in order to eliminate any possibility of a nuclear counterattack.

The argument concerning damage to the environment might seem to favor the second rule. A full-scale nuclear exchange by both superpowers would be more devastating than an attack by the Soviet Union. On the other hand, we have already seen that the likelihood of a Soviet attack is increased by unilateral American nuclear disarmament. When the greater likelihood of some nuclear devastation of the environment is balanced against the

---

[5]James P. Sterba, "How to Achieve Nuclear Deterrence without Threatening Nuclear Destruction," in James P. Sterba, ed., *The Ethics of War and Nuclear Deterrence* (Belmont, Calif.: Wadsworth, 1985), p. 62.

[6]Samuel Huntington, "Conventional Deterrence and Conventional Retaliation in Europe," *International Security*, Vol. 8, No. 3 (1983–84), p. 38. Cited in Josef Joffe, "Nuclear Weapons, First Use, and European Order," *Ethics*, Vol. 95, No. 3 (April, 1985), p. 613. See also Richard Ullman, "Denuclearizing International Politics," *Ethics*, Vol. 95, No. 3 (April, 1985), pp. 567–588.

potential for greater damage under present conditions, it is less clear which rule is more desirable.

The argument about the chances of starting an accidental war is also difficult to evaluate. The claim that the Soviet Union would believe that a non-nuclear United States would have no reason for starting a war is probably correct. But there is perhaps more reason to believe that the Soviet Union would take more chances that could lead to an accidental war against a non-nuclear United States. Therefore we shall consider this argument inconclusive.

The argument that the Soviet Union would not use its nuclear arsenal to intimidate the United States and other Western countries is also open to criticism. Virtually all strategists are united in their belief that the Soviet Union is a formidable adversary that will exploit every opportunity for advancing its own interests. Hence the United States must occupy a position of strength with reference to the Soviet Union.[7] The period from 1945 to 1949 probably does not provide historical evidence against the belief that the Soviet Union would not use its nuclear strength to influence the policies of the United States and its allies. During this period the United States lacked sufficient nuclear weapons to stop what would almost certainly have been a massive Soviet conventional response to any American nuclear first strike.

4. The foregoing arguments are little more than illustrations of the kinds of utilitarian considerations that are relevant to this difficult and complex issue. Nevertheless we shall offer a tentative conclusion that utility favors the first rule rather than the second. Unilateral American nuclear disarmament would probably dramatically increase the chances of war, and there might be few other compensating goods. The arguments about damage to the environment and the possibilities of starting an accidental war seem to be inconclusive, and the argument about the likelihood that the Soviets would use their superiority to intimidate and manipulate other nations seems to favor the first rule.

5. If utilitarian considerations justify a policy of nuclear deterrence, the United States would have to make the threat convincing. If the threat were known to be a mere bluff, it would not be effective, and the Soviets would almost certainly eventually learn that our intentions were not sincere. Therefore the United States would have to find a way to make the policy of nuclear retaliation almost automatic. Applying this policy to the original scenario, we would have to conclude at least tentatively that, from a rule-utilitarian perspective, nuclear retaliation is obligatory.

[7]Russell Hardin and John J. Mearsheimer, "Introduction," *Ethics*, Vol. 95, No. 3 (April, 1985), p. 412.

A Respect-for-Persons Analysis. The final type of ethical analysis that we shall use involves the two versions of the moral standard of the ethics of respect for persons.

1. We can formulate the moral rule presupposed by the attack on the Soviet Union in the following way:

> A nation should threaten to engage in nuclear retaliation against an attack with nuclear weapons.

2. This rule would pass the self-defeating test, because it would not prevent the United States from retaliating against a nuclear attack if other nations adopted a policy of retaliating defensively in the same way.

3. The negative test of the means-ends principle requires us to ask whether the general policy of deterrence treats others as mere means by overriding their freedom and well-being. Using the concept of expected deaths developed in the previous section, we can say that, although the policy of deterrence decreases the expected deaths of citizens of the United States and perhaps other Western nations, it increases the expected deaths of the citizens of the Soviet Union. Furthermore, Soviet citizens are innocent, having done nothing to forfeit their right to life, even though their leaders would not be innocent if they started a nuclear war. Therefore the principle of forfeiture does not apply, and the only way to justify the policy of deterrence is by appealing to the principle of equality. However, using the reasoning we gave in the respect-for-persons analysis of retaliation, we shall conclude that the principle of equality does not justify the policy of deterrence. Soviet citizens would not die if they were not attacked, and it is important to keep in mind that large numbers of innocent civilians are involved. Therefore we shall conclude that the rule does not pass the negative test.

4. If we assume that leaders of the United States have an obligation to preserve the freedom and well-being of U.S. citizens and that a policy of deterrence decreases the chance of nuclear war, the rule passes the positive test.

5. Because the first rule does not pass the negative test, we shall conclude that so far a policy of nuclear deterrence is morally impermissible. Now we shall look at the alternative rule, which can be formulated in this way:

> A nation should not threaten to engage in nuclear retaliation against an attack with nuclear weapons.

This rule would also not violate the self-defeating test, because other nations' adopting this policy would not preclude its adoption by the United States.

A rejection of the policy of deterrence does not directly cause the deaths of citizens of the Soviet Union or the United States, even if it does increase the probability of war. Therefore we shall conclude that the alternative rule does not violate the negative test.

We have already decided that the leaders of the United States have a special obligation to preserve the freedom and well-being of U.S. citizens, so we shall conclude that the alternative rule violates the positive test.

Because the first rule violates the negative test and the second rule violates the positive test, we shall conclude that morally both rules are permissible according to the ethics of respect for persons. We cannot argue that one violation is more serious than the other because we are balancing innocent lives that might be lost if deterrence is followed against innocent lives that might be lost if deterrence is not followed.

Conclusions

First let's survey the results of our analysis of the morality of nuclear retaliation and deterrence, beginning with the issue of retaliation in the scenario we have described. We have seen that the egoist would probably favor retaliation as the course of action that would be most compatible with his self-interest. The natural-law theorist would say that retaliation is immoral because it requires an unjustifiable killing of innocent human beings. The act utilitarian would conclude that greater overall utility is produced by not retaliating. Finally, the advocate of the ethics of respect for persons would probably find an act of retaliation a more serious violation of his moral position than nonretaliation.

The four theories do not yield the same conclusion. Egoism justifies retaliation. Natural law and act utilitarianism make retaliation impermissible. We also concluded that, on balance, respect-for-persons morality makes retaliation impermissible. We have decided to give egoistic considerations less importance, and the other theories agree that retaliation is impermissible. So we shall conclude that retaliation, considered as an isolated event and apart from any general policy of deterrence, is impermissible in the scenario we described.

Turning to the question of nuclear deterrence, egoism justifies the policy of threatening to retaliate and even actual retaliation. A natural-law analysis would find a policy of actual retaliation immoral, but a threat to retaliate with no intention of carrying it out would be morally acceptable. This position might not provide an effective basis for national defense, because our lack of serious intentions to use nuclear weapons would probably be discovered by the enemy. A rule utilitarian analysis would justify a policy of deterrence and the execution of that policy if certain controversial factual assumptions are made. A respect-for-persons analysis would find both deterrence and nondeterrence permissible and so provide no definitive moral guidance. Because we have given more weight to the utilitarian and respect-for-persons analyses and the respect-for-persons analysis is not decisive, we shall conclude that some form of nuclear deterrence can be morally justified. The determination of the particular type of deterrence that is most desirable from a moral standpoint would require further analysis.

The difference in the moral assessment of a particular act of retaliation and a general policy of deterrence may be surprising. If nuclear retaliation is wrong, how can nuclear deterrence be right? The advocate of deterrence can point out, however, that if nuclear deterrence is justifiable, it may be necessary to make nuclear retaliation virtually automatic to convince the enemy of our serious intent and thereby render the policy of deterrence effective. In this way actual retaliation might be justified as an implementation of the general policy of deterrence. The advocate of deterrence can also point out that a rule utilitarian believes that many actions are justifiable as implementations of general policies that would not be justifiable from the perspective of act utilitarianism. Whether or not this response is adequate will be left to the reader to decide.

The foregoing analysis still leaves many questions unanswered. We have not, for example, considered the moral questions that arise with nonnuclear forms of retaliation and deterrence. Also, we have not considered the argument that in the conditions that prevail between the United States and the Soviet Union, the ordinary rules of morality may not apply at all.[8] The problem deserves more extensive analysis, but the four moral theories can be useful tools in understanding this moral issue, as well as others.

CONCEPT SUMMARY

It is helpful to lay out a moral issue like nuclear retaliation and deterrence into factual, conceptual, and moral components. The factual issues have to do primarily with the enormous destructiveness of nuclear weapons. The

[8]See Christopher W. Morris, "A Contractarian Defense of Deterrence," *Ethics,* Vol. 95, No. 3 (April, 1985), pp. 479–496.

conceptual analysis shows that the issues of retaliation and deterrence are distinct enough to deserve separate treatments. The moral issue focuses on the prohibitions of killing innocent human beings. The analysis of nuclear retaliation shows that, in the scenario described and apart from any general considerations, retaliation is morally impermissible. The analysis of the policy of nuclear deterrence shows that certain forms of deterrence can be justified, all things considered, if certain factual assumptions are made.

INDEX